LIES

MY

MOTHER

NEVER

TOLD ME

ALSO BY KAYLIE JONES

Celeste Ascending
A Soldier's Daughter Never Cries
Speak Now
As Soon As It Rains
Quite the Other Way

LIES

MY

MOTHER

NEVER

TOLD

ME

a memoir

Kaylie Jones

wm WILLIAM MORROW *An Imprint of* HarperCollins*Publishers*

All insert photographs, unless otherwise indicated, are from the Jones family collection. Page 1, top, right: photograph by Patt Meara; page 4, bottom, and page 9: Loomis Dean / Getty Images; page 5, top, left, and page 6: reprinted by permission of Columbia Pictures; page 5, bottom: reprinted by permission of Twentieth Century Fox; page 11, bottom: photograph by Michel Ginfray/Gamma; page 13, top and bottom: photographs by Anthony Harvey; page 14, middle: photograph by Deborah Purcell; page 15, middle: photograph by Scott Andrew Christiansen; page 16, top: photograph by Susan Wood; page 16, bottom: photograph by Lisa Harsh.

The names and identifying characteristics of some of the individuals featured throughout this book have been changed to protect their privacy.

An edited version of chapters one and two was published in *Epiphany* magazine's January 2009 issue, under the title "City of Lights." Sections of chapters fourteen and seventeen were published previously, almost unrecognizably, in the January 2005 issue of the *Los Angeles Review*, under the title "Taekwondo Master."

HarperCollins books may be purchased for educational, business, or sales promotional use. For information please write: Special Markets Department, HarperCollins Publishers, 10 East 53rd Street, New York, NY 10022.

FIRST EDITION

Designed by Joy O'Meara

Library of Congress Cataloging-in-Publication Data has been applied for.

ISBN 978-0-06-177870-4

09 10 11 12 13 OV/RRD 10 9 8 7 6 5 4 3 2 1

To Eyrna
My best teacher

CONTENTS

PART I

I used alcohol as the magical conduit to fantasy and euphoria, and to the enhancement of the imagination. There is no need to either rue or apologize for my use of this soothing, often sublime agent, which had contributed greatly to my writing. . . . I did use it—often in conjunction with music—as a means to let my mind conceive visions that the unaltered, sober brain has no access to.

—WILLIAM STYRON, *DARKNESS VISIBLE*

"I'm All Alone"

My mother was a renowned storyteller. She was hilarious, irreverent, capable of Chaplinesque self-deprecation as well as boastful self-aggrandizement, depending on her audience. She was known for shocking the gathered company into paroxysms of uncontrollable laughter, or horrified silence.

Here is a story my mother loved to tell, which ended up, in a slightly different form, in my novel *A Soldier's Daughter Never Cries*.

⤜⤜   ⤛⤛

One night when I was perhaps two, I stood up in my crib when my parents came in to say good night and announced, "I'm all alone."

"No, no," my father explained, "you're not alone. You have us."

"No. You have each other," I told him, "but I'm all alone."

Apparently my father sat down in a chair and burst into tears. My mother used to say that these words of mine convinced them to adopt my brother.

Why had my statement made my father cry? Perhaps this is only wishful thinking on my part, but I hope that on some unconscious level, he knew my words were true.

When I was little my mother often told me, "If I had to pick between having your father or having you, I would pick your father." This seemed to me a perfectly reasonable and honest statement because, given the choice, I also would have picked my father.

CHAPTER ONE

⤜⤜ City of Lights ⤛⤛

IN 1958, FOLLOWING IN THE footsteps of his writer heroes, Hemingway, Fitzgerald, et al., James Jones decided he wanted to live in Paris for a few years, and so my parents, newlyweds still, moved there, neither one of them speaking a word of French.

This was seven years after the publication of *From Here to Eternity*, a novel based entirely on my father's own experiences in the peacetime, pre–World War II army. The book, which won the National Book Award in 1952, sold more than three million copies in the United States alone and was published worldwide, including in Eastern Europe and Asia. The film, starring Montgomery Clift, Frank Sinatra, Deborah Kerr, Donna Reed, Ernest Borgnine, and Burt Lancaster, won eight Academy Awards in 1954.

By the time they moved to Paris in 1958, he'd written two other novels, *Some Came Running* and *The Pistol*. While all three were bestsellers, and *Some Came Running* was made into a Vincente Minnelli film starring Frank Sinatra, Shirley MacLaine, and Dean Martin, the novel had been savaged by critics. *The Pistol* fared much better with reviewers. Neither book reached the level of success of *From Here to Eternity*.

They moved into a little one-bedroom apartment on the quai aux Fleurs, a block from Notre-Dame cathedral. My mother was an excellent reader and offered insightful comments, though of a general nature. My father gave her the first 150 pages of *The Thin*

Red Line, his Guadalcanal combat novel, and she thought they were terrible. She didn't know what to say and finally she blurted, "It's too technical, there's no heart in it." And he burned the entire 150 pages in the fireplace. He started again, approaching C-for-Charlie Company as one collective, emotional consciousness, and he was off.

Over the course of their first year in Paris, my mother suffered several miscarriages, but eventually she became pregnant with me. Five months into the pregnancy, she had some complications, and total bed rest was recommended. My mother, for the next four months, had to give up the nightlife she loved so much.

My father was making progress on *The Thin Red Line,* so my mother, lying flat on her back, listened to him clacking away on the typewriter in the next room. One day, the laundryman arrived just as my father was writing one of the saddest scenes in the book. During an attack, Sergeant Keck, a die-hard, solemn, no-bullshit veteran, foolishly pulls a hand grenade out of his back pants pocket by the pin. Realizing this terrible mistake, he rolls away, onto his back, not wanting to upset, or hurt, his men.

My father got up and opened the door, and there stood the old laundryman, carrying their clothes. My father was shaking, his face twisted up, tears flowing; the laundryman could see my mother through the door, lying hugely pregnant in the bed. As my father reached for his wallet, the laundryman threw up his hands and said, *"Ne vous inquiétez pas, monsieur! Pas de problème!"* Don't worry, sir, no problem! And he refused to take my father's money. "You pay me next time!" My father, with his very limited French, couldn't convince the kind man to take his money.

In early August 1960, a few days after I was born, we moved into an apartment my father had bought and renovated on the Île Saint-Louis, which overlooked the quai d'Orléans, above the Seine. My father had furnished it himself—with mostly Louis

Treize, dark, shiny wood with red velvet and beige-toned upholstery. It was a strangely shaped apartment, since it spread out over two second floors in different buildings, and the buildings were not level. The living room/dining room was in one building, overlooking the quai and the Seine, while the bedrooms were in the back building, down a narrow hallway and shallow flight of stairs.

The Thin Red Line was published in 1962, and it was a critical and commercial success. The book was sold to the movies, and with that money, my father bought the ground-floor apartment in the front building, which became my parents' elegant bedroom. A curving, carpeted stairway was built, which led from the downstairs entryway to the high-ceilinged living room. He also bought the third-floor apartment in the old, musty back building, which became his office.

Like a king and queen holding court, my parents were soon surrounded by admirers, revelers, court jesters, and even the occasional spy. They had a cook, a housekeeper/nurse, and a chauffeur. They were wild and irreverent and defiant, and so hospitable to anyone passing through that you never knew who might show up. As a little girl, I met famous writers, actors, movie stars, film directors, socialites, diplomats, and even an emperor—Haile Selassie—who stood by my bedside while I was awakened from sleep, and blessed me in some incomprehensible language. Ambassador Sargent Shriver and Eunice Kennedy were frequent visitors, as well as the French writer Romain Gary and his then wife, Jean Seberg. My parents counted among their friends the writers Richard Wright, Irwin Shaw, James Baldwin, William Styron, William Saroyan, Carlos Fuentes, Françoise Sagan, and Mary McCarthy.

Their parties went on all night, sometimes into the next day. Both my parents escaped oppressively religious mothers—my mother's was deeply Catholic and my father's was Methodist turned Christian Scientist. Both came from small towns—my father was raised in Robinson, Illinois; my mother in Pottsville, Pennsylvania—and both claimed to be atheists, though, if pressed, my father would admit to being agnostic. They derided ignorance, intolerance, and narrow-mindedness.

My father's father, J. Ramon (pronounced *Ray-mon*) Jones, had been a dentist but became the town drunk, losing all his patients and his high standing in the community—absolutely everything. His wife, Ada Jones, died of diabetes in March 1941. My father was already in the army in Hawaii and did not request a leave to return home for her funeral. After the Japanese attack on Pearl Harbor in December that year, while my father and the rest of his infantry company were building pillboxes on Oahu to hold back a Japanese invasion, Ray Jones, a World War I veteran, went down to the closest U.S. Army recruiting office to enlist, but he was drunk and was laughed out into the street. He went back to his empty office, sat down in his dentist's chair, and shot himself in the mouth. He was found by my sixteen-year-old aunt, Mary Ann, on her way home from school.

The bar in our Paris apartment was an antique eighteenth-century carved wooden pulpit from a French village church. My father had seen a pulpit bar at a friend's apartment and for several years had searched for something similar. He finally found ours at the Village Suisse antiques market and installed it, complete with prayer stools, as the centerpiece of the living room. To him, this was the greatest of ironies, the most irreverent of jokes he could pull on his Christian forebears; it was as if he were thumbing his nose at all of it—the hypocrisy, the sexual repression, and the beatings his mother had given him in the name of God.

The pulpit bar became the scene of many political debates. Occasionally things got so heated fistfights broke out, candlesticks were thrown, and lamps overturned. As a result, my father, the supreme ruler of his fortified castle, created the Ten-Minute Rule. Anyone could take the pulpit, but after ten minutes, the person had to step down and give someone else a chance. James Baldwin loved to take the pulpit and was often found there in the early-morning hours putting forth the proposition that all white Americans, by the mere nature of their being white Americans, were racist. This would throw my dad into a rage.

Paris had its first big American civil rights march in the early sixties, and my mother took me along. I was not old enough to walk, so I was carried on Jimmy Baldwin's shoulders, all the way from the U.S. Embassy on a corner of the place de la Concorde, up the wide and tree-lined Champs-Élysées, to the Arc de Triomphe. I don't know if I remember the day, or if I remember my mother and Jimmy telling me about it. In my mind I see the backs of thousands and thousands of heads moving up the avenue, everyone singing songs. No one seemed afraid. Every time in my life I saw Jimmy, he would remind me of that day. He almost single-handedly turned me into a raving liberal.

In 1962, when we spent the winter living in a beach house in Montego Bay, Jamaica, my parents became friendly with a British couple, Michael and Pheobe, who ran an upscale hotel where my parents liked to hang out. Michael and Pheobe were fostering a little French boy they'd named Ambrose and were apparently trying to decide whether or not to adopt him. My mother, upon seeing the little blond baby frolicking in a shallow pool with his nurse, said to Michael, "Oh, how I wish I could have a little boy like that. If you don't want to adopt him, we will."

Pheobe committed suicide in 1963, and Michael, who was already in his late forties, felt he could not handle raising the little boy on his own. Ambrose's biological mother did not want him back, so he was temporarily placed in a French orphanage. Michael called my parents in Paris and told them what had happened. By this time, my mother had had two more miscarriages and an ectopic pregnancy, and did not think she could conceive again. It took almost a year for the paperwork to clear, but Ambrose came to live with us.

He arrived a month before his fourth birthday, in September 1964. I'd just turned four in August. He spoke only French, having forgotten his English completely during his time in the orphanage.

I have an image in my mind of the day he came to us, a little blond boy with a downcast look, in shorts and jacket too small for him, tightly gripping a small, battered suitcase, the only thing he owned. In it, he had a change of clothes and a few pairs of underwear and socks, and stained old footie pajamas. My mother went through the suitcase and promptly bought him a whole new wardrobe of beautiful, expensive clothes. Even so, he kept that suitcase, with its original contents, and took it with him everywhere he went, and slept with it under his bed. He must have thought he was going to be taken back to the orphanage at any moment.

Ambrose ate and drank everything put in front of him, quickly and efficiently, bent over his plate, never looking up. Everything except fish. No one could get him to eat fish, even under threat of punishment and even when Judite, our nanny, stood behind him at the little kitchen table and smacked him on the back of the head. He did not react, he just sat, his cheeks glowing, a glassy expression veiling his eyes, as if this was a normal part of life, something children had to endure. I knew this was wrong of her but did nothing to stop it. Ambrose's arrival did not alleviate my loneliness, but rather added to it, because now, while our father tried to remain impartial, our mother took Ambrose's side in every argument and defended him like a mother bear with a cub. To me, Judite was the only person in the whole house who was completely on my side.

When we ate dinner formally with our parents a couple of

nights a week, our dad would get annoyed at Ambrose and tell him to stop swallowing his food like a savage. Apparently none of us considered where he'd been. He'd spent close to a year in that orphanage, and who knew how much they were given to eat, or if there were bigger kids who tried to grab his food away from him.

For the first few months, my brother sometimes woke up crying in the middle of the night, begging someone called Tante Hélène not to beat him for wetting his bed. He'd been completely alone in the world, and now he was not. But he did not know this yet. And though I resented his arrival into our home, when he woke up sobbing, I helped him change his pajamas and invited him to share my bed, and told him he had nothing to fear ever again from Tante Hélène or anyone else, because our daddy would kill anyone who tried to hurt him.

Around this time, our old black-and-white TV broke three times. The TV repairman couldn't figure out what was wrong. One afternoon I heard a loud banging and came running to see. Ambrose was hammering the back of the TV with a long, flexible plastic rod with some kind of heavy magnet at the end, probably a piece from some board game.

"Mais qu'est-ce que tu fais?" I asked him what he was doing.

"I want to open it up to see the little people inside."

Judite swooped down and backhanded him across the head. "Ah, you little bastard," she shouted in French, "I knew it was you!"

My mother showered her little boy with gifts. She threw the biggest birthday party we'd ever had at our Paris apartment, inviting every child she could think of, ranging in age from toddlers to teenagers. She ordered a two-foot-high cone-shaped cake made of little cream-puff balls, glazed with honey. His eyes practically popped out of his head when he saw the pile of presents, all for him. It took him two days to open them, which horrified me. If

I'd had that many presents, I'd have torn the wrappers off in a matter of minutes.

Not for one second did my parents differentiate between us. He was ours now, for the rest of his life, and apparently he realized this himself pretty quickly. Shortly after his birthday party, my brother gave his suitcase to our father and told him he wanted to change his name to Little James. Our father named him Jamie.

Jamie learned to speak English in a matter of months, and then took on the task of Americanizing himself, refusing to speak, read, or write in French in our kindergarten class at the École Alsacienne. One day, while standing in the school yard, the teacher told my mother that her son was retarded. My mother promptly threw sand from the sandbox in the teacher's face. We ran away and never went back, but the next week we started at École Active Bilingue, a French school where English was taught. Unfortunately, this move didn't help Jamie much.

By the age of six, Jamie could give our dad a run for his money in a game of chess, and beat both our parents at gin. Our mom said, "Retarded, my ass! Now, stop acting like a jerk and start focusing in school."

An extremely expensive psychiatrist gave Jamie a battery of tests and reported that the only thing wrong was that he wanted to be American, and suggested Jamie be enrolled in an American school. He went to Pershing Hall School in Auteuil for the next eight years and never had a problem again. According to our dad, the only problem was that the "god damn school is going to cost me more than a fucking yacht."

Recently, my brother told me a story I'd never heard before. Just around the time my parents were adopting Jamie, his biological father, a wealthy playboy who lived in Monte Carlo, wrote a letter to our father, offering to subsidize the boy's education, right up through college. Our dad wrote him back and thanked him, but turned down the offer. "Jamie," he wrote, "will have to take his chances with us."

My mother adored dancing, and my fondest memories of her are of us kicking up our heels in our long, cream-colored, sunny Paris living room. My father had purchased a state-of-the-art stereo system, and sometimes in the afternoon, she'd decide to put on music, and it would fill the house, echoing off the walls and making the tall French windows rattle.

While Jamie sat on the couch, observing with a bemused expression, my mother and I and whoever else was over would dance to the Beatles, the Barry Sisters from Israel, Simon & Garfunkel, The Kingston Trio, Harry Belafonte. She taught me to walk up and down the stairs with a book on my head, which forced me to find my center of gravity and to move my hips while holding my torso still; the rest was easy—she taught me the twist, the waltz, the fox-trot, the two-step, and the Charleston. She even got her Israeli friend to teach us the hora.

"Come over here and dance, you pain in the ass!" she'd call to Jamie, but he would not budge from the couch.

When the Styrons or the Shaws were visiting, my mother would play The Writer Fucker Club anthem, "Take Him," by Rodgers and Hart, sung by some famous Broadway star. The wives would put on a little show, linking arms and kicking their legs out like chorus girls.

> *Take him, I won't make a play for him*
> *he's not for me. . . .*
> *His thoughts are seldom consecutive*
> *he just can't write.*
> *I know a movie executive*
> *who's twice as bright!!*

Everyone would howl with laughter, but I didn't get the joke and found myself cringing on the couch, next to Jamie.

Once, my mother played a classical record, and I recognized the tune from a little song we'd been taught in Chant, our singing class at school. I flew around the room, jumping and pirouetting, singing, "Up in the treetops / A birdie sang to me / It's springtime / It's springtime / And all the birds are singing!"

Jamie threw himself back into the couch and covered his ears, muttering, *"Au secours!"* Help!

"Bravo!" cried my mother. "You're singing to Beethoven's Sixth Symphony."

She had also made my father go up and down the stairs with a book on his head, and as a result, he'd become an excellent dancer. Watching the two of them moving in fluid rhythm, as one being, was a beautiful thing to behold.

For Jamie's first Christmas, our mother bought a large, fresh pine wreath, and piles and piles of candy and chocolate, which we spent hours tying to the wreath with gold and red ribbon. Then we hung the wreath on the outside door of the apartment with a little pair of scissors, an invitation for people to take what they liked. Merry Christmas! But some *voyoux,* young neighborhood thugs, pulled all the candies off, then rang the doorbell and fled, laughing and jeering. We opened the door and found the wreath all broken, branches lying on the floor in a carpet of pine needles, as if it had been attacked by dogs.

"Come back here, you little shits!" our mother yelled as she shook her fist at their fleeing backs. She kicked the door and started to cry. I was stunned into immobility. I had never seen her cry.

The day before Christmas, the doorbell rang, and it was two deliverymen from Au Nain Bleu, the fanciest toy store in Paris. They rolled a huge canvas container into the living room and unpacked a mountain of colorfully wrapped gifts. Jamie stood back and stared at this pile in complete shock.

"Is . . . is all that from *le père Noël*?" he stammered.

"There is no *père Noël*," our mother told him, tipping the two deliverymen. "*I*'m the *père Noël* around here!"

At Easter we boiled eggs and our mother's friend Addie Herder helped us paint them. She was an extraordinary collagist, and was also now Jamie's godmother. We made Addie paint the faces of everyone we knew on the eggs, complete with cotton hair, so that every time we walked by, it looked like a party was in full swing on the large silver platter. My mother bought big chocolate rabbits with bows, which she placed on the platter among the eggs. Jamie picked the one he wanted, which had a blue bow, and eyed it with the same pained devotion our German shepherd, Sir Dog, had for his steak bones. Knowing this was the rabbit Jamie wanted, I decided it was also the rabbit *I* wanted, and an enormous fight erupted. Of course, my mother took Jamie's side and I had to pick another rabbit with a different-colored bow.

I was convinced that planet Earth had never seen a more stubborn boy than Jamie. When I insisted, quite reasonably I thought, that Jamie's G.I. Joe should reciprocate my Barbie's affection and they should get married (of course Barbie really wanted G.I. Joe's Jeep—boy, what a great Jeep that was!), Jamie would get that glassy look in his eyes and refuse. "No," was all he would say. There was no point in taking this up with our mother, because she would only say, "Oh, for God's sake, stop acting like Lucy from *Peanuts*, you mean little girl, and leave him alone!"

With him, I could scream, yell, threaten, stomp my feet; nothing worked.

It still doesn't.

. . .

As a child, I suffered from insomnia, especially on Sunday nights when Judite was off. Jamie could fall asleep anywhere, and now that he no longer suffered from nightmares, he slept like a stone, undisturbed by noise or commotion. I hated that he could do this.

Sundays started around eleven, when our parents awakened. We'd have a family outing, lunch at the Lido Club, or the Brasserie Lipp, or our dad's favorite Vietnamese restaurant, then we'd go see an American movie with French subtitles. By 5:00 P.M. we'd be back home so that our mom could prepare the one dish she knew how to make—spaghetti Bolognese—for the fifty or so people who'd be stopping by in a couple of hours. My mom would have several scotch-and-sodas on the rocks, getting ready for the evening.

A seed of anxiety would sprout in my stomach while we were in the kitchen chopping garlic and onions for the sauce. By eight, which was our bedtime, this feeling would have bloomed into a huge, many-tendrilled, man-eating plant.

I clung to my mother as she put me to bed, and I loved the tingling, sweet and cool smell of scotch on her breath and the smoke of Marlboros on her clothes as she held me against her large, soft breasts.

"Okay, enough." She'd push me off. "Go to sleep."

At first, I cried and beat my fists against the mattress and shouted for Judite. "I want my Didi!"

My mother said, "Your Didi gets paid to watch you. She needs a day off, like anybody else. Now go to sleep."

This is how I learned to stay quiet, and wait in bed, staring at the dark corners of the ceiling for a long time, listening to the laughter and shouting and music coming from the living room, up a flight of shallow stairs. Right next door, Jamie was snoring away, sound asleep.

Then, after an appropriate amount of time, I would climb the stairs, dragging my leopard print blanket behind me, and my parents would let me stretch out on the couch and observe the raucous goings-on. One night, a tall and elegant lady whom I didn't know—clearly a newcomer—approached my father and said, "You shouldn't let your little girl see and hear all this. You should send her back to bed." Everyone tensed.

"If you don't like it, you can goddamn well get the hell out of my house," he said, and stormed off to another corner of the room.

When I finally fell asleep, my father would carry me back down to my bed. Sometimes their high-stakes poker game went on so late, they'd still be playing the next morning when Jamie and I left for school, the living room filled with a gray fog of smoke, ashtrays overflowing on every surface.

My father swore like the common foot soldier he'd been and didn't care who heard him. By the age of six, Jamie and I knew every gruesome and colorful swearword in the American lexicon.

About Mme. Cohen, the headmistress at my French school, our dad would say, "That mean old cunt couldn't tell her own ass from her elbow."

Or upon returning from a fancy party, "There were more famous people in that room than I could shake my dick at." (I promptly repeated this to my best friend, Lee Esterling, the next morning at the École Bilingue.)

I also told Lee's mom about my dad's nose: "My daddy says he has a nose like a douche bag." I had no idea what a douche bag was, but I was proud of my enriched vocabulary, and I couldn't understand why the comment received such a cold response from Mrs. Esterling.

Only one word was whispered in our house, as if it were

the worst insult in the entire world you could call somebody—
alcoholic.

My father, in a low, measured tone, admitted to me once, when
I was perhaps six or seven, that my grandfather Ray Jones had
been an *alcoholic*.

Alcoholic was a word my parents reserved for the most appalling and shameful cases—drunks who made public scenes or tried
to kill themselves or ended up in the street or in an institution.
If you could hold your liquor, you were not an alcoholic. If you
could get up in the morning and go to work, you were definitely
not an alcoholic. No matter how much my dad drank the night
before or what time he'd gone to bed, he got up at six every morning, made himself a pot of coffee, and climbed the two flights of
stairs to his office. Every day but Sunday, he wrote for six to eight
hours straight.

Most people were astounded by the amount of alcohol my father was able to consume and yet still retain his composure. He
appeared to judge people he just met by their capacity to imbibe.
The more they were able to drink without falling over or making
a fool of themselves, the better he liked them. One Sunday night
someone brought Jerzy Kosinksi, the author of *The Painted Bird*.
My father distrusted him and his wife, Katherina Von Fraunhofer
(known as Kiki), practically on sight. He told us later he thought
they were "phonies"—and interestingly neither one of them
drank; Jerzy never touched a drop of alcohol. Jerzy and Kiki
became regulars for a while at my parents' Sunday-night parties,
and my father tolerated their presence but never considered them
friends. Years later, when Jerzy was accused of inventing his
own biography, of plagiarizing his work, and of not having spent
World War II as a Jewish orphan wandering alone around Po-
land, I realized that my father's built-in bullshit detector had been
functioning perfectly, despite his inebriated state.

· · ·

One afternoon, perhaps a Saturday, I found my father sitting alone at the head of the long dining room table, looking worried. I asked him what was wrong. I must have been in second or third grade.

"We're going broke," he muttered. "We can't go on living like this. We're going to end up in the fucking street."

I put my hand on his large, tight shoulder and patted him there. "It'll be okay when you finish your next book," I gently offered.

"I can't write 'em fast enough," he replied. "It's these goddamn French taxes."

I thought for a moment and then said, "Why don't you go work for IBM, like my friend Lee Esterling's dad? Mr. Esterling gets a paycheck every two weeks. That way you could get paid every two weeks and you wouldn't have to write so much."

My dad threw his head back and guffawed. He leaned back so far that the Louis Treize chair he was sitting on groaned and threatened to crack in two. "Ah, shit," he said, wiping his eyes, "that's the funniest thing I ever heard in my life." For the next month or so, he told everyone this story, and they all thought it was hilarious.

I couldn't understand what was so funny. I was only trying to give him sound advice.

My greatest childhood terror, besides insomnia, was the last hour of school each day, when my anxiety built to the point that I felt I might pee in my pants. When the final bell rang and we thundered down the stairway like a herd of antelope, I searched the faces of the parents and nannies crowding the echoing, vaulted outdoor hall that in the old days held the horse-drawn carriages, hoping to see my mother or Judite. If I did not find one of them immediately, that meant my mother had told Judite she would pick me up today but had then forgotten to come and get me.

Now I had to wait, and wait, and wait some more as the last private taxis took my classmates home, and the janitors in their blue jumpsuits came out with their pails and mops, and the headmistress, Mme. Cohen, and the assistant headmistress, Mme. de la Marselle, clacked down the stairs in their sharp suits and heels, briefcases in hand.

"Mais qu'est-ce que tu fais là, toi?" What are you still doing here, you?

By then I had to pee so badly I had to ask them for permission to go to the toilet, even though we were not allowed back upstairs. Mme. de la Marselle, huffing and sighing, took me up and went back to her office to call my house, but of course no one was home, because Judite was out running errands. Even though I was crying hysterically by now, it never occurred to me, not once, to call my father on his private line in his office upstairs. In my estimation, this was not an emergency big enough to disturb his work.

My mother was probably still sitting at Brasserie Lipp or the Deux Magots or La Coupole, having another glass of wine or brandy or whatever it was she and her friends drank after lunch, having totally forgotten that she'd told Judite she'd pick me up.

By the time we got someone on the phone, it was close to dinnertime and Judite, harried and tired, rushed over in the family station wagon. It was pitch dark outside and I was so relieved I felt drugged, but I was also so angry I could not speak to her.

"Bien, c'était ta maman qui devait venir." Eh, it was your mommy who was supposed to come today, she said in her singsong voice, abdicating all responsibility.

Back home, not remotely calmed, I went downstairs to my parents' room to confront my mother. She might be lying back on her round bed with its faux fur cover, her eyes closed; or taking a bath, getting ready for her evening out.

"You forgot to pick me up at school again!" I shouted.

"Absolutely not!" she retorted, offended. "And don't talk to me that way. God, you're so neurotic!"

At eight years old, I asked my father to call Mme. Cohen and tell her that if no one showed up to get me, I had permission to go home by myself on the public bus. He agreed to this, with the usual warnings about bad men and crazy people. He taught me how to kick a man in the balls and break his nose with a well-aimed cross punch, something no one, especially not a dirty old Frenchman, would expect from an eight-year-old girl.

Several "dirty old Frenchmen" did expose themselves to me on my way home over the years, but in my opinion, that was nothing compared with being left at school when night was falling and the echoing old building was closing down and even Mme. de la Marselle was in a hurry to get home.

"You Ever Finish That Book You Were Writing?"

Here is a famous story of my mother's that has been described in at least two other books.

→→   ←←

While he was writing *From Here to Eternity,* Jim worked for a bit in a trailer park in Arizona. The book took him four years to write. He had a $500 advance from Maxwell Perkins at Scribner's, and to make ends meet, he helped move trailers around the park.

Years later, perhaps in the late fifties, while he and Gloria were in Los Angeles on a business trip, they went to a fancy party at an elegant restaurant with valet parking. The valet who took the keys from my father suddenly said, "Jim, is that you?"

"Hi, Fred," Jim answered evenly, as if they'd seen each other yesterday. They shook hands, and Jim introduced his young wife to his old friend. It turned out they'd worked together in the trailer park.

"Hey, you ever finish that book you were writing?" Fred asked.

"Yeah, Fred, yeah, I did."

"Well, did it get published? What's it called?"

"It's called *From Here to Eternity,*" Jim said.

CHAPTER TWO

⇥ Fiction ⇤

ONE EVENING, AFTER DINNER, AS Jamie and I were about to ask our parents to be excused, our father held up a hardcover edition of *Stuart Little*, by E. B. White, and announced that he was going to read us a book. We were only six years old, but we were not surprised, for our dad had a habit of making plans on the spur of the moment and then following through on them right to the end. No one except perhaps our mother knew what sparked these sudden decisions of his. But having his undivided attention was a momentous treat, almost as exciting as taking a trip to a foreign land.

For several weeks we remained at the dinner table after Judite had cleared the dishes, and we listened to him read in his deep, deliberate voice. Our mom sat quietly drinking wine, and listened too.

Generally he read a chapter at each sitting, but sometimes, if we begged hard enough, he read two.

I have never forgotten the scene in which the mouse Stuart Little leaves his loving, doting family of humans and sets out into the vast and scary world with his suitcase, chasing after the sparrow who has stolen his heart. My brother and I were perplexed while our big, strong, grown-up father's voice broke, and tears fell from his eyes.

"Oh, Daddy, don't cry!" my brother said. "It'll be all right, he'll find her!"

Our dad sighed, then said in a calm, fatalistic tone, "Well, maybe not . . ."

This was the first time we were faced with the possibility of loss and the reality of sad endings. Stuart does not find the sparrow, but he goes on, wandering purposefully down the road with his suitcase.

To this day I cannot look at a copy of *Stuart Little* without thinking of my father and the lesson he tried to impart to us for our future years. Just looking at the book today in Barnes & Noble makes me so choked up I can barely speak.

Apparently our dad had enjoyed reading to us, because the following summer, in 1967, we went to Skiathos, a small Greek island where there was no nightlife to speak of, and during our two-month vacation, he read to us, from a huge and imposing cloth-bound volume, the entirety of Homer's *Odyssey*. First, he prepared us by recounting a visually precise and detailed version of *The Iliad*, strong on character and motivation, which to this day has influenced my readings of that great, wondrous book. Our father told us, his eyes shining in the golden light of the hurricane lamp he'd set beside him on the table, that Achilles, while being the greatest warrior who ever lived, was also vain and therefore easily insulted, as most vain men are. He was angry over a woman slave who'd been taken from him by King Agamemnon, and now Achilles refused to fight. So the Greeks were losing the war. His best friend and lover, Patroclus, goes off to fight in Achilles' stead and is killed in hand-to-hand combat by Hector, the best of the Trojan warriors. Achilles loses his mind with rage and grief and goes on a killing rampage that scares even his own men half to death.

My brother looked a little disconcerted. "They *loved* each other?" he asked. "Two men? They were like . . . like you and Mommy?"

"Well, yes," our father explained. "Back then, it was considered normal. There was nothing wrong with it."

Jamie did not seem convinced, but soon, as our dad continued, Jamie lost his perturbed look and an expression of utter absorption took over—the same one he got when watching a cowboy movie on TV.

Our Paris apartment was filled everywhere with books. Once our dad had filled the wall-to-wall bookshelves in the living room, he filled the ones in my room, which climbed the wall surrounding my bed, right up to the ceiling. Jamie and I would climb the shelves like a rock wall and jump off, onto the bed below, hollering like attacking pirates. This was one of our favorite games. There were so many books that we simply took them for granted, never looking past their spines.

I remember James Joyce's *Ulysses* lay on the living room coffee table for several weeks. After that, it was *The Rape of Nanking*. This is still one of my greatest regrets—it never occurred to me to ask my dad what he was reading, or why. Once, many years later, when my father had been gone almost twenty years, I found his old, cumbersome *Columbia Encyclopedia* up in his dusty office, with a piece of paper stuck in it somewhere in the *C*s, and on it, in his bold, careful print, were the words *Council of Antioch*. What on earth could this mean? No one was able to tell me.

Almost all of my parents' friends who were present during my childhood have told me how much my mother adored me. I was the apple of her eye, they say. She constantly bragged about my accomplishments and said how proud she was of me. My godmother, Cecile Bazelon, an exceptional artist who was my mother's college roommate at Syracuse, tells me all my mother's letters from Paris raved about how intelligent and beautiful I was.

Yet, from the moment I was capable of thought, I was certain that something was seriously wrong with me, because I annoyed and bored my mother to distraction, and elicited from her the most soul-shattering cruelty—the kind only a mother can inflict. There was no pattern, no rhyme or reason to her outbursts. I tried for years to uncover the secret to her mood swings, to understand what I did to set her off.

You're a mean, spoiled, ugly girl.

You bore me to death. I can't wait till you grow up.

You have no sense of humor.

I know you love your daddy but my daddy was much better than yours.

You're a klutz.

You have ugly legs, not like me. I have great legs.

Who is Fat, Fat, the Water Rat?

And later, as I grew older:

Mothers who are jealous of their daughters are sick in the head. I wouldn't want to be you for anything in the world.

I was much prettier than you when I was your age.

Your life is so boring. I had a much more fun life than you.

You're a whore, you know that?

You're a nut.

Your father would be ashamed of you.

Fighting back was like throwing oil on fire. She'd laugh and say, "Oh, shut up!" or, "I don't care!" At these moments, I could feel myself turning into a massive, hulking iceberg.

I can see my father sitting at the long, luminous, dark wood dining room table, and I'm hovering just behind his shoulder. I'm still quite young, because I am barely looking down at him. In my memory most of our talks take place here, but I'm not sure if they really did or not. This was where I knew I could catch him, on Saturdays or on school holidays, when he was eating his lunch alone, or sometimes at dusk, after a long day of writing, he'd be there, just sitting by himself, thinking.

"Your mother is the most honest person I've ever known. She could never tell a lie. And she loves you instinctively, without thought." I remember his words clearly, though I don't remember what elicited them.

"What about you, how do *you* love me?" I asked him.

"I think about how much I love you all the time. It's not in-stinctual, like she loves you."

For years, I interpreted this as a simple geometrical proof: My father always tells me the truth. He says my mother could never tell a lie. Therefore, my mother never lies.

So, clearly, all the terrible things she says to me must be true. I must deserve them.

"But she's so mean to me," I answered haltingly, afraid he might get angry. But he was a fine arbitrator; he didn't automati-cally take her side in our battles simply because she was the adult and his wife and I the child.

He responded quite calmly, "Well, you know she doesn't mean it, that's just angry talk. She says things she doesn't mean when she gets angry. You have to make an effort. You have to try to get along with her."

Now, in my fantasies of returning to a time in my childhood, this is it—that is where I am, standing by the dining room table in our Paris apartment. I take a seat, catty-corner to him, I place my palm over his cool hand, and I say in a calm, measured tone, "You know what, Daddy? I think you believe what you're saying, but it's not true."

For the summer of 1969, my parents rented a house in Deauville, a chic resort town in Normandy. I liked to watch my mother pack her hard-bodied Louis Vuitton suitcases. She'd roll two bottles of

Johnnie Walker scotch into sweaters—the first thing she'd take out when we arrived. When we traveled, sometimes she'd forget the tickets, or the visas, or the passports. But never—*never*—the scotch.

The lovely white-fronted Deauville house with cross-hatched dark wood beams stood in the first line of buildings, on the boulevard Eugène Cornuché, just a short walk from the Hôtel Royal and the Casino de Deauville. From its front windows stretched a view of open fields and the beachfront boardwalk in the distance. Deauville was the Hamptons of the Paris jet set, where vastly powerful members of the European nobility and famous actors like Brigitte Bardot and Audrey Hepburn, and directors like Roger Vadim came during the high season to hang out at the casino, the Clairefontaine racetrack, and the boardwalk cafés.

Two weeks before we left Paris, I'd gotten a cold and had overused the extra-strength nasal spray, and now, I couldn't go to sleep at night without it. For the first week I still had my spray, but I ran out. On this night, at bedtime, my sinuses exploded, and the pressure was excruciating. Bedtime was already traumatic for me—everything had to be just so, the sheet turned down a certain way, the curtains drawn tight, a light on down the hall, but not too much light, and total silence. These theatrics annoyed my mother, who was usually in a hurry to go out, or to return to her guests. On this night, both my parents were decked out in formal attire, de rigueur at the casino.

"Mommy," I said, nervous, upset, my voice shaky, "I can't breathe through my nose. I'm really not feeling well."

Sitting at the edge of the large, creaky, still unfamiliar bed, she said sorrowfully, "You're so neurotic," and shook her head. "It's because Judite isn't here, that's all. You never can sleep when Judite is away. One day you'll realize that Judite is only a maid, a servant. She's not your mother. I'm your mother. There's nothing wrong with your sinuses. Now go to sleep." And she stood up, smoothing down her luminous, silvery casino gown. I heard her elegant high-heeled sandals clicking down the hall and then down the wooden stairway, the sound growing fainter as my desperation increased.

How could I have let this happen? Get caught like this, unprepared? I had the feeling I was suffocating and couldn't get enough air in my lungs, even though I could breathe perfectly well through my mouth. I didn't realize I was hyperventilating, breathing too fast and getting too much oxygen, but breathing into a paper bag was not something I knew to do at that age.

The next day, exhausted and anxious, I went by myself on my bicycle to find a pharmacy. I had no problem buying whatever I needed at our local pharmacy in Paris, but here, in Deauville, the druggist asked me if it was for me and I answered yes, when I should have simply said it was for my mother. He gave me some mild children's formula. I searched for another pharmacy within riding distance but couldn't find one.

I worried obsessively about whether or not I'd be able to sleep, and indeed, for a second night, my sinuses swelled and ached and blocked off the air. The mild children's spray had no effect. Why was this happening to me only at bedtime and not during the day? Was my mother right, and it was all in my head? For the summer my parents had hired a housekeeper named Madeleine, a very nice fat lady from Le Mans who'd spent the war hiding Jews and stranded American fighter pilots from the Nazis. She had the medals to prove it. She loved Americans and sometimes shouted out the expressions she'd learned from the pilots, such as "Hi there, beautiful!" or "That's swell!"

I liked Madeleine a lot, but I wasn't about to go find her in her little, alien-smelling bedroom under the eaves and explain my problem. Finally, sitting up in bed, I heard the first birds beginning to chirp and was relieved that dawn was nearing. The darkness began to turn blue, and I thought, It'll be daytime soon and everything will be all right. Finally I dozed off before my parents returned from the casino.

That morning, I decided to go to my father. This was not a decision I made lightly. I was keenly aware that his writing came first, and that we were never to disturb him while he was working. He could be interrupted in an emergency, of course, and this, certainly, was not a normal emergency. But I was scared enough, and upset enough, to climb the stairs and knock timidly on his closed door.

He probably hadn't gone to sleep at all, I now realize.

He'd taken over one small room under the eaves, as was his wont. He'd turned the desk to face a blank wall, away from the window with the magnificent view of the open field that led to the boardwalk and the golden sand and the red beach parasols and blue Channel beyond. He wasn't sitting at the desk, I remember, but reading in an armchair and balancing a large mug of black coffee on the armrest with two fingers. The room already smelled of him: pipe smoke, the black coffee, and 4711 cologne, a scent that still causes a knot in my throat.

"Why don't you put the desk in front of the window?" I asked him.

"It's too distracting," he said. "What's up?"

I told him the whole truth—how I couldn't go to sleep without the adult nasal spray from Paris; that I'd gone to the drugstore but the man wouldn't give it to me and I couldn't find another drugstore. I told him I was really, really scared because I *needed* the spray. I tried to keep my composure and not burst into tears. He looked at me, concern written in the wavy lines of his forehead.

"What you need is to clean your sinuses out," he pronounced after thinking it over for a minute. Then he told me that when he'd been a boat hand on a yacht in Florida back in the forties after the war, he'd caught a terrible cold. One of the yachtsmen was a doctor and told my dad to get in the ocean and tilt his head back and let the ocean water fill his sinuses, that it would cure his cold in a day. And by God, my dad said, it did!

I considered this doubtfully. There were few things more terrifying than jumping into a pool or the ocean and having your nose fill up with water. It was uncomfortable and unpleasant. "But doesn't that hurt?"

"Not really." He said he'd take me down to the Piscine de Deauville, an Olympic-size, heated saltwater pool just down the street, when he quit work in a couple of hours.

At the pool, in the shallow end, we were the only ones in the water. "Lie back," he said, "like this, and hold your breath, but let the water flow right up your nose. If you relax and just stay calm, it won't hurt. And I'll be right here, holding your hand. Here, watch. I'll do it first."

Scared as I was, I watched him do it, then did exactly what he had done. It didn't feel good, was unpleasant and frightening, but it didn't *hurt*, especially with him standing right there next to me.

"Do it a few more times," he said. "Then we'll go to the drugstore and buy that spray. You'll have it if you need it, but you probably won't. And if your sinuses don't get better quick, then it means you have some kind of infection and we'll go see a nose doctor."

He made it a point to go back to the same pharmacy and order the spray from the same pharmacist, taking his time, reading the labels, speaking to me in English and asking me which one I wanted. The pharmacist didn't say a word but looked miffed as he rang up the sale.

I did not need the spray again. But now I had the little white plastic bottle with a blue label, right on the bedside table, just in case. That night, I slept like a stone, feeling safe and protected and that all was right with my world.

. . .

In Deauville, on August 5, my birthday, my father gave me my mint-condition first edition of his newest book, *The Ice-Cream Headache*. He had all of his books bound in leather with gold lettering—blue for Jamie and brown for me—and gave them to us on birthdays and other holidays. In this one he wrote: "To Kaylie—on her ninth Birthday. Hoorah! A new one is almost finished! And so am I."

My bound editions went high up on a shelf next to my brother's, to save until we "grew up." All his books except for this one were big and fat and frightening. I knew that *The Ice-Cream Headache* was a collection of stories, so I asked my father if he thought I was old enough to read it. He considered this for a moment and said, "Sure—go ahead and start with the childhood stories." And he told me their titles: "Just Like the Girl," "The Tennis Game," "A Bottle of Cream," "The Valentine," and "The Ice-Cream Headache."

My father rarely talked about his childhood. He was eight years old in 1929, when his family lost everything in the Great Depression. Now, to prepare me to read the stories, he told me they were based on his own childhood in Robinson, Illinois, and that the grandfather in "The Ice-Cream Headache" was his own grandfather, George Washington Jones, a lawyer who was a quarter Cherokee and had written a book himself, a treatise on why Christ's trial was illegal. My father had loved and admired his grandfather, adored his own drunken father, whose best advice had been to always tell the truth, and hated—passionately hated—his mother, Ada, on whom the mother in the stories is based.

"Why did you hate her?" I wanted to know.

"Because she was a self-pitying, sanctimonious, self-righteous bitch." And that was all he would say on the subject.

• • •

I was taking riding lessons and swimming in the ocean every day, living a dream life of privilege, far from Robinson, Illinois, where I'd never been. I'd never met a single relative on my father's side. His childhood was far removed from anything I knew, but his writing was so straightforward, so honest, the details so clear—the oppressive midwestern summer heat, the small backyard, the public school's hallways, the mother's sweating back as she toils over the kitchen stove—that I felt I was there with him, witnessing his childhood as an invisible onlooker. His mother beat him mercilessly and then demanded that he feel sorry for her, because her life was so hard, being married to the town drunk. He knew how to appease her with loving words of pity and compassion, when what he felt was revulsion and terror. And I knew that even if some of the details were changed—my father often said that's what a writer did, fool with the facts—the little boy was my father, and he'd lived through this. It was almost impossible to imagine this powerful, decent man in the care of such ignorant, self-centered adults.

In "A Bottle of Cream," the cruel, angry, self-pitying mother sends the little boy out to return a bottle of spoiled cream. He's angry too, because she's interrupted his imaginary championship tennis game, in which he plays both sides, hitting the ball against the garage door. On the way, he breaks the bottle by accident and sits down on the sidewalk to cry, because he knows she'll beat him. A notorious local outlaw named Chet Poore appears out of nowhere and asks the little boy what's wrong. Poore's impatient goon friend wants to take off, but Chet Poore kneels down and listens to the boy's story. Poore takes him to the store and explains the situation to the shop owner. But the man won't replace the spoiled bottle of cream. " 'All right then, damn it, *sell* me a bottle of cream,' Chet Poore said irritably, 'you tight bastard.' " And just like that, the little boy's problem vanishes.

My father's world, it seemed to me, was upside-down. The

hero was an outlaw, and the villain was a fine, upstanding, churchgoing mother. Chet Poore probably had a mother or a father just like Ada Jones too. No wonder my father had helped me with my swollen sinuses. He remembered.

I ran to him and threw myself into his arms. "But, Daddy, these stories, they're not true, right? They're not really true?" I wanted him to reassure me.

"They're all true," he said in a quiet tone, "I just had to change things sometimes, you know, lie a little, to make them better stories."

I pressed my forehead against his thick, reassuring neck, and his calm and even voice explained to me that the world was not always a nice place and that people were sometimes pretty awful, even though they usually thought they were doing the right thing—and he wished it could be otherwise and that he could tell me it wasn't so, but there it is.

"What happened to Chet Poore?" I asked him.

"Oh, he died in jail, I guess," my father said wistfully. "That wasn't his real name."

"What was his real name?"

"I don't remember," my father said. "I don't remember if it really happened that way at all."

"The Best Cocksucker in New York City"

This story my mother reserved for special occasions. It was usually delivered in a confessional tone, her voice deep and somewhat reticent. She might share it with a person she admired greatly, whose moral fortitude and intelligence she did not question.

→→   ←←

In the spring of 1957, Jim brought Gloria, his bride of a few weeks, back home to Marshall, Illinois. He had built his new house, with his *From Here to Eternity* money, right next to the Handy Colony grounds. Lowney and Harry Handy had supported Jim through his writing of *From Here to Eternity*, and after the novel's success, he had tried to repay them by pouring money into a writers' colony Lowney wanted to run. During all those years while he wrote *From Here to Eternity*, while Lowney had mentored and edited and encouraged Jim, she'd also been his mistress. But Jim had neglected to tell Gloria this. He'd told her that Lowney was his foster mother. Apparently Lowney didn't know her love affair with Jim was over until she received a telegram from him stating that he'd gotten married. How he planned to pull this one off is anyone's guess, but he brought his shining, long-legged, beautiful blond bride back to his ex-mistress's home turf.

At night, Lowney tried to scare Gloria by wearing a sheet, stalking and *whoo-whooing* her way across the lawn. Gloria, looking out the window, said to Jim, "What's wrong with your foster mother? Is she crazy?"

One afternoon, Gloria was at the sink washing the lunch dishes. Her two young cousins, Kate and Joanie Mosolino, twelve and ten, had come from Pennsylvania for a visit. Lowney appeared at the screen door, brandishing a large carving knife. She slashed her way through the screen and came at my mother.

"You think you're something special, don't you? He tells everybody you're the best cocksucker in New York City."

Gloria grabbed Lowney by the wrist and they struggled, banging around the kitchen. The two little girls stood there, paralyzed with fear. Gloria screamed for help, and Jim came running from his office, where he'd gone back to work after lunch. He separated the two women and grabbed the knife away from Lowney.

Catching her breath, Gloria said to Lowney, "First of all, that's not true, Jim would never say that. I'm a terrible cocksucker, I have buckteeth."

CHAPTER THREE

⇥ Love ⇤

WHAT MY MOTHER EVEN MORE rarely told anyone was that this lie of my father's almost caused my parents to break up. In my mother's version, five minutes after Jim threw Lowney out of the house, he admitted to having been her lover, and Gloria demanded a divorce.

He said, in a surprisingly calm voice, "Take what you need. We're leaving."

According to my mother, she grabbed a few things—my father's manuscript of *Some Came Running*, his big, chunky Navajo silver and turquoise jewelry, and his mother's silver tea set—and threw them into the trunk of the car. He took nothing but a change of clothes, turned his back on all his collections—guns, knives, bows and arrows, handmade western boots, chess sets, books, not to mention the house he'd just built —pushed Gloria into the car, got in, turned the key, and sped off.

They drove across the Midwest, down to Florida, then back up through the South, fighting and yelling the whole way. They arrived at some kind of truce before they reached New York, making a solemn vow never to speak of it again.

My father never returned to Illinois.

But what happened to cousins Kate and Joanie? How did they get home? How come we still have my father's first editions of

Wolfe, Hemingway, and Fitzgerald? Did *he* throw those into the trunk of the car? Why did my mother throw his manuscript and silver into the trunk if she was going to leave him?

These questions would make my mother's mouth pucker up tight as a change purse, and she'd turn stone-faced and silent. Afraid of displeasing her, I stopped asking.

Recently, I brought up the matter with Cousins Joanie and Kate, who remember the day with absolute clarity. They were nice Catholic girls from Pottsville, P.A., who'd never left home before. They'd never seen anyone brandishing a knife, nor heard the word *cock*. Later that day, when things calmed down a bit, they asked Gloria, "What's a cock?"

Gloria responded in a grim, preoccupied tone, "A man's thing, I guess."

Neither Kate nor Joanie remembers my mother, during the altercation, saying anything about her own talents, or lack thereof, as a cocksucker.

"Are you sure?" I asked them, perturbed.

Both insisted my mother never said anything to Lowney in response to the cocksucker accusation. I asked them how they got home. They said they'd taken the train from Pennsylvania to Illinois, but Gloria and Jim sent them home on the first available plane from Indianapolis, which was not until the next day.

My mother never said the name Lowney Handy without a high-pitched, nasal, midwestern parody of Lowney's voice. If anyone else brought up Lowney Handy in my mother's presence, that person went to her shit list, exiled forever. She would also use her wheedling Lowney Handy tone whenever she was angry at my father: *"Jeee-i-um,"* she would call across the apartment. This drove my father to shatter more than one glass against the wall, as well as expensive candlesticks.

Lowney Handy died of a drug overdose in 1964, four years after I was born. And, according to my mother, *because* I was born. "She waited for him, but then you came along, and he still didn't come back, and she realized he never would," she told me. Apparently, at the news of Lowney's death, my father displayed not the slightest emotion. The only thing he ever said to me on the subject was, "Don't ever let anyone make you feel guilty for anything. I'm done feeling guilty, and I'm glad."

When he closed the door on her and on his past, he never looked back.

Recently, for the first time in thirty years, I went back and looked at my father's novel *Go to the Widow-Maker*, a thinly disguised account of how he and my mother met and fell in love and were married within six weeks. I felt like a child entering the forest primeval, afraid of what I would find on every page. The experience gave a whole new meaning to not being able to see the forest for the trees.

The dedication reads:

THIS BOOK IS DEDICATED
TO MY DAUGHTER
KAYLIE
WITH THE INFORMATION THAT THE
REASON HER FATHER NEVER TRIED TO WRITE
ABOUT A GREAT LOVE STORY BEFORE WAS
BECAUSE HE HAD NEVER EXPERIENCED ONE
UNTIL HE MET HER MOTHER.

It's the only book he dedicated to me, his love song to my mother.

From the time they met, they were never apart, except for the month he spent in Vietnam in 1973, writing for the *New York Times Magazine*. His descriptions of Lucky, my mother's doppelgänger, are painted with careful, loving, precise brushstrokes.

This is the scene in which he meets her for the first time, arriving at her apartment for their blind date. "Her shoulderlength champagne-colored hair was combed straight back above the smoothly rounded forehead in a sort of lion's-mane effect. She had high slightly prominent cheekbones that slanted her eyes the least tiniest bit. But beneath the short straight nostril-flaring nose, her mouth was her most attractive feature. It was wide enough that it seemed to go all the way across her face although it didn't and the full sweet upper lip was so unusually short that it appeared unable to cover a perfect set of prominent upper teeth except by an act of conscious will on the part of its owner."

His perception of their early days together is highly romanticized and sexually explicit, and he holds nothing back, trying to be as straightforward and honest as he can, showing both of them at their best, but also at their worst. This is very brave, but reckless too. He was so intent on throwing off the shackles of sexual repression and hypocrisy he'd been subjected to as a young man, he went to the other extreme, being as open—not just in his writing but also with me and my brother—as he could.

Now, thirty years later, still uncomfortable with his descriptive sex scenes, I skip over them, just as I did the first time I read the book, at seventeen.

Using Jamaica as the setting for the novel, he condensed what took place over four or five years—in New York, Haiti, Illinois, Paris, and Jamaica—into a six-week period in New York and Jamaica, which includes my parents' courtship and marriage, and the tumultuous rupture of his relationship with the Handys.

I found the scene of Lowney Handy crashing through the screen door, and it is almost identical to my mother's version, except it takes place in Jamaica; there is no knife; no little cousins there to witness; and no retort from Lucky.

Yet even before she learns of his longtime affair with his "foster mother," Lucky threatens Ron Grant with betrayal: "One day

I'm going to cuckold you." And he tells her to go right ahead and do whatever the hell she wants to do. This battle for dominance between them reminds me of a late-night poker game in which the last two players keep raising the stakes, hoping the other will fold before the bluff is called. My father, on some level, must have felt that way about love affairs in general, for he always said, only half in jest, "In any love affair or romance, the one who quits first wins." Meaning, the one who cares least wins.

Who cared least between the two of them? I have no idea.

In 1962 to 1963, while my father was writing *Go to the Widow-Maker,* we spent the winter in Montego Bay, and Judite came with us. My father did a great deal of scuba diving and skin diving and other research for the book. Many years later, Judite told me that in Jamaica, my parents had been befriended by a very rich and good-looking English lord, and my mother liked very much to flirt with him. *"C'était pas sérieux,"* Judite added quickly—nothing serious, of course. One night, my father came home without my mother, at around two in the morning. Steaming drunk and in a rage, he threw open my mother's closet and with a razor-sharp diving knife, sliced up all her clothes—everything—to ribbons.

"Were you scared?" I asked Judite.

"Un peu." A little, she said. "He never raised a hand to me, you know, nor to you. We just hid in a corner, you were in my arms.

"Then, a while later, your mother came back with the English lord. I thought your father was going to kill them! But five minutes later, they're all sitting at the kitchen table, having a drink!" With that, she laughed, blushing, as if she'd said more than she should.

She waited another fifteen years to tell me the rest: "You know, out on that diving boat in Jamaica, your daddy was doing his diving and you and me we were just sitting there, playing on the deck. Your mother got out of the water and took off her bathing suit right in front of that English lord. He was right below us, in the water, watching her. The look in his eyes . . . I could never forget it. *J'étais écœurée*," she said, a hand on her sternum. "It made me sick to my stomach."

In the novel, my father compares the effect of Lucky's cruel and threatening words, "'Would you like me to have an affair with Jim [a scuba diver]?'" to the echo that hangs in the air "like the end of the stanzas in Yeats's *Innisfree*, going on and on in silence after the words themselves have been said and have faded away. Grant felt almost exactly as he had felt [on a spearfishing expedition] when he watched the shark's flank going on and on and on past him and then the numbing jerk on his hand."

What is Yeats's poem "The Lake Isle of Innisfree" doing here? This feels to me like a secret key to my father's psyche, for the last message he left on his tiny tape recorder in the Cardiac Care Unit of Southampton Hospital—which I have listened to only once, and still have but cannot bring myself to hear again—was a slow, deliberate recitation of this poem, followed by a long, piercing yell, like a Native American war cry, that faded only when his breath ran out.

I will arise and go now, and go to Innisfree,
And a small cabin build there, of clay and wattles made:
Nine bean-rows will I have there, a hive for the honey-bee,
And live alone in the bee-loud glade.

And I shall have some peace there, for peace comes dropping
*   slow,*
Dropping from the veils of the morning to where the cricket
*   sings;*
There midnight's all a glimmer, and noon a purple glow,
And evening full of the linnet's wings.

I will arise and go now, for always night and day
I hear lake water lapping with low sounds by the shore;
While I stand on the roadway, or on the pavements grey,
I hear it in the deep heart's core.

And why does my father compare love, and the fear of losing it, to being next to an enormous shark in the murky blue depths of the sea?

Was my father describing that half-beat of time between the absence of fear, and fear? The moment just after disaster strikes, but before the adrenaline has kicked in? Or is it the numbness that sometimes takes over and paralyzes the emotions in the face of great danger? This explanation may only partly answer my question, but it is important: most alcoholics, if not all alcoholics, suffer from an abnormally pronounced fear of abandonment, which they unwittingly pass on to their children. They also suffer from a fundamental terror of intimacy, which is disguised by the false intimacy that develops between people when they're drinking excessively. I know it was true for me, and in rereading this novel of his, I see it was also true of both my mother and father.

A few years ago I saw a film clip taken of me in Jamaica in 1963. In it, I'm two and stark naked, and it's so sunny the light is blinding. I'm on the house's stone terrace, very busy filling an aluminum basin with water, which I then get into with my German shepherd puppy, Sir Dog. My mother is in the foreground, sitting in a deck chair. This film was a window onto my own childhood, and I watched her intently. Who is this young, golden, incredibly beautiful woman? In a moment she raises her hand and takes a sip of a drink and I realized—like a blow to the head—that in 90 percent of the candid photographs and film clips I've ever seen of her, she is holding a drink.

. . .

My father must have seen me as the perfect product of their unbri-
dled love for each other. But I always felt more like Athena, born
from the head of her father, than the product of my parents' great
romance. I know he worried about me. Perhaps he recognized in
me the same loneliness he had felt as a child, the same isolation
and constant anxiety. He gave me more of his time and patience
than most of the fathers of his generation gave their kids. He
tried to compensate for what he could see did not naturally exist
between my mother and me—and had certainly never existed between my mother and her mother, or his mother and himself.

My father first found out in the summer of 1970, when we were
visiting Bill and Rose Styron on Martha's Vineyard, that he had
congestive heart failure. The experts believed it was congenital,
exacerbated by the malaria he'd caught in the Pacific during the
war, and, of course, by his years of heavy drinking. His doctors
told him to stop drinking. He switched from scotch to white wine.
By 1974, he knew it was only a matter of time before his heart gave
out, and he wanted to be treated in the United States, by American
doctors. Also, by 1974, he realized that he was getting deeper and
deeper into debt, and that our lifestyle had to change radically.

He was offered a high-paying job as writer in residence at
Florida International University in Miami. My parents decided
to try it for a year, so they rented our Paris apartment to a rich
American couple, and off we went with our three cats and a
couple of suitcases each. Although it was never explicitly stated, I
knew that we would never be coming back to Paris.

The four of us, who had never spent more than two or three
hours a week together, moved into a small, unassuming ranch
house on Key Biscayne. My father had always loved Florida and
would probably have been content in a trailer, but my mother
immediately hated everything about Miami and spent the entire

winter sitting alone in the house, sipping scotch or white wine, in a kind of low-grade depression that nothing, other than visits from friends from New York and Paris, seemed to shake. Gloria hated the people and hated the weather. She hated the flat, hot beach and the closed-in feeling of the small ranch house. Even the pool was enclosed by mosquito netting, and all day every day lawn mowers disturbed the silence. By the end of our stay, she had gained over twenty pounds and was drinking all the time.

My dad, when he wasn't teaching, remained sequestered in the dark garage, which he'd turned into his office, using an old pool table as a desk on which he spread out his research materials. He'd been paid a sizeable sum to write the text for a book on World War II art, which he would call, simply, *WWII*. That, along with a new three-book deal from Delacorte Press, put us back in the black. "Jim wrote us right out of debt," our mother would proudly say.

When his class was finished in June, we rented a house in the small hamlet of Sagaponack, two miles east of Bridgehampton, New York. Bridgehampton was still, in 1975, a rural, quiet farming community that in the summer attracted a more "artsy" New York crowd. Several of my parents' writer friends had already moved to the area. At the time, it was not unusual to walk into Bobby Van's, the local pub, and find Willie Morris, Truman Capote, Irwin Shaw, John Knowles, James Jones, Kurt Vonnegut, Peter Matthiessen, Winston Groom, George Plimpton, or any number of other writers, sitting around shooting the breeze.

Bridgehampton was close enough to the city for my mother, and far enough away for my father, who was trying to finish *Whistle*, the third novel of the World War II trilogy he'd begun with *From Here to Eternity* and *The Thin Red Line*.

That summer, Willie Morris took Jamie to his first major-league baseball game; a friend had given Willie seats behind the dugout. He said to Jamie, pointing toward a man sitting nearby,

"Look, Jamie, look! There's Willie Mays! We'll get his autograph after the game."

Jamie said, "Who's Willie Mays?"

"Who's Willie Mays? *Who's Willie Mays!*" cried Willie. "Why, you're just a Frog, boy! I'm gonna make it my mission to teach you about this great country of yours."

Willie started a local softball league called the Golden Nematodes, named for a potato-destroying bug that was the bane of the local farmers' existence, and put Jamie to work as an outfielder. "You! Frog! *Throw* that ball to first base!" Willie would shout, and Jamie would laugh and do his best.

My father talked me into trying out for the local community theater group, the Spindrift Players. The group's director was an accomplished actor who was also the nighttime bartender at Bobby Van's. I landed the part of the little Catholic nurse in their summer production of *One Flew Over the Cuckoo's Nest*. The play was a big success and had sold-out performances six nights a week for a month. Just fifteen, in my stage makeup, I looked twenty-four, and soon realized that if I didn't wash it off after the curtain, I could go out drinking with the other actors and stagehands. I asked my father's permission, and he let me go; I'm not entirely sure why. He didn't seem worried. Maybe he made some kind of arrangement with the director; someone always made sure I got home. Personally, I never had so much fun in my life, and decided that I wanted to become an actress. For the next two years, I tried out for every Spindrift and school play and focused entirely on this goal.

In September, my parents bought an old, run-down farmhouse that sat at the top of the only hill in Sagaponack. My father started to design his renovations while my mother went back to Paris to pack up our apartment. Our Paris apartment had huge double doors, but it turned out my dad's beloved pulpit bar didn't fit through the Sagaponack house's doors, so he had the construc-

LIES MY MOTHER NEVER TOLD ME   49

tion crew take out a whole wall and add twelve feet to the small living room to accommodate it.

Growing up with a writer is a strange thing. I competed for his attention not only with the other family members and my parents' various friends, but also with all of my father's characters. At dinnertime during that cold and lonely first winter in Sagaponack, he'd come down from work exhausted and tell us what was going on with his characters, as if they were real people who hung out with him upstairs in his attic office.

The common foot soldier Bobby Prell, who began his literary career as Robert E. Lee Prewitt in *From Here to Eternity,* and was reincarnated as Bob Witt in *The Thin Red Line,* now, in *Whistle,* was languishing in a VA hospital with severe gunshot wounds in both legs. The doctors were considering amputation. My father was very upset.

"See," he told us, "he's up for the Congressional Medal of Honor, but if they amputate his legs, he won't get it. They never give it to cripples."

"Can't you just make it so he doesn't lose his legs?" Jamie asked, perplexed.

"Well, it's not really up to me," our father said, struggling as if his own best friend were lying in the hospital and he couldn't do anything to help him.

After several weeks of vacillation, he came down, looking relieved and happy. "They took away the sulfa drugs and his legs are beginning to heal! He's going to be okay!" he told us. "He ain't going to lose them after all and he's going to get his medal."

"Yes!" we shouted. That night, Willie Morris came over for dinner and we had a party, with champagne and ice cream for dessert.

• • •

I found in *Go to the Widow-Maker* a strange refrain—Lucky, while keeping up with Ron Grant's drinking, warns him to watch it, that if he doesn't, his drinking could become a problem. Any normal person reading the book will be stunned by the amount of alcohol the characters consume.

My father always thought he was watching it, aware of the dangers, since his own father had died as a direct result of alcoholism. But when people admire you and circle around you and compliment you and you have money and you can live in the most wonderful places on earth, and you adore your family, there could be no reason in the world to stop.

He was slowly dying of congestive heart failure and he knew it. And he continued to watch it but did not stop, long after it had already affected his health and, consequently, his work. Soon he could no longer climb the stairs to his office. He had elevator chairs installed on both staircases to carry him up and down. He worked tirelessly and without self-pity, right to the very end. And yet he never finished *Whistle*, his last and most important novel.

Many years later I found a little red spiral stenographer's notebook in the back of a drawer filled with papers, in my mother's house. It's my father's meticulous record, written in pencil in his familiar block letters, of everything he ate and drank during the last year of his life. The first date is June 20, 1976, and the last is May 1, 1977, eight days before he died.

From that day in June until January 14, 1977, when he was admitted to Southampton Hospital for the first time and stayed there two weeks, the word *wine* is written at every meal, even breakfast, followed by a 0.

What prompted this meticulous record keeping?

In Willie Morris's memoir of my father, *James Jones: A Friendship*, Willie describes a day in 1976 when he drove my father to Southampton Hospital for tests. My father didn't need a specialist to tell him he was getting worse, that it was going to be bad news. On the way to the hospital, Willie writes, my father wanted to stop in a bar, empty at that early hour of the afternoon, and have a few drinks. My father ordered a bottle of white wine, and, concerned, Willie asked him if he was sure this was a good idea. My father said to Willie, "I can't drink no more, goddamnit," and these glasses of wine were his last.

In his stenographer's notebook, my father even recorded how many cigars he smoked each day (usually four or five); but why did he include the word *wine* if he wasn't drinking in the first place? Perhaps he felt it was important that he wasn't drinking *at all*, as if each meal without alcohol could remedy his failing heart. He was watching it for real now. Meticulously, with an iron-fisted resolve. Right up until he was admitted to the hospital for the last time.

His last entry, on May 1, 1977, reads:

	5:30 P.M.	1 PIECE WHITE TST.
		(MUCH DSCMFT.)
145¼ LBS	6:50 P.M.	CALLED DR. DIEF.
	7:20 P.M.	DSCMFT. CLEARED
	8:20 P.M.	LEFT. FOR. HOSP.

"Who Do You Think You Are, Frank Sinatra?"

This story of my mother's is hard to beat.

⤛⤜   ⤙⤚

Once, during their many visits to New York during the sixties, Jim and Gloria met Frank Sinatra for a quiet drink in the dark bar of the Blackstone Hotel on East Fifty-eighth Street, where they always stayed. Sinatra had appeared in the film version of *From Here to Eternity*, and in many ways it had resurrected his career. Afterward he remained friends with Jim and Gloria, and they got together periodically in New York.

On this occasion, there was a fire or a bomb threat on the street, and the hotel was evacuated. A huge crowd formed inside the police barricades, and Frank Sinatra grew very anxious. He walked up to a uniformed policeman and quietly asked, "Hey, buddy, do you think you could let me through?"

And the cop answered, "Who the fuck do you think you are, Frank Sinatra?"

CHAPTER FOUR

⤜⤜ Birth of a Student ⤛⤛

I'VE NEVER SEEN ANYONE WORK as hard as my father did through his last winter and spring, trying to finish *Whistle*. Meanwhile, I was applying to colleges, and he was concerned I wasn't sufficiently prepared. He decided to give me a reading list and got out his old first editions, the ones he'd read himself as a young man. I read *A Farewell to Arms, For Whom the Bell Tolls, Light in August,* and *Pale Horse, Pale Rider,* all books with terrible endings. He was planting the seeds for my future education, knowing he most likely wouldn't be around for much longer to help me.

During my dad's last hospital stay the first week in May 1977, one night, his heart stopped several times. Dr. Diefenbach could not believe he had survived to see the morning. The next day, my father was serene yet seemed somewhat distant and bemused as he told us, his family gathered around his bed, that he'd had a vision the night before of his own death.

He saw himself lying in the center of an object shaped like a giant vegetable steamer, and as each leaf of the object opened, he'd felt his body floating upward, unmoored. He knew instinctively that if the last two leaves, the ones behind his head, opened, he would die. With all his will and strength, he mentally forced the leaves to close over him again, and he knew he would not die that night. He told us it had not been a painful experience, and he had not been afraid.

Upon hearing this, my only thought was for myself, But what about me? How am I supposed to deal with this?

Later, sitting in the waiting room in shock, in despair, my mother told me that while Jamie and I had been home asleep the night before, our father had suddenly sat straight up in the Cardiac Care Unit, tried to pull out the IV tubes, and shouted for her to get him a glass of scotch.

"What did you do?" I asked my mother.

She told me she poured him a big glass of scotch, because at that point, with only hours left, what damage could it possibly do him?

He lived another two days.

But he was no longer himself. He continued to talk into his little tape recorder, leaving explicit directions for Willie Morris, who was going to write down the end of *Whistle*. But he was slipping away. I felt a marked change in him, felt he no longer cared, really. He tried, and it took great effort, to focus and listen to me when I came and sat by his bedside and talked about school and what I was feeling. I told him our lilacs were in full bloom and tomorrow I'd bring him a bouquet. He said, "No, don't. I hate to see flowers cut. . . . My mother used to cut roses and leave the petals in a bowl of water in her parlor. God, I hated that smell. . . ." His voice drifted off. That was more than he'd ever told me about his childhood home. I swallowed hard to stop myself from bursting into tears.

Then, on his last day, he made a strange request: "You've got to get your mother to stop drinking so much."

"I will, Daddy," I said, nodding quickly. I would have done anything—anything—for him. I had no idea what I was promising.

He died later that day. Dr. Diefenbach helped him along with a massive injection of morphine. I watched the light go out of my father's eyes. He arched his back, squeezed my mother's hand until their knuckles turned white, and the heart monitor took much too long to flatline. I was overtaken by nervous laughter, and Dr. Diefenbach pulled me out of the glass room and gave me a 20m Valium. The image of my father's green eyes clouding over has haunted me all my life. It was 7:00 P.M. on May 9, 1977. I was sixteen years old.

Television stations interrupted their broadcasts with the announcement. People called from all over and showed up for days. The writer Harold "Doc" Humes, whom my parents hadn't seen in years, arrived in a flatbed truck with a rock that had a history somehow tied to Buddhist belief. It took four men to lift it and place it in our garden.

James Jones's lengthy obituary in the *New York Times* was written by one of the most acclaimed critics of our time, Herbert Mitgang. In a slightly begrudging tone, he focused on the critics' dismissal of my father's novels, especially those not dealing with war and warfare, and intimated that James Jones had sold out. "Unlike Hemingway, Mr. Jones continued to be criticized as a writer, regardless of his themes. Unlike Hemingway, he did not avoid writing for films and turning out books clearly designed for the commercial market. And unlike Hemingway, he had gone to Paris, not in his youth, but in his flourishing mature years."

I was so incensed I called the *New York Times* and complained. The gentleman on the other end of line listened to me, then offered his sincerest apologies. Somehow, Liz Smith heard about my call, and, herself displeased with the obituary, she wrote about it in her *New York Daily News* column.

Many years later, my mother told me that back in the sixties, in Paris, there had been some trouble between Herbert Mitgang and William Styron, apparently over a woman. My father, naturally, had taken his good friend Bill's side, and Mitgang had never forgotten it.

. . .

My mother collapsed on the living room couch and lay prostrate for days with a bottle of scotch on the floor beside her, while worried friends stood vigil. In a kind of twilight state, she ranted that she was going to walk into the ocean and drown herself. "Where's my daddy?" she kept saying. "I want my daddy." Her daddy had died of a heart attack on New Year's Eve when Gloria was nineteen years old. But this wasn't *her* daddy, this was *my* daddy who had just died.

I thought shouting this at her would make her snap out of it. I told her to pull herself together. When that had no effect, I went out to the local bars where by now everyone knew me quite well, and sometimes I didn't come home until after sunrise. I felt like I had a category 5 hurricane raging inside me, which seemed to quiet down only after many, many, many drinks, when I was calmed enough to feel the intensity of my grief. I'd lie under the hammock on the wet grass in the garden and cry until I was wrung out. I did not eat a solid meal for eight weeks, because every time I brought food to my mouth, I saw my father's green eyes looking up at us as the light slowly left them. No religion, philosophy, or any other type of belief system had been imparted to me in childhood, and after my father's death I had no idea where to look for solace.

The one thing my father had always been adamant about, the one plan he would never diverge from, was that Jamie and I go to college. He'd finished only two semesters of college himself. He'd studied at the University of Hawaii for six months, before Pearl Harbor. And after the war, in 1945, he took advantage of the G.I. Bill and came to New York to study writing at NYU. When he told his literature professor that he wanted to be a writer, the man tried to talk him out of such a hopeless aspiration, and suggested journalism school. My dad had hated New York, been desperately lonely, and couldn't wait to go home. So he quit school, went back to Illinois, and wrote *From Here to Eternity*.

I knew my father had been a good father and a kindhearted and wise man. But now that he was gone, now that he was no longer there to protect me and teach me about life, I wanted to know: How good was he, as a writer? What would people say about his work in, say, fifty years? Would he be dismissed? Or would people still be reading him when his great-grandchildren went to college? I decided to read his books.

That spring and summer, I read his big novels, beginning with *From Here to Eternity*. I had no concept of literary technique and read strictly for story. In my narrow view of things, *Jaws* and *Moby-Dick* had quite a lot in common. Both were about crazy men chasing after huge white malevolent predators from the deep, and *Jaws* was a lot easier to read. But I could hear my dad explaining that just because *Moby-Dick* was harder to read, did not make *Jaws* a better book.

In *From Here to Eternity*, the common foot soldier, a thirty-year man, Robert E. Lee Prewitt, a dirt-poor boy from a long line of western Kentucky coal miners, is good at two things—both of which he learned in the army—playing the bugle and boxing. He is so good a bugler that he played taps at Arlington in front of presidents. He's a world-class boxer too, but he won't box anymore, because he blinded a man in a match.

Sergeant Warden, Prewitt's superior, despises everyone equally, but in secret, he tries to protect his men from their officers, men like Captain Dynamite Holmes, who wants to win the boxing championship more than anything, because it will advance his career. Captain Holmes orders the company to give Prewitt The Treatment, and they punish him mercilessly. But Prewitt still refuses to fight. He will not break the solemn vow he made to himself. So he suffers The Treatment in dignified silence.

Staff Sergeant Warden watches all of this, doing what he can when he can to protect the stubborn, prideful, ignorant soldier in his care, who hasn't learned yet that he is nothing but a number. Warden despises Captain Holmes, and thinks one day he'll make a fine general.

"Good generals had to have the type of mind that saw all men as masses, as numerical groups of Infantry, Artillery, and mortars that could be added and subtracted and understood on paper. They had to be able to see men as abstractions that they worked on paper with. They had to be like Blackjack Pershing who could be worried about the morality of his troops in France so much he tried to outlaw whorehouses to save their mothers heartache, but who was proud of them when they died in battle."

Here, I thought, as my heart started to pound inside my chest, was a tiny corner of James Jones's Higher Truth revealed.

When Prewitt, after suffering The Treatment for several weeks, plays taps at lights-out in the Schofield Barracks quadrangle, the hairs on my arms stood up, as if electrified.

"This is the song of the men who have no place, played by a man who has never had a place, and can therefore play it . . . This is the song you drink five martinis every evening not to hear . . . This is the song you'll listen to on the day you die. When you lay there in the bed and sweat it out, and know that all the doctors and nurses and weeping friends dont mean a thing and cant help you any, cant save you one small bitter taste of it, because you are the one that's dying and not them."

Was that how *he*'d felt, lying in the hospital those last few days?

A few weeks after my father's memorial service at the Bridge-hampton Community House, I received a phone call from Leo Bookman, an agent at the William Morris Agency. He'd seen my picture in the *New York Times*, taken with Lauren Bacall when we were coming out of the service. He told me he'd discovered Candice Bergen and thought I had "that look." Would I come to New York to meet him?

I look attractive in that picture. I'd lost twenty pounds over the preceding two months and weighed less than a hundred pounds. Being too thin is usually a good thing for photographs.

I took the train into the City by myself and went to the William Morris offices on Sixth Avenue. Leo Bookman had a corner office with floor-to-ceiling windows overlooking the New York skyline. He asked if I'd give up my plans to go to Wesleyan if I got a part, say, on a soap opera—I could perhaps take a couple of night courses at NYU if it meant that much to me. Without even thinking about it, I balked. I told him I'd promised my father I'd go to college and that was what I was going to do.

"Too bad," he said with a rueful smile. "I could have made you a star."

On the train going home, I put *From Here to Eternity* down on the seat beside me as the conductor, an aging man in a blue uniform, probably a veteran, came over to punch my ticket.

"Great book," he said, handing me back my ticket and nodding toward my book on the seat. "Best book I ever read."

He moved away, down the corridor between the seats, punching tickets, talking to passengers, his hips bouncing against the backrests. I was so stunned I couldn't find the words to tell him my father had written it.

Next I read *The Thin Red Line*.

Private Bell, missing his wife, wanting to survive, after his first combat experience on Guadalcanal, reflects, "Nothing had been decided, nobody had learned anything. But most important of all, nothing had ended." He suddenly understands with soul-shattering clarity that there is no way in hell he can survive. He is only a number, a statistic, and his individual life counts not at all.

And yet—every one of them, the common foot soldiers, including Bell, soldier on. They know, they understand now, that the individual does not count, and has not counted since rich men figured out how to send their minions into battle to gain more riches. The buck-ass privates, as James Jones called them, were not fooled into believing for a second that what they were doing was fighting for Freedom, or Liberty, or The Pursuit of the American Dream. Their pointless pride, their self-annihilating loyalty, is not for their superior officers but for their companions.

Bell and his buddies throw themselves in front of bullets to protect one another, and to prove to themselves that they are not cowards. And the truly best fighting machines, the fearless ones, are the sociopaths, the ones who see the whole thing as a child's game of cowboys and Indians, who've never had so much fun or been given so much power in their lives. They try to one-up one another, for a stripe, for a promotion, for a medal—some of them even collecting enemy trophies, like ears—and their commanding officers stare at them with distaste, and a certain begrudging admiration.

Jamie had asked our father once, "How come you never show us your medals, Daddy?" He went up to his office and dug them out. He had two medals. A Purple Heart, for the head wound he received on Guadalcanal; and a Bronze Star. He explained, in a strange, distant, hollow tone, that they were not for display. Common foot soldiers never wore their medals, only their Combat Infantryman Badge; it was a matter of pride. He showed us that too. A plain, thin, rectangular blue pin with an embossed rifle, surrounded by a laurel wreath.

We knew the story of the Bronze Star—not from him but from our mother. A soldier from his company had taken machine gun bullets to the stomach. He lay in plain view of the Japanese pill-boxes, screaming, trying to hold in his intestines with his hands.

Two medics who'd tried to assist him had already been killed. My father, furious, ran from his position of safety, zigzagging like crazy until he reached the poor soldier and shot him up with the medics' morphine. For this, he'd been awarded the Bronze Star.

I found the scene in *The Thin Red Line*. It is not a private but Sergeant Welsh, our old pal Warden from *Eternity* in his new, crazier, meaner, drunker incarnation, who runs down to the screaming soldier. When Captain Stein tells Welsh he's going to recommend him for the Silver Star—a higher medal than the Bronze Star—Welsh replies, "If you say one word to thank me, I will punch you square in the nose. Right now, right here."

Neither of the two biographies of my father that came out in the early eighties mention this Bronze Star—nor do any of his papers—though the medal rests in its original box in the James Jones archives at the Harry Ransom Center at the University of Texas in Austin. My father wrote a sentence or two about it in *WWII*, saying it had been given to him randomly and arbitrarily. But when it had been offered, he'd taken it, not like his character Sergeant Welsh, who says Fuck You to the entire world.

When he was on Guadalcanal, my father killed a man in hand-to-hand combat. This scene is also in *The Thin Red Line*. In the novel, the calamity happens to the skinny, terrified Private Beade. It is the only documentation of the event in existence, as far as I know.

By the time my father's division, the Twenty-fifth Infantry, showed up on Guadalcanal, the U.S. Marines had already beaten the Japanese back and broken their supply lines. They were starving to death and dying of malaria by the thousands. But they still held on, hiding in bunkers and in the jungle, fighting on, unwilling to retreat, refusing to surrender. The starving Japanese soldier crept out of the jungle in his filthy fatigues and attacked my father while he was squatting to relieve himself. My father was forced to kill the soldier by wrenching his bayoneted rifle from his hands and bashing him in the head and chest with the butt. They were both afraid to shoot the gun, which might draw more soldiers—Jap or Yank—lurking in the dense, almost impenetrable jungle.

My father found the soldier's wallet in his pocket, a small, slim, red false-leather wallet with a thin black-and-white photograph of a young Japanese woman holding a baby in her arms. I had seen the wallet once, perhaps ten years earlier in Paris, when in a mournful and fragile moment, he'd taken it out of its hiding place and sat at the dining room table, looking at it.

For the rest of my father's life, he was haunted by the killing of this Japanese soldier. After he was sent back to the States for surgery on some torn ligaments in his ankle, he told his superior officers he would not fight anymore. They threw him in the stockade. They thought he'd lost his mind.

So what happens to these soldiers, if they survive, when they go home? That is the subject of *Whistle*, the last book of James Jones's trilogy, which I did not read in its entirety until it was published, much later in the fall of my freshman year of college. That book is about the return to the States of his four main characters, wounded during the fighting in the New Georgia campaign.

While they all recover from their physical wounds, none of them is able to survive his experience of war, and his reentry into society.

I went off to Wesleyan on Labor Day weekend and realized, after talking to other students, that I knew very little about anything. I believed I'd gotten into Wesleyan because of who my father was, not because I deserved it. My dad had even written my college application essay. I'd sat next to his big leather office chair, engulfed in the smoke from his fat Cuban cigar, watching him type it out on his IBM Selectric II. He used the word *avocation* when describing my interest in stage acting. "Do you know what that means?" No, I didn't know what that word meant. "Well you should. It means an interest outside of your main line of work. Like acting, for you."

I timidly asked if it was okay for him to be doing this.

"Those goddamn New York millionaires probably hire people to do this shit for their kids. Why shouldn't I help you?"

But now he was gone. During my first few months of college, I felt like a person wandering around in the dark, fumbling for a light switch. I got plastered every night, but was up at eight in the morning to make my Russian language class at nine. Some weird fuel made up of rage and fear kept me going, and constantly on my guard.

As the orphaned child of a renowned doctor might search for answers in the pursuit of medicine, I was naturally drawn to literature and immediately registered for a course in twentieth-century literature. On the first day, a gentleman with a graying goatee and little glasses got up before the class of a hundred students and recited a poem:

> *Others because you did not keep*
> *That deep-sworn vow have been friends of mine;*
> *Yet always when I look death in the face,*
> *When I clamber to the heights of sleep,*
> *Or when I grow excited with wine,*
> *Suddenly I meet your face.*

By the fourth line, the professor's voice cracked. By the last line, a tear trickled down his face. "Yeats," he managed to say. Wow, I thought. How many years had this man been teaching kids who couldn't care less? Teaching the same poems over and over again. And yet, they still brought tears to his eyes. I knew he was the teacher for me. The next day I went to visit him during his office hours—Professor George Creeger, on the top floor of one of the old houses that made up the English Department.

I didn't see any reason to hold back, so I told him everything. I told him who my father was, and how I'd decided to stay home with him and go to public school in East Hampton rather than go away to prep school, because he was sick and I wanted to be near him. I explained that my first written language was French, that I'd gotten into Wesleyan because of my acting background but that I no longer had it in me to act, and that I didn't know how to write a literature paper, but if he'd show me, I'd do my best. He spent several hours with me, explaining the structure of a three-page paper. My first effort was on Hemingway's "Big Two-Hearted River." He gave me a B+. On my next one, I got an A.

I found several such brilliant, kindhearted guides that year, and under their mentorship, I began to read in earnest. For an entire semester my sophomore year, I studied Tolstoy with my Russian language professor, Duffy White.

One evening in the library, lying in a big, square fauteuil with my feet up, I was reading the scene in *War and Peace* when Prince Andrej dies, and it was as if Tolstoy had reached out to me personally, across a continent, an ocean, and more than a century, and touched me on the shoulder. It was another light twinkling through the darkness.

During the 1812 battle of Borodino, Prince Andrej is wounded in the thigh, and an infection develops. He is taken in by the Rostovs and spends his last days surrounded by his beloved Natasha Rostova, her parents, his own sister Princess Marya, and his little son from his first marriage. Feverish and weak, Prince Andrej slowly begins to slip away from them.

He dreams he is lying in the room he is lying in, when the heavy double doors begin to open. Prince Andrej knows it is death trying to get in, and in the dream, in abject terror, he gets up and with all his will and might, attempts to push the doors closed. He is unable to lock them, and after a last valiant effort, "It entered, and it was *death,* and Prince Andrew died.

"But at the instant he died, Prince Andrew remembered that he was asleep, and at the very instant he died, having made an effort, he awoke."

But he awakens liberated from his body and his bodily concerns, and while he attempts to show interest in his family, he is simply going through the rituals required of him before his heart stops beating forever. He is released from his earthly cares, and feels only lightness, and an overwhelming love for all of humanity. He becomes a part of the greater firmament, and no longer feels anguish, fear, or pain.

I read the passage again, and remembered what my father had told us as he lay in his hospital bed after that terrible night, two days before he died. After I'd read the scene for a third time, and stopped the crying that had overwhelmed me, my first lucid thought was, How did Tolstoy do this? This Russian count who had about as much in common with me as an airplane had with a fly, had obviously lost someone and knew what it was to grieve; he had thought long and hard about it, and sometime between 1863 and 1866, he had written it down.

And I understood why my father had been so distant and vague his last few days. He had finally been at peace, and it was not that he didn't care or love us, but that he was letting go. I felt an enormous sense of relief as I realized—it is those who are left behind who suffer, not the person who dies.

I could feel the hairs on my arms standing on end, as if I'd been plugged into a wall socket. It was a feeling I continue to have to this day when I stumble upon a great truth, revealed on the page by a great mind.

Now I had a direction. I would follow the writers who had come before my father, and the ones who would come after. They would have to take his place as my guides. I began to feel a tenuous sense of hope.

I called my mother the next day and asked what my father had thought of *War and Peace*. She said he'd read it several times and had studied the battle scenes in careful detail while he was writing *The Thin Red Line*.

My senior year, I applied for a coveted spot in a literature seminar called War as Told, taught by the renowned scholar Khachig Tololyan. *The Thin Red Line* was on the reading list, at the time the only course at Wesleyan that included any of my father's works.

On the first day of class, when Dr. Tololyan handed out the syllabus, I saw he'd changed the reading list. Now, instead of *The Thin Red Line*, we would be reading Norman Mailer's *The Naked and the Dead*.

Obviously, Dr. Tololyan had been forewarned.

On the very last day, we had a party. After several glasses of wine, I started to feel brave and righteous. I went up to Dr. Tololyan and asked, "Did you change the reading list on my account, sir?"

He responded that he'd thought it would be too difficult for me if people didn't like the book. That it might get too personal. He opted against provoking any possible friction or emotional scenes in his class.

"I think it's a better novel than *The Naked and the Dead*," I said.

"Do you, now?" he said with a slight smile.

"I do. And I could have told you things about the book and what he was thinking when he wrote it that might have interested you."

He did not look pleased, but it was the last day of class, and I didn't really care if I got an A or an A- (he gave me an A-). So I smiled and turned away, in search of another glass of wine.

Several years later, I met Herbert Mitgang at the poet William Jay Smith's apartment on East End Avenue in New York. I was holding a vodka on the rocks, and the impulse to throw the drink in Mr. Mitgang's face was so strong my hand started to tremble. He looked questioningly into my eyes as he shook my other hand, and I stared back at him with all the pent-up rage I'd bottled up over the years.

I didn't do it. I didn't do it because I didn't want to embarrass my kind host, nor his son Greg, who was a good friend of mine.

I got blind drunk that night and then went home and cried, because I hadn't had the courage to defend my father.

"And for God's Sake Don't Fuck Frank Sinatra"

Here is the only humorous anecdote surrounding my father's death my mother ever told.

→→   ←←

My mother adored Lauren Bacall, known as Betty to her close friends, and they had been good friends for many years. Gloria thought Betty Bacall was the most beautiful woman she'd ever met, and she admired Betty because Betty was completely down-to-earth and suffered no flattery from sycophants.

For several days after my father died, my mother, lying with a bottle of scotch on the couch in the living room, refused to budge. Someone called Betty Bacall, who arrived like the cavalry. Taking the situation in hand, she said to Gloria, "All right, Moss. You don't have to get up now, but you will soon. I went through it with Bogie and I know exactly how you feel. Here's what you do: nothing. No impulsive decisions, no rash moves. Don't start giving stuff away that you'll regret later. Don't sell the house. Don't do anything stupid and for God's sake, don't fuck Frank Sinatra."

Betty was of course referring to her own disastrous rebound relationship with Sinatra in the wake of Humphrey Bogart's death. Gloria started to laugh. She laughed so hard she had to sit up to avoid choking, and from there, she finally got up and had something to eat.

Two days later the phone rang. Gloria picked up.

"Hi, Moss, it's Frank."

"Frank who?" she said.

"Frank who the hell do you think? Sinatra." They had been friends for many years, but it seemed absurd to her that he'd automatically assume there were no other Franks of importance in her life.

After a pause, he said, "I called to say I'm so sorry about Jim. Do you need me to come out there?"

"Uh . . ."

To his great astonishment, she started to giggle, and couldn't stop.

CHAPTER FIVE

⇢⇢ Birth of a Writer ⇠⇠

AS A CHILD AND TEENAGER, I wanted to be an actor, and my father had been all for it, but he urged me to get an education first. He believed that knowledge was the greatest weapon against hypocrisy and cruelty. The problem was, the older I got and the more I learned, the more hypocrisy and cruelty I saw, and the less protected I felt, for he, my father, had always shielded me from hypocrisy and cruelty, and now he was gone.

I have a framed, yellowing copy of my first published oeuvre, a poem called "Fresh Fruit of Autumn Leaves," which at five years old I had composed for my mother while we were having a bath. I was standing in her sunken tub, covered in bubbles. The idea came to me from the bubbles dropping slowly from my outstretched hands like leaves falling from a tree. My mother jumped out of the tub, grabbed a pen and paper, and asked me to repeat what I'd said. I was just learning to read and couldn't write yet. My father, so moved by this effort, sent my poem to the *Carolina Israelite*—why this publication, I'll never know—and they published it. Even at age five, I was not so easily fooled; the poem is no doubt a fine effort for a five-year-old. But I knew it never would have gotten published if my father hadn't been James Jones.

. . .

My eighth-grade English teacher at the École Active Bilingue, Mrs. Kessler, is also responsible for fueling my desire to write. At the beginning of the school year, she announced a short-story contest and said she would read the two winners aloud in class. I was one of them. My story was about a little girl's stuffed animals coming to life during the full moon and revolting against her cruel treatment by attempting to run away. The other winner was Peter Calahan, who wrote a story about two boys playing war with toy rifles the afternoon they find out their older brother has been killed in Vietnam. His story was much better than mine.

But mostly I like to blame Daniel Stern, the novelist and short-story writer who taught writing at Wesleyan. He was an old friend of my parents, and having taken a personal interest in me, he suggested Wesleyan as a good college for me. Once I was there, he urged me to register for his Composition 101 writing class. My first effort was a sensory exercise in which I wrote about walking to the school bus early one morning in Miami, and smelling the first raindrops hitting the hot asphalt. I was overcome by a feeling of lightness and warmth, before I realized it was the smell of Paris on a warm spring day, which just as quickly dissipated as I approached the school bus and found myself standing in a cloud of mosquitoes.

Danny pulled me out of the class and said, "You don't need Comp 101. I want you to write fiction."

During the fall semester of my junior year, in 1979, I hit an emotional wall. But giving a psychological label to this beast—"depression"—doesn't begin to describe it. The cold sweats, sick stomach, dry mouth, shaking hands, emotional paralysis, and intense agoraphobia perhaps parallel most closely the downward turn of a cocaine binge, when the gathered partiers start running around frantically, looking under the sofa cushions and then through their wallets and then pooling their pennies to buy more.

Strangely enough, with cocaine, I could go right to bed when the drugs ran out, while my friends would gnash their teeth and be brought to tears by the need for more. For me, running out of coke was nothing—*nothing*—compared with this dread I lived with.

I decided to go back to Paris for the spring semester, thinking being back home would help me. But Paris was no longer home. The hostage crisis in Iran was at its peak. Everyone hated Americans. The exchange rate for the dollar was the lowest it had been in my lifetime.

I met a lovely Frenchman, a banker who could have solved all my problems. But on our second date in a restaurant on the quai across from Notre-Dame, after a little too much wine, he seemed to forget I was American and launched into a tirade about Americans being imperialists with a fascist agenda. Furious, I told him that the U.S. Army lost more than three thousand men on Omaha Beach alone on D-day. "And what for?" I said. "To save your sorry French asses because you couldn't do it yourselves." His tough countenance collapsed, and the look of hurt and shame on his face made me feel suddenly terrible. I apologized, but it was too late. He never called me again.

It was a bad time to be in Paris, and I was running out of money. I called my mother and she called our good friend William Styron, who was coming to Paris to see his French editor about *Sophie's Choice*. She asked him to bring me $3,000 worth of American Express traveler's checks.

A year before, while Bill, Rose, my mother, Jamie, and I were sitting in the back of a limo on our way to the L.A. premiere of the *From Here to Eternity* television miniseries, Bill turned to me and asked, "I need to know something for my book. How do you say 'you have a hard-on' in French?" Eighteen years old, I promptly responded, without blinking an eye, *"Tu bandes."* No one in the car seemed to find this exchange inappropriate; when it came to literature and the writing process, art came first, above propriety and decorum, and everything else. Later, I found the reference in *Sophie's Choice*. Sophie says this to young Stingo, who gets a hard-on while lying next to her bathing-suit-clad form on the beach.

In Paris, Bill took me to dinner at a small, darkly lit *auberge*-like restaurant and ordered a bottle of expensive red wine. We drank two of these, and our conversation during the meal is hazy in my mind. He had been one of my father's closest friends, and I basked in a feeling of safety just being in his illustrious company. To eat well, drink well, and be cared for was a momentary reprieve in a raging storm. Toward the end of the evening, when we were sipping cognac, he asked me to go to bed with him. I laughed and said lightly, "But, Bill, I really think of you as family. And my father would roll over in his grave!"

And he replied, completely serious, "Let him roll."

I didn't want to hurt his feelings, but really, sleeping with him was not something that had ever even fleetingly crossed my mind. "I love you and admire you so much, Bill, but really, that would be like incest."

It was all said in a bon vivant tone, but I was in the middle of the worst emotional crisis I'd ever faced. I was never able to completely understand or accept the ramifications of this strange exchange. For me, the aftershocks went on for years and years. What was he thinking about? Was it a compulsion, an addiction, that drove him to suggest such a thing? One thing I know absolutely: if my father had known that Bill was going to proposition his nineteen-year-old, grief-stricken daughter, he would have beaten the living shit out of him, sick or not.

This was a turning point because I understood now how completely alone I was. My father's memory was not powerful enough to protect me. I longed to go home to Sagaponack.

. . .

It is worth going into more detail here on the way Gloria ran her household. After our father died, my brother and I were spoiled rotten in many ways. We didn't have to pay for anything or answer to anyone; on any summer weekend, we would throw all-night parties, free-for-alls with the inevitable skinny-dip in the pool, or dancing in the big kitchen with the music blasting, which didn't bother Gloria in the least because she'd be out at her own parties, or dancing right along with us, or passed out upstairs.

My mother was also capable of amazing generosity. In the summer of 1980, Max Mosolino, the second oldest of Gloria's nephews, who was around the same age as Jamie and me and had been living in a sleeping bag on the beach in Florida, called my mother in desperation. He told her about the unrestrained physical and emotional abuse he'd suffered at the hands of his mother, who was a serious drunk. Then his father, my mother's brother, Mark, left his wife and married another woman who was even worse, and that was who Max was running from. Gloria immediately wired Max money, and he arrived on a Greyhound bus. Max at the time was into bodybuilding, so his smallish head looked tiny on top of his massive shoulders and arms. Gloria helped Max get into Southampton College, got him a job as an apprentice on a local building crew, and just like that, he became a member of our family. A little while later, his youngest brother, Michael, who was around fifteen, showed up at Gloria's door, and she took him in too and got him registered at East Hampton High School. Not long after that, Anne, the youngest sibling and the only girl, moved in as well.

Michael and Anne, as the youngest, seemed to have suffered the most as their mother's drinking progressed. I told my mother I thought they needed therapy, but she thought that was a ridiculous overreaction and simply let us all run wild through her house. My mother was wonderful at grand gestures but truly abominable at follow-through.

Someone had to feed all these people, and my mother, while happy to pay the bills, wasn't volunteering, so with the help of Craig Claiborne's *New York Times Cookbook*, I took on the task. As soon as my mother saw I was preparing a meal, she'd pick up the phone and start inviting people over for dinner. For a long time I thought Claiborne's portions were all wrong. It took me years to realize that Jamie, Max, and Michael ate like six people by themselves. So I simply tripled Claiborne's recipes, but no matter how much food I made, it was all gone by the end of the evening. My ability to estimate portions when cooking has never completely recovered.

Eventually, Max moved to Connecticut and began to make a living as a foreman in a major construction company; and Michael and Anne moved into a small house down the street. But they were constantly over. Michael, who wanted to become a chef, would walk in and "borrow" cooking utensils and pots and pans, and never return them, so that, in the middle of boiling spaghetti, I'd be searching for the colander, and my mother would say, with total indifference, "Michael took it." From then on, whenever someone couldn't find something in the house, someone would say "Michael took it," and everyone would laugh.

Sometime in 1980, Nelson Algren moved into a little house in one of the less elegant neighborhoods of Sag Harbor, about five miles from my mother's house in Sagaponack. Nelson's illustrious career had spanned many decades. He'd written novels and short stories about the downtrodden, the poor, the merciless, and he was a World War II veteran. Today he is perhaps best remembered as the passion of Simone de Beauvoir's life. When he moved to Sag Harbor, he was alone and penniless.

The local writing community took great pains to make him feel welcome. He came to Christmas dinner at my mother's house that year. He was a heavy, red-nosed, balding, morose man, and it was hard to imagine him eliciting such passion in Simone de Beauvoir. Recently, I found a picture on the Internet of Nelson Algren in his thirties. What a good-looking, strong, intelligent face! He resembles the young George C. Scott. No wonder Simone fell for him. Sartre looks like a pansy by comparison. But maybe Simone had had enough of sexy, brawny, tough young Americans by the time she got to Sartre.

In any case, I had just submitted my application to the Columbia MFA program in writing, and this became, for a while, the topic of conversation at the Christmas dinner table.

My mother's house was very popular with my friends and Jamie's, as well as with the older set, because my mother was an equal opportunity drinker—everyone was welcome to imbibe as much and stay as late as they wanted, and the next morning it was not unusual to find people passed out on the couch. That night we got blasted on excellent martinis, the Stolichnaya vodka a Christmas gift from a guest. Quite late, it was discovered that Nelson's ride had departed, and someone had to drive him home. Jamie was already asleep. Since I was the best drunk driver of the group and could still see somewhat straight, I was conscripted. Someone helped him into the car and I got in behind the wheel. That someone got in back, but for the life of me, I can't remember who it was. I can, however, remember what proceeded almost perfectly.

As I concentrated on the dark road that twisted through scrub oak woods, Nelson suddenly broke the silence. "Why do you want to be a writer?"

"I don't know if I want to be a writer," I told him.

"Good," he muttered. "Don't become a writer."

"I'm just going to study writing," I said, feeling that this was a worthy pursuit and who was he to tell me what to do.

"Good. Study all you want, just don't become a writer. It's a lousy, stupid thing to do. You start out thinking people are going to admire you and love you and respect you but really nobody gives a shit. It's a terrible life. And look at you, you're young, you're beautiful. First of all, what the hell do you have to write about?"

I began vaguely, through my drunken haze, to take offense. I hated when older people who'd done things like survive wars told me I hadn't suffered enough, hadn't felt enough pain to have anything to say. Fuck them and their wars anyway!

"Well, I could write about losing my father at sixteen and what that was like," I retorted, my voice getting a hard, defensive edge.

"Yes, that was terrible. But you don't want to stay in that for the rest of your life, do you? Why, you could do anything you want!"

"Well, but what if writing's the only thing I'm good at?" I responded, starting to cry now, feeling sorry for myself. "What if I do have something to say?"

"That's what they all think," he mumbled, leaning up against the window, his breath fogging up the glass. "And even if you do, who's listening? Who cares? The novel is dead."

By the time we pulled into his driveway, I was sobbing. "The novel isn't dead! The novel is not dead!" I kept muttering. He fumbled for the door handle. My friend in the back and I got out and came around to help him. I tried to wipe my face with my coat sleeve. I cried so easily when I was blasted; it was a great relief, unleashing all of my pent-up sadness.

"Don't become a writer," Nelson repeated, leaning against me with his index finger pointed toward my face. He stared at me with great solemnity as we walked him up the dark footpath. The entire house was dark, except for a lonely yellow light that cast a small half-circle at the foot of the door.

"Well, then." He turned away and started to climb the front steps, his back stooped, his steps heavy and labored. "Then go ahead and write, see if anyone cares."

That was the last time I saw him. I went back to Wesleyan for my final semester. Nelson died on May 9, 1981—four years to the day after my father—having made no provisions for himself.

My mother told me over the phone that she was paying for Nelson's funeral. He had absolutely nothing left.

In the spring, right around the time I received my acceptance to Columbia's MFA Program in Writing, I got another call from Leo Bookman, the William Morris agent. He'd tracked me down in my student residence at Wesleyan. "Hi, Kaylie, it's Leo. Remember me?"

How could I forget?

"What are you doing for the rest of your life?" He'd been waiting for me to graduate from college so I could take up my acting career in earnest. I told him I'd meet him and talk it over in a month or so, when school was over.

In July, we met for drinks on the terrace of a brilliantly white, sprawling estate in Southampton that belonged to a friend of his. He was in tennis whites, and I wore a long and not too revealing sleeveless summer dress and espadrilles.

"So, are you ready to start taking this seriously?"

This estate, with its expansive, emerald green lawn and a view of the sand dunes and shimmering ocean beyond, made my mouth water with a vague but sharp feeling of longing. Perhaps I longed for my childhood, for exquisite meals on the bright, parasol-clad terraces of glamorous European hotels, or the feeling of safety when I remembered the summer and winter vacations we took, the hilarity of long meals at tables crowded with luminaries of the literary and film worlds. I had lost that life when I lost my father. Without him, those worlds had come to mean absolutely nothing to me but loss. And what would it cost me, to get it all back? My dad had warned me a long time ago that in show business, people would flatter you, and if you were vain and stupid, you'd buy their lies.

I blurted out, "I'm going to Columbia for graduate school in writing."

I could see that Leo was not impressed and probably thought this was an utterly ridiculous waste of time, but he tried to be patient with me. "Well, at least you'll be in New York. No reason you couldn't do both."

Under his direction, in the early fall, I had some head shots taken, and went on a couple of auditions for commercials. One was for an acne cream, and as the bright lights and the merciless black eye of the camera trained on my face and I was asked to show great enthusiasm for how clear my face had become, I started to giggle.

I went home and called Leo Bookman. I thanked him profusely for his time and kindness, but told him I was going to stick to writing.

My mother was pleased that I was accepted into Columbia, and she urged me to "get around campus a little, meet some future doctors and lawyers." When I pointed out that my father had once been a struggling writer who'd lived in a trailer, she looked at me as if I were completely insane. She fiercely distrusted anyone who had the hubris to even consider trying to make a living in the arts, except, of course, if they'd already found success. Then they were exempt from this harsh judgment. She was still convinced, and told me so at every possible occasion, that I'd never be able to take care of myself and was heading for a miserable life of drudgery and want, from which I could only be rescued by a very rich man. My mother, at this time, was financially secure, but she feared poverty obsessively. My father had indeed "written us out of debt," and Gloria was able to live quite comfortably on my father's literary estate, augmented by her salary at Doubleday, where she worked as an acquisitions editor. My mother always gave me money when I needed it. Always.

When it was time for me to start thinking about where to live in New York City, my mother did an incredibly generous thing: she lent me her one-bedroom apartment in the Delmonico on Park and Fifty-ninth Street, and for the three days a week she worked in New York, she stayed with her new boyfriend, Walker, in his mansard room in the Hotel des Artistes on West Sixty-seventh Street. She even allowed me to share her apartment with my college friend Carol, who had just started working for a Wall Street bank.

My mother's apartment was furnished with her friends' cast-offs—a brown velour fold-out love seat; a dry-bar made of some flimsy, pale wood; someone's old armchair; a large rectangular table of a light, lacquered wood and four caned chairs that looked like they'd come from some factory; and a few leftover odds and ends that had been stored in the basement of the Sagaponack house. It was a strangely appointed space, as if the persons staying there were only stopping by on their way to somewhere else.

For the next nine months, Carol and I turned the Delmonico apartment into party central, with people stopping by at all hours of the day and night. I'm still amazed we didn't get evicted.

I was certain I'd gotten into Columbia because I was James Jones's daughter. But at least graduate school would buy me two more years of study, to figure out what I wanted to do with my life. I would continue to have health insurance, and as long as I stayed in school, I received more than $500 a month from my father's Social Security benefits.

On the day I registered for classes, the secretary in the MFA office told me that the acceptance committee read the applications blind, with no names attached. I'd been awarded a $2,000 fellowship on the basis of my stories, which the kind lady now tried to talk me into giving up, since she figured James Jones's daughter must be rolling in dough. At the time, I had what was left of my share of the money Hollywood had paid us in 1978 for the television miniseries of *From Here to Eternity*, starring Natalie Wood as Karen Holmes, and the then-unknown Joe Pantoliano as Angelo Maggio, which had aired in the spring of 1979. The money had paid for three of my four years of college and was also going to pay for my $8,000-a-year graduate school. But it was dwindling quickly, and I refused to give up my fellowship.

When asked to choose a writing workshop, I checked off Richard Price because the name sounded vaguely familiar. I hadn't done my homework and confused him with Reynolds Price.

Straight out of college, and barely twenty-one, I walked into my first class in Dodge Hall on the Columbia campus with my new notebooks and a dark and loose, unassuming shirt over jeans, and waited patiently for the teacher to arrive.

"Okay, then, let's get started." This came from a pale young man sitting under the blackboard at the front of the room. He was very young, younger than at least half the students, and was wearing an old red T-shirt with one sleeve rolled up over a pack of Marlboros, his curly hair uncombed, a three-day growth of raggedy beard on his chin. We all stared at him. This was Richard Price?

Richard Price, who was barely thirty, had hit it big with *The Wanderers*, a first novel about the South Bronx. Of course, I didn't know this until I went to the bookstore later that day.

It was immediately apparent that he wasn't going to teach some wimpy college writing workshop; we were in the big leagues now. He was uproariously funny but mean as could be when he didn't like something. When he encountered what he saw as bad writing, he bit to the bone, without an ounce of compassion. Once, he held up a student's story—not mine, thank God—and shouted,

"This, this—*out the fucking window*!" And we all sat there in stunned silence as he chucked the pages across the room.

Two of the students he seemed to think the least of were Susan Minot and me. He seemed to think our privileged backgrounds had given us nothing to write about. He called our work "all dressed up and nowhere to go."

Richard's attitude was reverse prejudice, as far as I was concerned. I thought Susan Minot was the best writer in the program. Her short story "Lust," which later was published as the title story of an excellent collection, is still the best short story I've ever read on a young woman's search for compassion and intimacy in sexual encounters that do nothing, ultimately, but grind away at her soul.

My best friend at Columbia was Beverly Donofrio. We met at the first gathering, a party, and ended up as the only two dancing. Eleven years my senior, she was at thirty-two the mother of a fifteen-year-old boy, Jason. Bev was working on a book about growing up the nice Catholic daughter of a conservative Connecticut town sheriff, and getting pregnant and having a baby at seventeen. This book became the critically acclaimed memoir *Riding in Cars with Boys*, which later was a Hollywood film starring Drew Barrymore as Bev.

Bev and her son, Jason, lived on Avenue A and Twelfth Street, a drug-infested, perfectly terrifying neighborhood as far as I was concerned. When she invited me over for dinner, I would take a cab, have the cab drop me a block away, and pretend I'd taken the subway. Her buzzer was broken, so I had to call from a filthy pay phone on the corner, and she'd throw the key out the fourth-story window. An old gym sock would come spiraling down with the key in the toe, like a paratrooper with a broken parachute. One night, having had numerous bottles of wine with our pasta, Bev told me, "I was second in line for this two-thousand-dollar fellowship. They tried to get this rich girl to give it up but she wouldn't. You think it was Susan Minot?"

I felt so guilty it took me twenty-four years to tell her it was me.

At the end of our first semester at Columbia, our friend Dennis, who had the biggest apartment, threw the class party. I had terrible bronchitis, but there was no way I was going to miss the class party. I drank half a bottle of Mount Gay rum and pineapple juice before leaving (lots of vitamin C in pineapple juice) and brought the rest with me. Richard Price was sitting in the back room that had once been a maid's room, and like a psychologist receiving patients, took us in one by one for our end-of-term evaluation. I stood in the kitchen awaiting my turn, and drank several more Mount Gay rum and pineapple juices (for the vitamin C), then screwed up my courage and went in to talk to him.

I sat down in a chair across from the single bed where he was sitting and launched into my prepared speech.

"Listen, Richard, just because you had a hard childhood and came up on your own from nothing doesn't mean you have a right to judge everyone who didn't. I've had enough of people taking their shit out on me because I'm James Jones's daughter." As this came flying out, it occurred to me that I'd had a few too many Mount Gay and pineapple juices, but it was too late now. "You didn't give me a chance," I concluded in a softer tone, backpedaling furiously now. I opened my mouth to apologize, to explain that I was sick with bronchitis, when Richard said:

"You're right."

All I could do now was sit there, mouth agape. Maybe he was just tired and didn't feel like arguing, because this capitulation was very unlike him.

He said, "Take my class again next fall. I promise I'll give you a chance."

. . .

That summer I waitressed in a trendy restaurant called The Laundry in East Hampton. I was lucky to get the job. When I went for my interview, about nine people were waiting in line ahead of me. I knew the woman who was doing the hiring from the Spindrift Players, the theater group I'd been a member of all through high school. She gave me the job on the spot, even though I was much less qualified than most of the other applicants.

I was a lousy waitress and I didn't like the clientele, who were for the most part on the make, and cheap with tips. The depression I was now suffering from was as bad as any I'd experienced before. I began to drink even more because I couldn't stand the way I felt, but this did not help much.

My senior year of college, I had fallen in love for real, for the first time in my life. I had never truly believed that this could happen to a person in five minutes, and last for years and years, like being struck by a devastating illness. This young man, Aidan, this boy, really, was two years behind me at Wesleyan, though we were the same age. We'd met in September, in a mutual friend's dorm room during a party. He was little, only an inch or so taller than I. We sat down against a wall and started talking as if we'd known each other before, though we'd never met. A big guy bellowed, picked up a chair, and threw it across the room and I muttered, *"Quel con."* What an ass. Aidan answered in perfect French, *"C'est vrai, il est con."*

He told me he'd spent his childhood in French Africa and later in boarding school in Switzerland. The party was too loud so we moved out into the lobby of the dorm and sat there talking until the next morning. He told me his father was in the State Department and they'd lived in some pretty hairy places, countries on the verge of revolution and collapse. Once, they'd gotten thrown out of a central African nation, were given twenty-four hours to pack up their entire lives. They'd had to leave their dog, which had broken Aidan's heart. I could see the shadows of these experiences lurking behind his eyes, but his demeanor was calm and contained, and I thought, He's not afraid. When I started a thought, he finished it, as though he could see the pictures forming in my head before I could. He was not like anyone I'd ever been attracted to before. On Sunday afternoon, he called and told me in a low, calm voice he was feeling very strange. He hadn't slept and had butterflies in his stomach. "I think I'm in love," he said, as if he'd just witnessed a fascinating phenomenon, like a lunar eclipse. On Monday, I learned that he was a collegiate wrestler. He was in training, and his weight class was 125 pounds. To me this was totally unthinkable, appalling; this was only a few pounds more than I weighed. I was so afraid he'd get hurt I refused to go to his matches. He said he didn't mind. His old girlfriend went, though, and told everyone she thought I was a selfish bitch. On the days he wrestled, I walked around in a daze, praying to every god I could think of to protect him from harm.

I was going to wait for him to finish college; I wanted to be with him for the rest of my life. But two years is a very long time when you're in your early twenties. Now I'd been out of college a year, and he was finding his own way, making different friends. The more independent he became, the worse I acted. Now he was slowly cutting ties, and the love story was coming to an end in a miserable, slow, grinding way, and neither Aidan nor I had the courage to walk away.

Every evening, as the sun began its slow descent and The Laundry's utensils and glassware glowed like dying coals in the fading light, the bartender would play a Stevie Wonder song that made me want to bolt out the door screaming.

> *You've made my love a burning fire*
> *You're getting to be my one desire*

If only I could have said these words to Aidan, rather than punishing him for being two years behind me in college, for not wanting to spend every single weekend with me. I was cruel and acted out in ugly ways. I slept with strangers. I slept with friends. I said terrible, unforgivable things to him on the phone and then hung up. I couldn't seem to get control of my emotions or my behavior.

I was overwhelmed by a feeling of exhaustion similar to what one might experience with a low-grade fever. I felt a constant, gnawing fear, as if I were back in third grade in Paris and no one was there to pick me up. And no matter how many drinks I had after my shift was over, or if I went out dancing with my girlfriends or not, or if I went to bed with a stranger or not, the next morning the discomfort and fear was still there, gnawing at me from the inside, augmented tenfold by the alcohol I'd consumed the night before.

One evening, the wait staff was all abuzz because John Irving, who'd recently moved to the area, was having dinner there with his girlfriend, Rusty Unger, whom I'd met several times through my mother. She waved to me now across the crowded and noisy restaurant and I waved back.

Toward the end of my shift, as I was standing with my arms crossed waiting for my last table to leave, John Irving approached me. He was dark haired, tanned to the color of cured tobacco, of medium height with wide shoulders and muscular arms.

"Hi, I'm John Irving." He put out his hand and I shook it. "I just wanted to tell you that I loved your father's books, and it's an honor to meet you."

I almost fell over. The Laundry was always crawling with movie-star hopefuls, directors, producers, all kinds of people who wanted to be seen at one of the "in" restaurants of the Hamptons. Which of them would ever go up to a waitress and say something like that?

Another night in mid-July, Richard Price came in with a friend, quite late. I waited on their table. Richard looked right at me and didn't recognize me as he ordered a bottle of champagne. Perhaps it was the uniform—white shirt, black pants, an apron—and the fact that my hair was tied back in a tight bun. He seemed to have dressed for the Hamptons, wearing a button-down shirt, the first I'd ever seen him in.

I brought their champagne and said, "Hi, Richard."

He stared at me, dumbfounded.

"It's Kaylie," I said. He continued to stare at me. Nothing was registering. "Jones," I added, laughing, and took out my hair clip. "Recognize me now?"

"Holy shit," he said. "You got me totally out of context here." He introduced his friend. "She's one of my writing students at Columbia."

I couldn't have invented a better scenario for myself. Before him stood a poor girl, struggling through this miserable job to make ends meet. And here he thought I was an overprotected rich kid. I gloated to myself at this amazing stroke of luck.

I got the phone number where they were staying, and after discussing it with my mother the next morning, we invited Richard and his friend Bob for dinner that night.

My mother's boyfriend Walker had recently moved in with seven birds—two macaws, an African grey, and four green finches that woke up the whole house every morning as soon as the sun rose. The African grey had spent the first year of its life in the laundry room of Walker's East Hampton house, and the parrot would imitate the machines' cycles, running through the *chugga-chugga-chugga* of the washer's watery spinning, and the *beep, whoosha-whoosha* and *wheeeep* of the dryer.

Three of us kids were living in my mother's house that summer—Jamie, who was getting ready to start graduate school in Washington, D.C.; my mother's nephew Max Mosolino, who was attending Southampton College; and me. None of us could stand this boastful, arrogant Walker, but at least he kept Gloria from being lonely. Secretly, we'd each been attempting to teach the African grey new words.

When Richard and Bob arrived at cocktail hour, the macaws had been uncuffed from their perches and were striding importantly around the living room with their strange, awkward, splay-footed gait, staring threateningly at the guests out of the corners of their little black eyes, and squirting their weird, liquid shit that looked like Wite-Out all over my maternal grandmother the Dread Gertrude's very old and very bald Persian rug. Richard sat at the edge of the couch, and one of the macaws attacked his sneaker while the other tried to peck the Abyssinian cat, Pushkin, who fought back with a hiss and a left hook.

The African grey, stirred by the commotion, let loose in a bloodcurdling scream from its cage, *"SHUT UP, WALKER, YOU MOTHERFUCKER!"*

Richard threw himself backward into the couch.

Walker jumped up and went over to the cage to admonish the bird. He accused me of interfering with his bird training and told my mother to get control of her brood of brats. My mother laughed, lit a cigarette, and murmured to no one in particular, "I don't care," and sat there, giggling, her head enveloped in a shroud of smoke. This made me uncomfortable, so I lit a cigarette as well.

"I've seen a lot of things," Richard said in his deadpan way as he recovered his breath, hand over his heart, "but this—this is definitely new."

We stayed up talking late, and Richard told me to get a paper and pen, he was going to give me a reading list. He said, "You're educated, there's no question. You have a good grasp of the classics. Now I'm going to give you *my* reading list." He wanted me to read all these books between now and his workshop in the fall.

On the list were John Rechy's memoir of hustling in New York, *City of Night;* Toni Morrison's *Sula, Tar Baby,* and *Song of Solomon.* Also *Last Exit to Brooklyn,* by Hubert Selby Jr., who had been a mentor of Richard's; as well as *The Basketball Diaries,* by Jim Carroll, about his youth in upper Manhattan and his struggle with heroin addiction. The list was long—James T. Farrell's *Studs Lonigan,* William Kennedy's trilogy, *Legs, Billy Phelan's Greatest Game,* and *Ironweed*—all books I'd never read.

I went to the bookstore the next day and ordered them all. For the rest of the summer, I immersed myself in Richard's favorite books and found there were all kinds of wars raging on our planet, and there were as many kinds of cruelty and evil as paths to redemption and grace. My love for Aidan haunted me like a low-grade fever, and the only time I felt any kind of peace was when I was reading about other people's tragedies.

Aidan and I broke up for good in the beginning of October. For the first and only time in my life, I punched a girl in the face and knocked her down, on the corner of Sixth Avenue and Fifty-sixth Street, because she'd slept with Aidan and I'd considered her one of my best friends. I knew it was a revenge fuck on his part, but that didn't help. The next night I went out drinking with a Hamptons crew I knew from the summer. They were rich kids, just the kind of kids from famous, powerful families that my mother wanted me to associate with. I was not at my best. I was unbathed, in an old black T-shirt and black jeans, and already three-quarters tanked-up. We started at Isabella's, on the corner of Columbus and Seventy-seventh, and ended up many hours later barhopping up Second Avenue. One of their number, a fellow named Arthur, wore black lizard cowboy boots and an elegant sports jacket, and had cocaine, which he blew into my nose through a tiny cocktail straw in the stinky, hot, and close bathrooms of the various bars we visited.

When the bars closed we went back to his apartment and talked about death and the endings of relationships, and was suicide a viable option or not, until sometime the next morning, which was a Sunday. The garbage trucks were making their rounds, one of the most forlorn sounds I've ever heard. We took some Valium that he kept in the medicine cabinet, and before we passed out, I told him about Aidan and tried to explain that the pain of losing him seemed to me just as bad as when my father died, and I couldn't seem to separate the two events. Arthur dug through a drawer and pulled out a yellow legal pad containing his father's suicide note, written in a hasty and crooked hand. We both cried a little and I became afraid of this sudden, rushed intimacy.

Later, I went home and wrote, in one sitting, a story based on that night for Richard's next week's class. It was a blow-by-blow description of Arthur's and my all-night binge, and the feeling of running from one bar to the next and not being able to outrun the fear or the pain, and the sound of the Sunday-morning garbage trucks forcing us back to reality, like hitting a brick wall at full speed.

Our class met the afternoon of Halloween. Richard said my story was one of the best he'd ever read in a workshop, and gave me several names of magazine editors to send it to. For the first time, I believed I had a real chance. Richard had been my harshest critic.

I went straight from the workshop to a party at an apartment with a huge second-floor terrace overlooking the annual, wild Halloween parade on Christopher Street. All the people at the party were bankers, and I tried to explain what had happened to me that day, but their faces remained blank and mildly perplexed and they quickly changed the subject. So I found myself a folding chair, drinking my way through a bottle of Mount Gay rum as every possible costume pranced by below. There was a six-foot-four Grace Kelly in a silver evening gown with a diamond-encrusted tiara, a hairy chest, blood dripping from her temple, and a broken steering wheel around her neck. The entire crew of the original *Star Trek* Starship *Enterprise* marched by on stilts and I screamed down, "LIVE LONG AND PROSPER!"

Marvin Gaye blasted from outdoor speakers, and every time I hear certain Marvin Gaye songs even now I am transported back to that night. For a few hours I felt like I had crossed in victory some important finish line and now stood looking back over my shoulder at the past and forward into the future, and realized I'd become a writer. It also occurred to me that if my father had lived, I would never have written. His death had broken me, and it was only through reading and writing that I had begun to heal myself.

A few weeks later my mother and I had dinner with Rose and Bill Styron at Elaine's. I thanked Bill again for bringing the American Express traveler's checks to Paris, but my heart skipped a beat at the shrouded memory of what he'd proposed to me that night. I also realized that though I was angry at him, I still loved him. He was one of the few direct connections I still had with my father, and I had wanted so much to learn about writing. I hadn't told a soul about that night, certainly not my mother. Bill now said with a chuckle that bringing unsigned traveler's checks had been totally illegal, and the bank teller had had to get the manager, with whom Bill had gotten a little sharp.

I told Bill about the story I'd written for Richard Price's class. I told him how Richard had interpreted as sexual the cocaine being blown up the girl's nose through the tiny cocktail straw. "What's so strange," I told Bill, "is that never occurred to me at all."

He thought about this for a while, nodding, then told me the following story.

There was an expert on Faulkner who wrote a long, convoluted article about the wisteria growing up and around the house in *The Sound and the Fury.* The expert had gone on for dozens of pages on the symbolism of the wisteria, how it represented the disintegration of the family and how the family was choking itself from within. When Faulkner was asked about it, he replied, "There was wisteria growing outside the house I grew up in, so I put it in the story."

I often share this anecdote with my writing students because it illustrates perfectly the writer's unconscious mind at work, and what a mess critics like to make of it.

"This Is Not the Chesa Grischuna"

This is a story of my mother's that sometimes made people laugh so hard they fell out of their dinner chairs.

When my father went to Vietnam in 1973 to do a series of articles for the *New York Times Magazine,* my mother took Jamie and me to Klosters, Switzerland, for two weeks during our winter vacation. She booked two rooms in a quaint if not quite elegant bed-and-breakfast chalet at the edge of town. Gloria shared a room with me, and Jamie had one down the hall. The hotel had two entrances, one on the ground floor right off the main street, and one around the corner and up a flight of stairs that led into the second floor. Never one for details, Gloria counted the floors to our room and never looked at the number on the door.

One night, after having gone out partying with her very good friend Irwin Shaw and his entourage at the Chesa Grischuna, Irwin's favorite hangout, an old-style, more elegant and more expensive hotel in the center of town, she came back to our hotel very, very late and very, very drunk. She went in by the second-floor entrance. She counted two flights, slipped into the unlocked room, and dropped her mink coat, her boots, her après-ski wear, her bra and panties on the floor, and got into bed, totally bare-assed naked. I was a light sleeper ("You know, Kaylie is such a neurotic"), and she was afraid I'd wake up and never go back to sleep. After a little while she started to hear a very loud and guttural snoring and reached over to feel if I was all right, and instead, felt a man's hairy chest.

"Kaylie?" she cried out.

A German matron sat up suddenly on the other side of her husband, switching on the light. "*Was ist das?*"

The wife, upon seeing a naked woman lying on the other side of her husband, started screaming. Gloria tried desperately to explain that she'd made a mistake, but she couldn't speak a word of German. She tried English, then French, to no avail.

The Germans saw no humor in this. Finally, Gloria covered her large breasts with one arm, slipped out of the bed, gathered up her discarded clothes, put her mink coat over her naked body, and tiptoed quietly out the door.

Unfortunately, she forgot her purse, and was caught. While an hour earlier she'd been afraid to wake me up, she now woke me by shaking me wildly and, in fits of uncontrollable laughter, told me the whole story. For me, the funniest part was seeing her so vulnerable.

The next morning, the big-boned Switzerdeutsch *hotelière* said to Gloria in a thick accent, "Madame, zese sings may happen at other hotels, but not at mine. Ve have no zuch behavior here, this is not the Chesa Grischuna."

It took the careful diplomacy of Marian Shaw, Irwin's ex-wife who also still lived in Klosters, to intervene on Gloria's behalf and calm the *hotelière* down.

CHAPTER SIX

The Black Hand of God

I VISITED ROBINSON, ILLINOIS, MY father's hometown, for the first time in early December 1982. I went with Frank MacShane, who was researching his biography of James Jones. I was in my second year at Columbia. My mother didn't want me to go, but for the sake of the biography, she didn't try to stop me. She thought I was a very peculiar girl to want to go and learn about a part of my father's life that she'd spent the last twenty-five years trying to obliterate. If she could have, she would have erased all of James Jones's life before he met her, nuked the southern half of Illinois. But even that might not have been enough to quell the anger she still felt at my father's lie about his relationship with Lowney Handy.

My father's time with the Handys caused his own family split. There was a skirmish, then a war, some long-lasting feud. My father never discussed what had caused the rift between him and his brother, Jeff. It had happened before he married my mother, and perhaps had something to do with his notoriety in Robinson and his peculiar living arrangement with the Handys, and the writers' colony that sprang from their relationship. Or maybe it had to do with my uncle Jeff also wanting to be a writer, and after the success of *From Here to Eternity*, my father tried to help Jeff get a novel published at Scribner's, but the book was turned down. I did not know this in 1982 but learned it from their letters, which I read for the first time many years later.

There was no question that the Handys' unorthodox colony fueled fear and resentment in the community. Lowney had even been accused of running a satanic cult. After my father was world famous and no one could touch him, he told a local newspaper, shortly after his marriage to Gloria, that they planned to start a Haitian-style voodoo church in Marshall, like the one in which they'd been married in Port-au-Prince. I'm amazed that people in Robinson and Marshall actually took his joke seriously.

I wanted to go to Robinson to learn about my roots, but I also wanted to help Frank MacShane write the best biography he could. I thought that by my accompanying him, the Robinson population might talk more honestly with him about my father's childhood and youth.

When Frank and I pulled into Robinson's town square, I found myself reliving the opening pages of my father's second novel, *Some Came Running*. It was like returning to a place I knew well, so vivid was the square in my mind—the utilitarian red-brick courthouse with its flat roof, surrounded by small stores, including the jewelry store, The Lobby bar, and the bank, all three important settings in the book.

After my father's discharge from the army hospital in Memphis in 1943, having blown all his back pay on a fancy suite in the Peabody Hotel and booze and girls, he received his papers to return to active duty, and went AWOL. Soldiers were being shipped off to England to prepare for the Normandy invasion, and he had no desire to kill anyone ever again. He also believed absolutely that his luck had run out, so he took off. Bumming around was not new to him. After he'd graduated from high school in 1939, he'd hit the road, hitchhiked his way to Canada.

As a twenty-one-year-old veteran, in 1943, he bummed around the country, jumped on freight trains, hitchhiked, and got along by doing odd jobs and hanging out with other wounded veterans, discharged or on the lam. One day, after a major drinking binge,

he woke up on a bus headed for Robinson. And this is exactly
what takes place in the opening of *Some Came Running,* except
in the novel, the war is over, and our protagonist, Dave Hirsh, is
returning home from the European Theater.

Once, when I was quite little and wouldn't eat my dinner, my father told an appalling story, which has stayed with me all my life.
When he was homeless, he'd go into bars and ask for a glass of
water, then fill the water with ketchup for something to eat. He'd
also stop at people's back doors around dinnertime and ask them
for their scraps. I was so horrified I cried for hours and I never
forgave him for telling me this, and it was on my mind when
Frank MacShane and I arrived in Robinson, population 6,700.
We parked in front of the *Robinson Daily News* office to meet the
publisher, Kent Lewis. As we stepped out of the car, the skies
opened up and it didn't stop raining for three days.

Lewis, a quiet, reserved, elderly gentleman, had a whole itin-
erary planned out for us. Within five minutes, the phone started
ringing. The entire town knew that the daughter of their prodigal
son had returned.

I met the old librarian, Vera Newlin, who had so carefully
guided my father's early reading. He'd arrive on his tricycle daily
and pester her for new books. By the time he was ten years old,
he'd read every book in the children's library and wanted access
to the adult books. Special permission was granted, and he was
allowed to read certain carefully chosen books, with no sex or
swearwords.

I was invited into the home of his longtime sweetheart, Annis
Flemming, the girl in his short story "The Valentine," who was
still beautiful, with exquisite black eyes and a fine, delicate bone
structure, though she was now in her midsixties. Her husband,
Hap, welcomed me with a gentle hug and a cup of tea. Annis con-
fided to me in a mere whisper that my grandmother, Ada Jones,

had been fed up with motherhood and had not wanted this second child, twelve years after Jeff was born. Ada had told Jim when he was little that she'd tried to kill him in the womb by throwing herself down the stairs. I realized, with a shiver, that my other grandmother, the Dread Gertrude, had told Gloria the same thing, except Gertrude had stuck a knitting needle up inside her. She told Gloria, "You were stubborn even then."

Later, when Jim was two or three, Annis said, Ada would tie him to a clothesline in the backyard and leave him there until nightfall. The neighbors, including Annis's mother, were concerned, but back then people minded their own business, and no one felt they had a right to interfere. "He was such a gentle, fragile boy." Annis took my hand in hers, which were warm and dry. "He was a bit of a show-off, but that was not really who he was inside. He was hurting so bad when he came back after the war," she said. "All the boys were like that when they came back."

My father's best and oldest childhood friend, Tinks Howe, and his wife, Helen, invited us to their house for dinner. They told the story of the day my father received the galley proofs of *From Here to Eternity*, and Burroughs Mitchell, the young editor who'd inherited James Jones after the death of the mighty Maxwell Perkins, asked my father to delete more than 350 swearwords from the manuscript. The publishers had already taken out most of the homosexual sex scenes, as well as the phrase *piece of ass*, substituting instead *piece of tail*. My father couldn't get the homosexual scenes back in, but he did put *piece of ass* back, in every case. Helen, Tinks, Lowney, and Jim sat around for days, going through each page, and while he was willing to negotiate on certain words, on others, he categorically refused to yield. During one of my dad's visits to New York, Burroughs Mitchell had told him that he'd been in the army during the war and he didn't remember the men talking like that at all. "Of course not," my father replied, "you were an officer."

Helen mentioned that when my father returned the galleys, he wrote a letter to Mitchell that said: "The things we change in this book for propriety's sake will in five years, or ten years, come in someone else's book anyway, that may not be as good as this one, and then we will kick ourselves for not having done it, and we will not have been first with this . . . and we will wonder why we thought we couldn't do it. Writing has to keep evolving into deeper honesty, like everything else, and you cannot stand on past precedent or theory, and still evolve. . . . You know there is nothing salacious in this book as well as I do. Therefore, whatever changes you want made along that line will be made for propriety, and propriety is a very inconstant thing."

My God, how did he know this? He was only twenty-nine years old!

Tinks Howe took me aside toward the end of the evening and murmured, "I never blamed Jim for leaving. I knew why he left and never looked back. I understood. And even though I never talked to him again, I always thought of him as my best friend."

The next day, as the deluge continued, Helen took me to visit an ancient woman with a pinched, parchment-like face, who'd been a friend of my grandmother's and a member of the Christian Science church Ada Jones had joined in middle age. There was something sanctimonious and frightening in the woman's glassy eyes as she told me with complete conviction that my grandmother had loved her little Jimmy and knew he was a special gift from God because God had come to her in a dream and told her so.

"Was that before or after she threw herself down the stairs to get rid of the pregnancy?" I asked the woman, my voice trembling with anger. Her eyes veered away from mine and off to the side, then up toward the ceiling, then came back at me, shiny and dense as marbles.

"Well that's just cruel gossip," she said. "There was never a finer, God-loving woman than Ada Jones."

She brought to mind another story, long forgotten. My father
had told me this, and I don't know what triggered it: when he
was about ten years old, his mother had caught him playing with
himself. Those were his words—"playing with myself." Ada told
him if he didn't stop he would turn black. He tried to stop, but it
was irresistible. While he was sleeping, she painted his right palm
black with indelible India ink. In the morning he tried to wash
off the spot but couldn't and was forced to go to school with the
telltale spot on his palm. He spent the whole day in an agony of
shame, trying to hide his hand in his pocket.

When he came home, Ada said, chuckling in a self-satisfied
way, "See, I told you, black as a nigger."

He'd told me he intended to write a short story about it, which
he would call "The Black Hand of God." He never did.

I asked Doug Lawhead, a young journalist and photographer for
the *Robinson Daily News*, if he could find out where my grandparents were buried. The next day, in the blinding rain, he drove me
to the cemetery. We stopped at the flower shop just beyond the
gates and I bought a bouquet of carnations and roses, the only
flowers they had that were not plastic. We got out of the car and
walked across the drenched grass until we came to a large, square
monument with JONES carved in the stone. Before the monument
were the graves of my great-grandparents, George W. Jones
and his wife, Christine. My father had told me a little about this
grandfather. He'd been a quarter Cherokee and had long black
hair that he only cut on the dark of the moon, which, he insisted,
is why it remained black till the day he died. He had been elected
town sheriff twice, and my father had adored him. About his
wife, I knew nothing at all. On the other side were my grandfather, James Ramon Jones; my grandmother, Ada Blessing Jones;
and Mary Ann Jones, my aunt who'd died in 1952, at the age of
twenty-seven, of a seizure brought on by night epilepsy.

The only information my father ever gave me on Mary Ann was that she'd died in her trailer on the Handy Colony grounds in Marshall, and that she'd "swallowed her tongue." He used to tell me when I was little, especially when Jamie and I fought, that he'd been mean to his sister and he regretted it every day. My father had put two stanzas of a poem by Edna St. Vincent Millay on her headstone: *Gently they go, the beautiful, the tender, the kind— Quietly they go, the intelligent, the witty, the brave . . .*

The Jones family monument had several empty plots, and I wondered for whom they'd been intended.

Standing there in the rain, I felt an enormous sense of responsibility. How did this boy, this strange, suffering boy, grow up here, flee, go to war, survive Guadalcanal, and return home to write not one, but four of the most important novels about World War II? Many soldiers had survived, and a few had written excellent books—but my father's were considered by common foot soldiers and war experts everywhere to portray the true experience of war. And I was his child, reared so far away from this place I had no connection to it, except for a few kind strangers, and five headstones in the town cemetery. I laid the flowers on Mary Ann's grave.

No one in Robinson wanted to talk about Mary Ann or her death. I was told during the next day, in a kind of indirect way, that some members of the Jones family, led by my great-uncle Charlie Jones, an upstanding, churchgoing, well-respected member of the community, had demanded an inquest. Uncle Charlie believed that Lowney had played a malevolent role in Mary Ann's death. People had hinted to me that Mary Ann was addicted to pills. My mother—not my father—had once told me that Mary Ann had married a black man, and the Upstanding Members of the family had stopped her estranged husband from attending the funeral. No one in Robinson would confirm anything about Mary Ann, except that she was kind, and pretty, and a complete mess. I have two sepia-toned photographs of my aunt. In them she is smiling, an overweight girl with the same pained eyes and square jaw and thin lips as my father.

The only fact I could ascertain conclusively was that the medical examiner had judged her death to be of natural causes, and no inquest was ever held.

I have a mimeographed letter from Uncle Charlie to my dad, dated shortly after Mary Ann's death. Its tone is so overblown, cruel, condescending, smug, and self-righteous that it is no wonder my father hated pretentious bores—he'd been forced to suffer this one for years.

I went to see my new friend Annis Flemming again, and she told me in confidence—and asked me not to tell Frank Mac-Shane—that my father had left town in 1939, in part because Uncle Charlie had "gotten into trouble with a young woman" and put the blame on Jim. I never found out any more, because every time I brought up the subject of "some kind of trouble with Uncle Charlie," I was met with that flat, blank, uniquely midwestern stare, as uninviting as a bramble-covered stone wall.

On Friday night, Frank and I went to check out The Lobby ("The Foyer" in *Some Came Running*), the long, loudly echoing bar and pool hall whose glass-fronted windows overlooked the square. After a while, Frank went back to the hotel and I stayed and drank and drank and drank. People came up all during the evening to shake hands, or to give me a piece of their mind. Some—the children and grandchildren of the characters my father had portrayed unfavorably in *Some Came Running*—wanted to pick a fight. I just gave them back their same flat, blank, midwestern stare—which I had seen my father use on more than a few occasions.

Twenty-five years later and the denizens of Robinson were still upset; my father sure must have hit a serious nerve, I thought.

The next morning, Frank MacShane and I drove the half hour to Marshall, to visit Lowney Handy's brothers, Earl and Andy Turner, and the house on the Colony grounds that my father had designed, and lived in, for most of the fifties.

Earl and Andy were strangely formal but generous with their time and their words about James Jones. They had a disconcerting parrot in a cage that kept screaming, "EARL! EARL!" as if the cage were on fire. They were, in fact, much kinder to us than I had any reason to expect. They still had the original manuscript of *From Here to Eternity*, but this didn't seem like the right moment to bring it up.

They seemed, like Tinks Howe, to understand very well why Jim had left. Lowney, they said, could be a very overbearing woman. The only thing they regretted was that Jim had not kept in touch.

My father's house in Marshall, which he built using his *From Here to Eternity* money, stood at the edge of the Colony grounds; the old wood cabins, now in ruins, still dotted the wooded landscape. Across the backyard, in the distance, was a brick fireplace—the only vestige of Lowney and Harry Handy's house, which had burned to the ground sometime in the sixties.

I noticed right away that my father's house had a similar feel to our home in Paris. He'd designed an enormous bathroom for himself, with a bare-chested mermaid on the shower glass, complete with a bidet, which, according to the present owner, was the first one in Crawford County. My father had also built a secret room behind a bookshelf. He'd always loved secret rooms and alcoves and large, extravagant bathrooms. It was strange to feel my father's presence so strongly in a house he'd walked away from with my mother in the summer of 1957, and never returned.

Frank MacShane's biography, *Into Eternity*, turned out to be a mediocre book. MacShane's research is for the most part competent, though he made some blatant mistakes. He found, and researched, the wrong Jones family in the Robinson courthouse archives, and therefore, all the Jones ancestry is incorrect. Ultimately, he seemed at a loss in understanding what made a man like James Jones tick. He divides my father's life into before and after his move to Paris, as if, somehow, by marrying Gloria, "a born party girl," and moving to Europe, my father had abandoned his old self and his midwestern ways and tried to climb above his station and become someone entirely different, someone erudite and suave. This view is nothing new—almost the entire Ivy League literary establishment took the same stance after the success of *From Here to Eternity*.

My father was absolutely and totally midwestern, and proud of it, and never for a second did he try to be anything else. What he had despised about the Midwest and wrote about in *Some Came Running* he had hated all along—the Puritanical hypocrisy, the greed and concern with upward mobility, and the social pretensions.

In Europe, my parents were free of all that, in a way that they were not in New York. He absolutely spent too much money living the high life. If Gloria wanted to spend the summer in Deauville or Biarritz, they did it. He was addicted to alcohol, yes. He worried constantly about money and what his next book would be. But he was deeply humble in the best ways a man can be humble—he felt he'd been lucky, and had been given a talent, and he worked harder and more constantly and consistently than anyone I've ever known, and he never took his good fortune for granted. He labored over his work, slowly, methodically; he wrote all of *The Thin Red Line* and *The Pistol* in France, as well as a good part of *Whistle*.

When I was in eighth grade at the École Active Bilingue in Paris, those of us who already spoke two languages were given the opportunity to study a third—Spanish, German, or Russian. I picked Russian because it was the weirdest and most alien, and had an incomprehensible alphabet that I thought would be fun to use for secret messages.

On the first day, a very old lady in a ratty sable coat and a tall, square fur hat walked in and introduced herself as Marina Zhukhovskaya. She told us her family had fled her beloved country when she was in her late teens, after those dirty Bolsheviks took over and destroyed everything. She spoke French with a heavy Russian accent and became teary-eyed as she described the snowy streets of Saint Petersburg and the winter droshky rides she'd enjoyed with her brother Petya, a real horseman, who'd been a lieutenant, killed fighting for the White Army during the Civil War. She recited Russian poems by heart in a fluid, deep voice and taught us how to speak and read from a funny children's book with colorful drawings. The first word I ever learned in Russian was *arbooz*—watermelon.

She took us out to a Russian Orthodox church service and then to lunch at a Russian restaurant on the right bank of the Seine. She ordered shots of vodka, and all six or seven of us twelve- and thirteen-year-olds had our first drink. We sipped carefully, as she instructed, toasting Russia and all things Russian—except those dirty Bolsheviks who had destroyed her glorious land.

When we moved back to the States in 1974, the high schools I attended didn't have Russian language courses, but Russian was the first class I signed up for at Wesleyan. I went to these classes religiously, even though they were at 9:00 A.M., and I was often more than slightly hungover. I studied Russian language and literature for more than ten years—in school, then college, then graduate school, and as a postgraduate at the Harriman Institute at Columbia University, and in Moscow for seven months, on two different occasions, at the Pushkin Institute.

During my summer of study in 1984, the American students at the Pushkin Institute threw a Fourth of July party for our instructors and monitors. Our own KGB Man, assigned to watch us and keep us out of trouble, brought a sleek, black air pistol to the party and set up some empty soda cans on a post about fifty yards off. He invited the American boys to try to shoot the cans, and they all dutifully lined up. None of them managed to make even one hit. I approached and asked if I could try. Our KGB Man was a self-proclaimed "old-fashioned Russian," which meant women should know their place and stay in it. He snickered politely as he handed me the pistol. He tried to show me how to hold it, and I just as politely declined his help. I aimed calmly, breathed deeply, as my father had taught me a long time ago, and fired. In three shots, I knocked over two of the cans.

"Daughter of a soldier," he said in Russian, with a smile. I nodded. He said he was the son of a soldier, and his father had fought in the Great Fatherland War.

"Mine as well," I responded.

"But our war was much worse than your war," he said. All Russians said this, and it was undoubtedly true. They lost 15,000,000 people (a low estimate), many of them civilians, while we Americans lost 405,000, almost all soldiers.

I stood there, remembering how my father could never sleep for more than a few hours at a clip and kept a loaded pistol in the bedside cabinet. He had nightmares and shouted in his sleep. You couldn't sneak up on him, because he always jolted awake. Once I managed to tiptoe right up to the bed—it took me close to half an hour. But then his body suddenly tensed, he gasped, and he stared up at me with a look of fright and rage that I didn't like at all. "Don't ever do that again," he said. "It's dangerous. I might hurt you."

I never did it again.

"True," I now said to our KGB Man. "But all veterans suffer equally when they go home." He nodded solemnly and patted my arm. We never found out if he *really* was KGB.

Later, I had a boyfriend from Texas who yelled out in the

midst of one of our arguments, "I can't fight with you, you fight like a man! You know, that's your problem, your father raised you like a son instead of a daughter." It struck me as peculiar that anyone would differentiate.

"My father," I responded proudly, "raised me as a soldier's kid. He just taught me to fight back."

In 1967, when my brother and I were six years old, my family spent the Easter holiday in a villa outside Florence, Italy. My father bought cap pistols for Jamie, his friend Jamie Bruce, and me. They were shiny black revolvers that you loaded like a real gun, and they sounded and smelled like firecrackers when fired. Seeing how much fun we were having, my father bought himself a pistol too and pronounced himself Sergeant Jones, leader of our platoon. He organized war games against the local Italian kids, taught us to salute American-style, positioning our hands at exactly the right angle so we wouldn't look like European soldiers; to fire searching fire and covering fire; and to belly crawl through tall grass. The feeling of excitement while we waited for the Italian kids' attack, the smell of the dust and dry weeds, has stayed with me to this day.

Perhaps my father's behavior seems strange, considering that he was an extreme pacifist, a man who abhorred killing and who sheltered draft evaders during the Vietnam War. "The War"—his war—loomed darkly over our lives, always present. In 1973, he took us to Normandy, Omaha Beach and Utah Beach. It was winter, the week between Christmas and New Year, and we walked through the perfectly tended American cemetery with its crosses and Stars of David in even rows, stretching to the horizon. He wept over the graves of unknown soldiers, unashamed of his tears.

One afternoon in the winter of 1985, my mother called and said, "Come over right now. There's someone here you have to meet."

She was, at the time, still living in the Delmonico during the week, working as an acquisitions editor at Doubleday.

She opened the door with a slightly frightened look in her eyes. Though I never understood her, I had learned to recognize her expressions. I walked in and found a scruffy man in a wheelchair looking up at me with a warm smile. It was Ron Kovic, author of *Born on the Fourth of July*. He had joined the U.S. Marine Corps and been deployed to Vietnam in 1965. During his second tour of duty, he had been shot in the spine and was now paralyzed from the chest down. As a college student, I had seen the movie *Coming Home* three times, and it is still one of the best antiwar films I've ever seen. The character played by Jon Voight is based on Ron Kovic, and Ron had in fact chained himself to several government fences in his protests against the war. He'd been beaten with billy clubs by riot police, teargassed, and thrown bodily out of his wheelchair, but he never quit, never backed down.

He'd shown up at my mother's door at the Delmonico, just wanting to meet the widow of James Jones and say hello. Though my mother was discomfited by his visit, she was also honored. I had never met anyone in a wheelchair and felt uncomfortable looking down at him. I promptly sat on the couch so we would be eye to eye.

His thoughtful, dark eyes told me he had seen a great deal and understood suffering on the most fundamental level, but they were also filled with a calm wisdom, as though nothing would shock him. And I could sense some fearless beast of rage below their surface, mastered now and under control, but always there. I found him hugely brave.

He took my hand and held it a long time, and told me what a great writer he thought my father was, and that he and many other Vietnam veterans consider James Jones's war trilogy to be the master work that any human being had to read if he or she wanted to learn the truth about war and warfare.

At some point, my mother jumped up, having decided to take us to Elaine's for dinner, always a good, fun place to go where she was bound to know half the customers. Elaine's was on Second Avenue and Eighty-ninth Street, a matter of ten minutes by taxi. Outside, on Park Avenue, it was very cold and damp, and cabs wouldn't stop for us. They probably thought Ron's wheelchair would be too much trouble. I felt like beating them up, the bastards.

"No problem," said Ron, "we'll walk." He navigated the streets and curbs and surly passersby and speeding traffic with good humor and a fierce resolve. At one point, he popped a wheelie, throwing himself back in his chair. My mother screamed, made a small and rapid sign of the cross, and murmured, eyes toward heaven, "Hail Mary, full of grace . . ." This made Ron laugh.

I had never realized how narrow the space was between the front tables and the bar at Elaine's. A lot of chairs and tables had to be moved around to accommodate Ron's wheelchair, and there was quite a bit of fussing from the maître d' before we were settled in. People kept bumping into the wheelchair. I felt so overwrought I proceeded to get totally blasted, and the rest of the night is a blur.

Two weeks later, my friend Dennis from the Columbia MFA program threw a huge party, and I invited Ron. Dennis lived on the ground floor of a building, and you had to go down about ten steps to get to the lobby. Three young men carried Ron's wheelchair down the stairs. Ron and I danced a lot, Ron popping wheelies and spinning around, and me spinning around him. Then he was tired and wanted to go home.

Someone called a cab company and told the operator we had a Vietnam veteran in a wheelchair and wanted a cab for him as soon as possible. Less than five minutes later a speeding yellow taxi pulled up with a dramatic screech of brakes. The driver, an African-American in his early forties, jumped out and came around to our waiting group.

"I gotcha, man," he told Ron. They started talking in some kind of Vietnam veteran patois we could hardly understand—something about where they'd been and what division they'd fought with. I heard Ron say something about two tours, and the cabdriver muttered a response that included the words "Khe San," and shook his head. Ron allowed the man to push his wheelchair and lift him into the cab, which I'd never seen him let anybody do. Then the man expertly folded up the chair and put it in the trunk, and they sped off together into the night.

I went to see *Born on the Fourth of July* on opening day in December 1989, with my Russian friend Natasha, a makeup artist in film and television who had emigrated from Leningrad. I was hungover and shaky from a Christmas party at the *Paris Review* the night before. The film of Ron's book practically knocked me out of my seat. Tom Cruise so perfectly embodied Ron that I felt I was watching my friend's life flash before my eyes. In the beginning of the movie, there's a Fourth of July parade, and the child Ron watches as the old World War II veterans are brought out and marched before the town. The real Ron was in that scene, in a World War II dress uniform, bemedaled, a broken veteran in a wheelchair who salutes the crowd. Then, a firecracker pops, and he cringes into himself in his chair. I started crying and couldn't stop.

At the end of the movie, I walked out of the Ziegfeld Theatre still weeping, with Natasha holding my arm and guiding the way.

"*Da*, but you know," said Natasha, in an attempt to calm me down, "our war was much worse. . . ."

"You Russians and your goddamn war." Now I was laughing and crying at once.

I found myself surrounded by concerned Vietnam veterans,

members of an organization called Veterans for Peace, who were handing out pamphlets. I blurted to one of them, whose name was Mike, that my father had been a veteran of World War II and had fought at Guadalcanal, and had since died and how lonely I felt; I told him Ron Kovic was a friend of mine but he'd gone back to Los Angeles and disappeared and I couldn't find him and how war was such a goddamn fucking waste. This veteran, Mike, told me that Ron had been in the mountains in northern California but was back in Redondo Beach and he could get me Ron's new phone number tomorrow.

Ron and I have not lost touch since. As a veteran's daughter, I'm proud to say, Mike gave me a special dispensation to join Veterans for Peace.

"Be Careful Where You Swim"

When I was studying at the Pushkin Institute in Moscow during the winter of 1987, my mother wrote to me frequently, but she was convinced the Soviet Authorities monitored her letters. This is from a letter I received in late February, when the thermostat reached minus fifteen degrees Celsius:

→→　←←

Dear Kaylie,

Don't forget to tell the Russians that your father was very famous and his novels were published in Russia and that he was a liberal and had nothing against them and I HOPE THEY WILL TAKE CARE OF MY BABY.

I read an article yesterday about an American student who went to Australia and went swimming and got eaten by a crocodile. Please be careful where you swim.

Love,
Mom

CHAPTER SEVEN

⇥ Powerlessness ⇤

In June 1983, I got my first (and only) full-time job, at Poets & Writers, giving away small grants to writers for public readings and workshops. Poets & Writers is a nonprofit organization funded by government grants and private donations, whose sole directive is to help writers. I behaved myself for the first week of work, drinking only a reasonable amount and going to bed at a reasonable hour. But then my mother called and asked me to meet her for dinner at Elaine's. My roommate Carol, who was still working at a bank, pointed out that I never came home early, or sober, when I went out with my mother. I knew I was in trouble. If I told my mother I couldn't go, she'd be angry; so I went. And I was late for work the next morning, stinking of booze and not a little hungover.

"What's wrong with you?" my boss asked.

"I went out with my mother last night," I mumbled.

"Oh," he responded with a knowing smile. My mother was friends with the founder of Poets & Writers, and her partying habits were legendary.

As I sat at my desk, trying to make sense of some paperwork, the thought crossed my mind that perhaps this nine-to-five life was not going to work out too well for me.

I finally handed in my Columbia MFA thesis in October, 150 pages of my first novel, which I intended to continue writing in my free time. But free time was scarce, what with the drinking and the full-time job. In fact, I lasted six months. I quit two days after Doubleday offered me an advance for my first novel, *As Soon As It Rains*, about a teenage girl overcoming her father's death.

I have to point out that there was a good deal of nepotism at work in getting my first novel published by Doubleday. Without telling me, my mother gave her copy of my MFA thesis to Carolyn Blakemore, her friend and colleague. Carolyn was an editor of the old school whose authors included such best-selling stars as Barbara Taylor Bradford and James Dickey.

I didn't know Carolyn had the manuscript until she called me in November to tell me that Doubleday was offering me a $6,500 advance. I was furious at my mother for having done this without telling me—it was a complete breach of trust; at the same time I was overwhelmed that Carolyn Blakemore wanted my book. But I was also fairly certain that I didn't deserve this chance—at least, no more than any of the other writers in my MFA program—and that I'd been given it only because I was James and Gloria Jones's daughter.

After I hung up with Carolyn, I immediately called my mother and asked her why in hell she hadn't *asked* me first if she could give my book to Carolyn.

"Because I knew you'd say no," she said.

"I'm not ready for this," I told her. "People are going to say I got published because of who I am."

"Oh, bullshit," she said. "You think the world doesn't work this way? You think there's *justice*? You're an idiot if you think other people don't take advantage of who they know. Just write the goddamn book and shut up."

Now, twenty-five years later, I'm starting to see her point.

But back then, if I'd felt before that I'd been harshly judged for being the overprivileged daughter of James Jones, that feeling was now magnified tenfold. Even if I wrote the absolute best book I could write, my classmates from Columbia and probably everyone else who gave a shit would think I'd gotten published because of who I was.

It would be five years and a whole novel later before I finally began to feel I was earning my own place.

Just before Memorial Day weekend 1988, I turned in my second novel, *Quite the Other Way*, to Carolyn Blakemore. The next morning, almost all of my mother's Doubleday allies were fired, including Carolyn. My mother, unsure of whether or not she'd been sacked, simply never went back to work. When someone called to ask her when she would be returning, she was reported to have said, "I'll come back when the new boss kisses my ass on Fifth Avenue."

My novel was passed on to a young editor, Shaye Areheart, who was a hands-on, nurturing, old-fashioned editor. This novel, which was quite a bit better than my first, included a good deal of Soviet history, specifically of World War II and the Stalinist purges. It received few, but excellent, reviews and little attention otherwise. The daughter of James Jones writing a first novel was news; the daughter of James Jones writing a second novel, about the Soviet Union no less, was of no interest to anyone except people who had an interest in the Soviet Union, and they were few and far between during those monstrous Reagan years.

From 1983 to 1989, I was embroiled in a relationship with Dennis, who was one of my closest friends and drinking buddies at Columbia. Dennis, five years my senior, was short and slight, with a devilish grin, blue eyes, and blond hair straight as rain. He couldn't have been less threatening, but beneath his boyish exterior and hilarious sense of humor lay a barely contained mean streak. He said my mother's boyfriend Walker was "so vain he's varicose." Dennis worked irregular hours for a moving company so that he could pursue his writing. His hands were bruised and sore, and he despised the rich people he helped move. He liked to make fun of successful writers. When Joyce Carol Oates came out with yet another novel, Dennis made up the moniker Joyce Carol Granola; Susan Cheever's biography of her father, John, one of his favorite writers, pissed him off too, and he took to calling the book *Daddy Queerest*.

Over those years, we broke up once every two or three months, and I would take off on a serious bender that usually involved payback with a third party, then waking up horribly hungover and shaking, assailed by dread.

In December 1986, Dennis moved to New Orleans to get out of the tug-of-war that our relationship had become. In February, I went back to Russia for six months and drank myself into a blind stupor. I started a relationship in Moscow, with an Iowan in my program who also liked to drink Stolichnaya vodka right from the bottle. Upon my return, I spent a week in Iowa with him in August. It was 104 degrees in the shade. We stayed in a house in the middle of wheat fields that stretched like a sea in every direction, no end in sight. At night, for entertainment we ate psilocybin mushrooms and watched eighteen-wheelers speed across the distant landscape, the ghosts of their lights trailing behind them for miles like party streamers. I felt squashed between the earth and sky and was terrified and thought, This is definitely not the place for me. I realized I wanted to be in New Orleans with Dennis, and I tried to send him telepathic messages and felt him thinking about me at that exact moment.

In September, I called Dennis from New York and asked him if he'd been getting my telepathic messages. He chuckled, said he'd felt something, but his drinking was kind of befuddling his mind. He was trying to finish his first novel. He invited me to come down to New Orleans.

"What's the matter with you?" my mother said when I told her Dennis and I were going to give it another try. "Why can't you find a guy that has a normal job? A grown-up who makes money? You have no goddamn common sense."

New Orleans had an end-of-the-road feel, even though miles and miles of bayou stood between the city and the Gulf of Mexico. The French Quarter bars that lined Bourbon Street on both sides were filled to bursting every night, and open all day. You could walk around with booze in open plastic containers. While I was in Russia, Dennis had gotten involved with a twenty-two-year-old bartender, and every time the doorbell rang, he turned pale and froze, refusing to open the door.

I couldn't really get angry at him; after all, I was on the run from my Iowan. I thought perhaps the problem was Stolich-naya vodka. So I turned to cognac—after all, wasn't that close to wine? But soon I was drinking almost a fifth of Courvoisier a night. After a month of living in New Orleans, my incipient ulcer was no longer incipient, and I took to gulping down Pepto-Bismol from the bottle as I walked back from the store. People passing me would cheer. In New Orleans, getting so blotto you had to chug Pepto in the street the next morning was apparently considered an honorable and brave pursuit.

I made several trips back and forth, finally returning to New York for good after Mardi Gras, because Jason Shinder, the founder of the Writer's Voice writing workshops at the West Side YMCA, offered me my first teaching job.

At the New Orleans airport, as Dennis and I sat in a row of cracked plastic chairs bolted to the floor, I set him free. He cried, and I cried, and then I got on the plane.

As the plane banked low over Lake Pontchartrain, I remembered how just a few days ago we'd gone sailing there with a couple Dennis and I had met in a bar, and how his eyes had been hollowed out by grief and confusion, and I'd realized something drastic would have to happen for us to sever our ties. Now, we would have almost half the landmass of the United States between us, but earthly distance had not in the past been efficacious in keeping us from tearing each other apart.

Teaching at the Writer's Voice opened a door onto a whole new world of hope for me. By helping other writers, I found a new direction. I've never stopped teaching since the day I walked into that first workshop. Jason Shinder had created the program by marshaling writers and using the classroom space in the West Side Y, and applying for funding from the New York State Council on the Arts. By 1988, when I started, the program had developed a stellar reputation, and the classes were filled almost entirely by word of mouth.

The Writer's Voice students were extremely serious and the talent level very high. Most everyone had a daytime job and other obligations, yet they showed up without fail. The age range went from recent college graduates, to young professionals, to octogenarian retirees. I found that several of my students were writing stories of publishable quality, and just needed direction and encouragement. I realized I was good at getting right to the technical problems, and explaining them clearly and succinctly.

At a pro-choice consciousness raising seminar at Gail Sheehy's house in East Hampton in 1988, I met a woman from the New York City Board of Education who agreed to let me volunteer as a creative writing teacher once a week in a public middle school in Morningside Heights. The students in this particular class were "at risk" eighth graders who were being held back an extra year before going on to high school. Their teacher, Anne Puddu, was trained as a gifted-and-talented teacher but chose to take on this class instead, for she felt she could do the most good here. Anne Puddu was the best teacher of children I've ever known.

Every week I had to find interesting subjects for the students to write about. I brought in *Life* magazine photographs of sad-looking dogs in cages; war-torn landscapes; refugees; people behind bars; kids smoking dope in alleyways; addicts shooting up; couples kissing. I played music, and sometimes tapes of sounds, like an Amazon rain forest, or a Sahara desert windstorm, and let them write whatever passed through their minds. I took no points off for spelling or punctuation. I never wrote on their papers in red but commented at length in green or blue ink. I read the best of their work aloud in class, week after week. They tried to shock me, but that wasn't easy, and this amused them no end.

When I taught them to write modified haikus, three lines with three words in the first line, five in the second, and three in the last, one boy wrote:

SEX
Ooh! Aah! Oh!
Oh, Baby. Faster! Slower! Faster!
Yes! Yes! YES!

I thought this was so funny and so smart that I wrote it on the board, while Anne Puddu sat there making a face and shaking her head, but I could see she was trying not to smile. The whole class started to crack up and then hoot and howl with laughter. The boy may have meant to shock me, but I told the class it was the smartest and funniest modified haiku I'd ever read.

Their stories and poems lacked all restraint and form; they just told things as they saw them. Once, I brought in a photo of Greta Garbo gazing adoringly at herself in a mirror, her face almost touching her reflection as it gazed adoringly back. One tough nut to crack wrote:

I am so fly no one as fly as me.
Wait! What's that on my face?
Oh, NO! A ZIT!
Quick! Gotta get me some of that Oxy-10!

When I read this aloud, the class cheered and the boy sat back proudly, arms crossed, taking in the applause.

I never drank on Tuesday nights, because I knew I had to be up at the school at eight on Wednesday morning, and those kids could see right through me. I had to be strong, I had to be awake, I had to be on my toes.

Recently I'd started having total blackouts, waking up in the morning uncertain of what had happened the night before, and shaking with fear. I couldn't determine what caused them and decided to stop drinking cognac. I switched to wine. My fear was not totally unfounded; I was running out of money faster than I could write. My advances and my now part-time job at Poets & Writers hardly covered my expenses. One day I broke down crying in front of my mother and admitted I was terrified. She rescued me with a $20,000 check. I didn't want to take it. She pushed it toward me, shrugging it off. "It's found money, anyway," she said. I don't know where she found it. I started blubbering, grateful and ashamed. Now I was no longer in a state of panic, but I still had no idea what the future would hold.

We all had read that horrifying 1986 *Newsweek* cover article which stated unequivocally that according to a recent Yale and Harvard survey, a forty-year-old, single, white, college-educated woman was more likely to be killed by a terrorist than to marry. All of my unattached girlfriends who were fast approaching thirty were freaking out. I thought it was some kind of right-wing conspiracy; yet, living in a crappy little apartment with cinder block and pine board shelves was not how I had envisioned my future, when I'd given my future any thought at all.

Such was my state of mind when I met Andrew, at a Hamptons literary cocktail party over the Fourth of July weekend 1988, on someone's wide, sloping, perfectly tended green lawn that was straight out of *The Great Gatsby*. As the saying goes—we headed right for each other and crashed like two garbage trucks in a head-on collision; recovering from the impact, looking around at the mess, there was no way to tell whose garbage was whose.

Andrew was handsome in a clean-cut, LL Bean sort of way, his thick black hair cut very short and perfectly in place, he wore little round glasses, and was not the least bit threatening. We quickly found out that we had a great deal in common, and before leaving the party, exchanged phone numbers. He was twenty-four and I was twenty-seven; but he seemed mature for his age.

"How come you don't have a girlfriend?" I asked him the next night, when he came over to my mother's house with his acoustic guitar and serenaded me under the grape arbor. My sixty-year-old mother was out at a party. Memorial Day to Labor Day for her was just one party after another, sometimes two or three a night. By the time she got home she was usually so blotto any attempt at conversation was impossible. At least she had the good sense not to drive.

"Oh, I do have girlfriends," Andrew said. "But they're indoor girlfriends."

"What's an indoor girlfriend?"

"Well, they're girls I like to have sex with, but that I'd never take out in public."

"Oh," I said. This seemed like a strange statement to me, but I put it out of my mind. After all, I'd heard stranger things.

My mother took an immediate dislike to Andrew. Softer, more sensitive souls ran for the door screaming when confronted by her ire, but Andrew had no idea he inspired such resentment in Gloria. She was an excellent holder of grudges, and she held a major grudge against Andrew's mother, Linda, a successful journalist and ghostwriter who lived down the street. In the early eighties Linda had written a nasty review of a fledgling local newspaper, the *Bridgehampton Sun*, that my mother had been hired to work on as the society page editor. The paper folded after one season. The review was pretty acerbic. Linda called Gloria a gossip hound, and the paper nothing more than a rag. My mother never forgave Linda. And, as any good Italian will tell you, that kind of grudge will be passed down from parent to child and across generations, ad infinitum.

But there was one thing you could count on with Gloria: she would never admit to having been offended. It was a question of pride; she would simply bad-mouth the persons who had insulted her behind their backs. So for the entire time I was with Andrew, she mostly sulked, ignoring him, as if he were beneath her contempt. And while I'm sure her close friends heard an earful, I was spared the worst of her tongue-lashings, and it felt wonderful—a bit like catching your breath in the quiet eye of a hurricane.

Gloria wasn't able to keep quiet about Andrew being a Republican. He believed in the death penalty but was pro-choice and campaigned tirelessly for a woman's right to choose. Just to raise his hackles, she would say things like, "Give them free abortions now, it's a hell of a lot fucking cheaper than paying for their trials and executions in eighteen years."

"Now, Gloria," he'd respond mildly, with a condescending smile, "there's no need for that kind of language."

This would make her bristle like an old tabby cat. No one who knew her, absolutely no one, had the nerve to speak to her that way, and I giggled secretly in horrified admiration, because Andrew was totally impervious to her underhanded, or sometimes not so underhanded, attacks. He was like the Starship *Enterprise* with its deflector shields up. He simply did not allow himself to consider anything that contradicted his view of himself or the world. This rare and amazing ability carried over into every aspect of his life.

Andrew's parents had gotten divorced when he was two, and several years later, his mother remarried a man who, according to Andrew, hadn't liked him very much. His mother had two more children, daughters, and Andrew told me he'd been forced early on to take care of himself. He'd also learned to never accept defeat.

He thought he could badger me into curtailing my drinking, as if I were a child who'd been given too much freedom and only needed more discipline. At the time *I* certainly didn't think I had a drinking problem, and I didn't like being badgered; I thought he was a square, a lightweight who couldn't see that a sensitive soul like me needed an outlet for emotional stress. Andrew was not a drinker; he might have a beer or two or a glass of wine on special occasions, but his drink of choice was Diet Orange Slice. We argued over what shows to watch on TV and could only enthusiastically agree on *Star Trek: The Next Generation*. He liked the gadgets; I liked the political message.

We went out to Sagaponack every weekend and stayed in my mother's house. The recent, messy breakup of her relationship with Walker, who'd left her for a younger woman, had shaken her up, though she would never admit it. She was still in love with my father—his ghost filled the rooms of her house—and that had not left much space for Walker, who'd tried his best to get a foothold. He'd even hung framed pictures of himself with his parrots wherever there was wall space.

The arrival of fall brought a radical change to the Hamptons, for almost everyone left, all at once, after Labor Day. With Walker gone, Gloria had nothing to hold her in check. The house seemed to be crumbling around her. The brick path from the driveway to the kitchen door was slowly sinking and became a river during storms, more frequent now at summer's end. The rugs smelled of dog and cat pee, the door handles fell off in your hands, and there were cobwebs hanging from the lamp shades and bronze Italian statuettes and vases that she'd brought from her own mother's house. When I mentioned the situation to my mother's live-in housekeeper, Mary, who was losing her eyesight from diabetes, Mary said, "I keep saying it, we got to get ourselves a maid."

Mary had come up from Georgia as a migrant worker in the early sixties, following the crops, and had ended up staying in Bridgehampton. During the Hamptons property boom of the early 1980s, she lost her modest rental off the Sag Harbor Turn-pike, and she'd been living with Gloria ever since.

As Andrew and I were returning to the city on the Hampton Jitney after one particularly difficult weekend, we hit some traffic. The sun was setting straight ahead, the same electric, vibrant red as the brake lights on the thousands of cars moving toward it in a slow, funereal procession. I saw in a flash the future unspooling like the highway before me. My mother was going to die—alone, drunk, with her house falling down around her, and I would not be able to stop it. Suddenly I felt I couldn't breathe and started hyperventilating myself into a panic attack.

Andrew took off his earphones and asked me what was wrong.

I told him I was scared, that I thought my mother was in real trouble, and the future seemed hopeless and terrifying. He sug-gested I give up my "crappy little bohemian apartment" and move in with him. "College is over," he said. "I'll build you real book-shelves. The second bedroom can be your office. We'll take care of your mother. Things will be fine." And then he added, as if it were completely simple, "I love you."

I loved the idea of him. I loved the notion that my fragility could be bolstered by his invulnerability. I loved the idea of no longer being alone, or lonely. His no-nonsense, slightly martial approach to life seemed to me the correct one; perhaps I was just seeing things all skewed. Maybe my mother really was fine and I was just causing myself anxiety over nothing. Immediately I felt better. He squeezed my hand. His common good sense seemed like a sensible reason to place all my fragile eggs in his shatter-proof basket. In a rare flash of insight, I thought, At least, if I go with him, I won't end up like her.

"I love you too," I said.

I moved into his apartment a few weeks later. No place felt safe to me, but his Upper East Side two-bedroom flat with central air and soundproof windows on a high floor seemed safer than most.

Andrew worked in the direct marketing department of one of the big banks. He was responsible for those mass mailings, which 90 percent of us threw away without opening, that we used to get before the Internet. His favorite writer was Dean Koontz, whose colorful, glossy hardcovers lined one small shelf in his closet.

He played the electric guitar and had a serious, sleek black "entertainment center" in his living room, including a huge TV with a zillion channels, a CD player, hundreds and hundreds of CDs, a guitar amp, and copies of the words to the songs he played so guests could sing along when he plugged in after dinner. He also had a smaller, older TV in the bedroom, which had a set of headphones attached, and I spent endless nights unable to sleep, watching *Miami Vice* reruns and other such emotionally calming shows until the wee hours of the morning.

He seemed to feel no differently about sex than he did about going to the gym, and I came to think of it as a forty-five-minute vigorous workout with an attentive, if a little overbearing, personal trainer. Soon, however, this grew annoying to me and became a chore. The only time I felt like having sex with him was when I'd had too much to drink, and that was the only time he had no interest in me.

And I drank much, much more than he suspected, or than anyone suspected. When he saw at a dinner party that I'd had too much wine he'd comment pointedly, "I see we're going a little overboard tonight. Might want to taper down," which would make me want to pummel him. Instead, I'd pour myself another glass. At least now I knew where I'd be waking up in the morning, and if I couldn't remember what I'd said the night before, Andrew would remind me in that mild, condescending tone he liked to use with my mother. He even wore the same small condescending smile.

Andrew asked me to marry him while I was standing behind my dad's pulpit bar, mixing a batch of martinis on New Year's Eve 1988. I was so baked I wasn't sure I'd heard him and had to ask him to repeat himself. I could feel my mother approaching from across the room. She had a peculiarly keen radar for drama, and this was high Kabuki indeed.

"Andrew just asked me to marry him," I told her in a neutral tone, just to see her reaction. For an instant, a look of such horror crossed her face that I felt scared, then suddenly thrilled. I felt, in a sense, as if I were running across a burning bridge that was about to explode behind me.

But then she lit a cigarette, took a deep drag, blew out the smoke that curled around her like a ghostly octopus, and said with a shrug and twist of her lips, "I don't care. Do what you want."

A prickle of heat started to spread through my chest, and I didn't like the way it felt. So I lit a Marlboro Light from my pack that was lying on the bar top. I turned to Andrew and said, "Yeah, okay, why not?" My heart began thundering in my rib cage. I had just committed an act of pure defiance and regretted it immediately, but come hell or high water, I was not going to back down.

Andrew's mother, Linda, was by now also standing just on the other side of the bar, and she, who'd been married and divorced twice, said with alacrity, "Well, if it doesn't work out, you can always get divorced!"

The wedding, on May 27, 1989, was a veritable Hamptons event. All my friends from college and graduate school came. My godmother Cecile and her husband, Buddy—Irwin Bazelon, a brilliant modern classical composer—hired a string quartet for the ceremony in my mother's garden, and Andrew's mother hired a twenty-piece Dixieland band for the reception at the Bridge-hampton Community House, where, incidentally, my dad's memorial had also been held. We were in the *New York Times* and all the local papers. It was a *Who's Who* of the Hamptons literary scene.

My brother walked me down the garden path, and I couldn't stop laughing. Jamie looked at me somberly and murmured under his breath, "You don't have to do this, you know."

The string quartet played on and for some reason I kept thinking about the orchestra on the sloping deck of the *Titanic*. I responded, as if in a fog, "But we've already opened so many of the presents."

Jamie's ears turned red but he didn't say another word. The ceremony is a blur in my mind. Later I watched the video with Andrew, sitting on his living room couch. It was a beautiful ceremony, bright, pale shimmering colors under the deep green trees of my mother's garden. But I had no idea who these people were or why they were getting married.

Andrew and I bickered. Not heated arguments, but nasty little squabbles. I was trying to finish *A Soldier's Daughter Never Cries,* the most autobiographical of my novels, the one that most closely reflected my own childhood experiences in France. It was sending me into another bout of weighty emotional malaise, and I had a hard time getting from bed to desk.

Andrew, preparing for work in the morning, all spruced up and rosy in his suit and tie, said, "Why don't you give yourself a page quota? Say, ten pages a day. Then just write ten pages. What could be easier than that?" Problem solved, he wished me a good day and was out the door.

During this period, I read Bill Styron's *Darkness Visible* for the first time and was amazed to recognize many of my own symptoms in the depression he describes in this memoir. He connects the onslaught of his first major episode of depression with his body's sudden rejection of alcohol, that "magical elixir," which he admits to having depended on for years, both for inspiration and to calm his anxiety. Yes, I thought, I do that too. I am a writer and I'm depressed and therefore I drink. Alcohol is a great thing, it gives me inspiration and quiets my fears. It is medicine and I need it.

But this time I was desperate enough to make an appointment to talk to our family friend, Ben Wolstein, a psychoanalyst. I tried to describe to him the terror that seized me at night, and the sleeplessness that accompanied the grinding anxiety I felt. He asked me how much I drank.

"Not that much at all, really. I might have a couple of glasses of wine every two weeks or so." This was, of course, a gross underestimation. Most people in the psychological field aren't trained to look for the symptoms of alcoholism, which is why, for the most part, patients talk and talk and talk and go right on complaining of their symptoms, without anyone picking up on them. In the meantime, the patients go right on drinking for years.

Ben nodded pensively and moved on to other subjects. I talked about my father, about how terribly his death had affected me. One day Ben said, "But what about your mother?"

"My mother?" I asked, mystified. "What do you mean?"

"Depression is anger turned inward," he explained. "Do you think you're angry?"

"Angry?" I repeated. I had no earthly idea what Ben was talking about.

Right before Thanksgiving, Jamie called to tell me he intended to ask his girlfriend Beth to marry him. He wanted to know if I would mind if he gave her our mother's Dutch Schultz ring, an exquisite diamond solitaire in an ornate, old-fashioned platinum setting. Sometime in 1946, Dutch Schultz had apparently bought the ring for his mother but lost it to our grandfather, Tony Mosolino, in a poker game on the Broadway Limited, the overnight train from Philadelphia to Chicago. Tony gave the ring to his eighteen-year-old daughter Gloria, to the great dismay of his wife, Gertrude. Gloria had given me the ring some years ago, and I had put it away.

Jamie's plan was to bring Beth out to Long Island over Easter weekend and take her down to the beach to collect seashells, which she loved to do. He was going to find two clamshells and put the ring inside. It was a lovely way to propose, and I was very happy for both of them. I had already told Jamie years ago that he could have the ring. I thought it was wonderful that Jamie wanted to give it to Beth.

When I hung up, Andrew was standing a few feet away, looking gloomy. I told him about the call, and he remained obstinately, gloomily silent.

"What?" I asked.

"Do you really want to give up your diamond ring?"

"I don't need it, I have the one you gave me. Why shouldn't Jamie have it?"

"Well, it's *yours*."

"It's not *mine*, it's the family's. I think it's great that Jamie wants it."

Andrew shook his head, clearly disappointed in my inability to see things his way. He seemed to place great store in what a person owned, and felt that material possessions reflected who you were. But there were very few objects I held so dear that I wouldn't give them up. My books, I wouldn't give up. And there was a South American silver bracelet, and a gold ankh ring my father had worn; also his National Book Award plaque, but none of these held any financial value. My mother had some artwork by old family friends that I hoped would stay in the family. It occurred to me, if only fleetingly, that I owned absolutely nothing, and Andrew's attraction to me suddenly seemed completely illogical. The thought frightened me, but I quickly pushed it away.

I remember sitting beside him on the couch one evening, watching some absurd sit-com he liked, and sipping Diet Orange Slice, which I hated. I had the terrifying thought, This is it. This really is the end of the road.

At least, this time I wasn't drinking. Well, I was only drinking once every two or three weeks—though getting potted is a better way of describing it. Therefore, I couldn't possibly have a problem. What was I worrying about?

I started watching *Oprah* in the afternoons while I cleaned the apartment or made dinner. I felt very domestic. One day, she interviewed the wives of alcoholics. There must have been ten of them sitting in a semicircle on the stage. They described the repetition patterns. They talked about promises made and broken; the impossibility of intimacy in such relationships; and the push-me, pull-you that keeps occurring. And, most staggering to me, the paralyzing fear of abandonment that kept them coming back, or staying, in the bad relationships.

I was so amazed I even told Andrew about it when he got home. I explained that I'd watched the most incredible *Oprah*, which described in perfect detail my relationship with Dennis, the only difference being that she was talking about alcoholics! Wasn't that amazing?

Andrew thought it was indeed amazing and moved on to the

more pressing issue of whether he should make his special Parmesan dressing for the salad.

On December 1, the Thursday after Thanksgiving, I went down to Wall Street to meet Andrew for lunch—something romantic and unplanned, for our life had already become totally ordinary and we were struggling not to bore each other to tears. We went to a sushi bar and had a fine lunch. I said something that annoyed him, something about being worried that my book wouldn't be as good as I wanted it to be.

"You're always worried about something or other," he said peevishly. "Why can't you just be happy?"

"I think it would be nice if you could be something *other* than happy all the fucking time."

"No need to use that language."

"I'll talk any goddamn way I want. Let's go."

Walking me back to the subway, out of the clear blue, he said, "I don't think this is working out. I think we should split up."

I went from terror to elation in twenty seconds flat. Exactly the feeling I'd had on the Coney Island roller coaster at the age of ten.

"Okay, fine," I agreed.

"I'm a much more sexual person than you are," he explained. "I need someone who wants to have sex much more often."

I started to feel that little prickle of heat below my skin, and my chest constricting. Could this be the anger Ben Wolstein had been talking about? All around us men and women in nicely tailored wool coats hurried along, clutching briefcases, their elegant shoes clicking purposefully on the sidewalk. In my long, flowing skirt and droopy chenille sweater, I felt like a hippie.

"You have to like someone to want to have sex with them, Andrew," I said, my voice hard and tight. "I don't think I like you all that much."

The next Saturday, we went to Sagaponack to tell our families. To say I wasn't looking forward to this would be an understatement. I wanted the whole thing over and done with. Couldn't we just pretend it hadn't happened? Andrew went to his mother's house down the street, while I went home to Gloria's. I dropped my bag at the bottom of the narrow stairs, a few feet from my bedroom door, and went up to her room.

She was lying on her bed, smoking a cigarette.

"You shouldn't smoke in bed, Mom."

She didn't say anything, just continued smoking. I took one from the pack lying beside the ashtray and lit it with her lighter. I inhaled deeply, blew out the smoke, and said, "I have something to tell you but I don't want you to get upset."

She sat up, her eyes suddenly wide and anxious. "What is it? You're not pregnant, are you?"

"Andrew and I are breaking up."

"I knew it. What happened?"

What happened, indeed. Where to begin? Since, clearly, no explanation would be satisfactory, I told her what he'd basically told me.

"He says I'm a lousy lay." And then I started to laugh, the ironic chuckle of a person about to climb the gallows steps. But really, I felt things were going to get much better now, as soon as the messy details could be cleaned up.

"A lousy lay?" said my mother. "A lousy lay? Jesus Christ."

"He's going to stop by later to pick up his stuff."

"A lousy *lay*?"

"I'm going downstairs now. You need to stay calm, Mom. I need you to stay calm."

While I was in my room packing up Andrew's belongings so we could get this part over with as quickly as possible, my mother went out to lunch. I knew for certain that by 3:00 P.M., every friend (and enemy) she had in the world would know. Fuck them. I didn't care. I just had to get out of it. Deal with the small details. Jesus Christ. We had to share the apartment for at least another six weeks. Andrew had told me on Friday, when he got home from work, that he'd been offered a job in an advertising company in Minneapolis, Minnesota, with whom he'd been doing business for more than a year. He'd be moving there sometime after New Year's.

I decided to make myself a drink and got behind the pulpit bar and poured a tumbler of cheap vodka. I rarely drank vodka anymore, but fuck him and his Diet Orange Slice. After I'd gotten ice from the fridge, I went and locked myself in my room.

A while later, I heard a commotion in the kitchen. There was shouting and then running, followed by a frantic banging on my bedroom door.

"Come here, you slimy little coward. You son of a bitch, you're not even intelligent. Lousy lay! I'll show you a lousy lay, I'm going to cut your balls off!"`

I rushed to the door and unlocked it. There was Andrew, pale and frightened, with my mother fast approaching, brandishing a long carving knife. I stepped between them, and he escaped into my room.

"Mom, you need to calm down. If you stab him, you're going to go to jail. It's not worth it."

"Get out of my way." Her voice was barely under control. "I'm going to cut his balls off."

I could smell booze, heavy on her breath. She'd gotten ripped at lunch, as expected. But this behavior was a little extreme, even for her.

"Put the knife down, Mom, before he calls the cops."

"This is my fucking house! I'll cut his balls off if I want to. This is *my* house!"

I pried the knife from her hand and told her to go lie down.

"In ten minutes he'll be out of here, and you'll never have to see him again."

"Lousy lay." She was stuck on this detail for some reason. Maybe I should have said something else.

In my room, I placed the knife on the dresser. Andrew was lying facedown on the bed, weeping uncontrollably, his shoulders shaking. I gathered he'd never been threatened at knifepoint before. I didn't feel like consoling him. Suddenly she was banging furiously on the door again, trying to kick it in. "Let me in! I want to cut his balls off, that lousy little coward!"

"I think you'd better go," I told him. All I could think was, Good thing there's a back door to my room. Otherwise she might really try to kill him.

He stood up, pulled himself together, and started gathering the garbage bags filled with his things.

"I'll need the engagement ring back," he said. "It's a family heirloom, after all."

I didn't feel like giving it to him. Anyway it was back in New York, in my jewelry box, along with the wedding ring.

"I'll give it to your mother next time I see her," I added coolly.

The hardest time I ever had to live through since my father's death was those six weeks when Andrew and I were separated but living in the same apartment. I moved into my office—the room where I wrote and where I kept my old futon—and went out every night, and drank until my mind became blank, and stayed out as late as I could, sometimes sleeping on a girlfriend's couch just to avoid having to face him.

Jamie stayed a couple of extra days in Sagaponack over the Christmas weekend, concerned about my state of mind. We did our Christmas shopping together in Southampton, braving a bitter, biting cold. Then, after Christmas Day, he reluctantly went back to Washington.

With nothing to occupy my overtaxed mind, I spent two drunken days holed up in an unheated pool house in Southampton with a blond Australian tennis pro I'd met on the Jitney coming out. I came home to my mother's a disheveled mess, only to learn that John Irving had invited us for dinner, in his pretty house in the middle of a potato field with its red barn imported from New England. I didn't want to go, but my mother insisted. I took a bath, washed my hair, put on a clean chenille sweater and black jeans, but I couldn't stop my hands from shaking.

John Irving gave us a tour of his barn, which he'd converted into a wrestling gym, complete with wrestling mat, dummies, heavy punching bag, and other equipment. He told us proudly that his older son was an excellent wrestler, just as John had been in high school and college. John was in amazing shape; rain or shine, summer or winter, you could always find him running the back roads of Sagaponack.

We moved into the living room for drinks. No one at the gathering mentioned my recent catastrophe, and I was grateful for their tact.

Peter Matthiessen, the writer and Buddhist scholar, was there, and I waited until he was alone and went over to him. Peter was tall and thin, and the older he got and the more lined his face grew, the more handsome he became. I told Peter I'd been volunteer teaching creative writing in a middle school, a class of troubled eighth graders who were at risk of not graduating. I told him, with all that was happening, I didn't think I could continue.

Peter said, "It's like feeding birds in the summer. If you put food out for birds in the summer and fall, they'll stay, they won't fly south, and then, if you suddenly stop, they'll starve to death."

I looked up at him, my throat tightening. "That wasn't exactly what I hoped you'd say," I said, and smiled shakily. Peter laughed quietly.

I called Anne Puddu and told her I'd be back the third week in January, that I needed a few weeks to pull myself together. When I knocked on the door and entered the classroom, those tough, hardened faces turned to me like a field of sunflowers and broke into wide-open grins. They started cheering and clapping and jumping out of their seats.

"The writer's back!" they shouted. "The writer came back!"

It took everything I had not to burst into tears.

Only a matter of weeks after Andrew had moved out of the apartment and resettled in Minneapolis, he sent his mother a FedEx package containing a binder that looked and read exactly like a business proposal. Linda called to tell me about it, utterly surprised. Since I needed to return her ring anyway, I went over to see her.

The binder had a title, which I unfortunately cannot remember, with photographs glued to each page. I barely glanced at the thing, I was so mortified. What Andrew was asking his mother to accept was a fait accompli. He had moved in with a woman ten years older (there was a smiling picture of her) who had two tween-aged children (pictured also) and a ranch house in a suburb of St. Paul. As soon as our divorce was final, he intended to marry this woman and raise her two children.

Andrew had been traveling to Minneapolis on business all through our relationship, but it had never occurred to me, until I saw the binder, that he'd probably set up the whole maneuver way in advance. The Minnesota woman may have been a backup plan all along; I'll never know for sure. Clearly, it had been important to him to gather whatever material spoils he could on his way out, and on that front, I'd been completely outplayed. I'd let him take anything he wanted out of the hundreds of expensive gifts. He took half the dishes, glasses, and silverware; the furniture; the bed; the two television sets (they were both his, after all). He wanted all the wedding photos and videos. Those, I was ready to throw down the garbage chute anyway.

For a long time after my visit to Linda, I wondered why on earth Andrew wanted any of these things, since he was moving into an already well-appointed household. Did he plan to show the videotape and photos to his new wife and children? Would they use those six Positano dishes and the Christofle wineglasses on special occasions?

When I called Cecile to tell her Andrew had taken everything, including both TVs, she turned to Buddy, who was standing nearby and said, "Can you believe it? He took *both* TVs!" I heard Buddy shout, "Call our TV man right now, Cecile! Get the girl a brand-new TV and VCR!" They were the first new TV and VCR I ever owned.

I decided not to fight Andrew on anything, and vowed never to speak to him again.

A Soldier's Daughter Never Cries was published in the spring of 1990, to very good reviews. I was still living in Andrew's apartment, now devoid of furniture, except for my old futon bed, my mother's old love seat, my books on the wall-to-wall bookshelves Andrew had built, and my new TV and VCR. The morning after the book party, sitting alone on the love seat in the otherwise empty living room, surrounded by overflowing ashtrays and empty glasses, I tried to assess what had gone wrong with my life, but I didn't have a clue.

I realized the first thing I had to do was move, find my own place. But I'd never looked for an apartment before; Carol had found the one we shared after college. How did a person go about finding an apartment? I called a friend, whose dad was a builder with connections, and in a day he found me a little ground-floor one bedroom in Yorkville that cost $750 a month, less than half the rent of Andrew's place.

Andrew called me in the spring to say we could get divorced over a weekend in the Dominican Republic, and would I like to fly down there with him for a romantic tryst for old times' sake, on top of a divorce? At first I thought I'd misheard him. No, I'd heard him correctly. I told him to fuck off and hung up. I sent him the weirdest postcard I could find, a picture of a Yemen camel market, and stated unequivocally that he could go to hell, and that I wanted him to stop calling me.

The Minnesota divorce papers weren't finalized until the following November. In them, he included as possessions not to be argued over, his new Nissan Pathfinder, in case I suddenly decided to get greedy.

I kept one photo of us scuba diving in deep blue water, taken on our honeymoon in Mexico. I cut Andrew out and in the gap glued a close match of tropical water from a travel magazine. There I am, at the bottom of the sea, floating toward the camera in full scuba gear, totally wide-eyed, and beside me is the ghostly blue outline of a human from, as if a *Star Trek* character had just been beamed away to some other, distant planet.

PART II

It was just before my birthday and I knew that Pappy was getting ready to start one of these bouts. I went to him—the only time I ever did—and said, "Please don't start drinking." And he was already well on his way, and he turned to me and said, "You know, no one remembers Shakespeare's child."

—JILL FAULKNER SUMMERS,
WILLIAM FAULKNER, A LIFE ON PAPER

"Votre fille est tombée sur son dos"

This is a story my mother liked to tell the gathered company on my birthday.

→→   ←←

In late August 1970, on the way back from the States, on the ocean liner *France,* Gloria met an old friend, Kitty Hayden, the actor Sterling Hayden's wife. Kitty was traveling in first class with her two sons, Andrew and David, who were around Jamie's and my age. They were on their way to join Sterling in Paris, who was living on a barge under the Pont Neuf. Gloria wondered aloud how Kitty was going to manage living on a barge, with two sons under the age of twelve.

I promptly developed a crush on Andrew, the older boy, who returned my affections. Coincidentally, *Johnny Guitar* was playing in the ship's movie theater, and Andrew and I sat alone for hours in the first-class balcony, watching his father kiss Joan Crawford, attempting to imitate them. Six hours later, our mothers found us there and had a good laugh at our expense.

Shortly after our return to Paris, Gloria went with a girlfriend to visit the Haydens on their barge under the Pont Neuf. Sterling Hayden, in leather sandals and dirty jeans, sporting a long white beard, brewed some hash tea. My mother and her friend drank it and got so stoned they lost their shoes and walked home barefoot along the quais, singing to the trees.

Jamie and I were invited to the barge to play with the boys the following Sunday. Gloria sent us over, warning us not to drink the tea. At four o'clock that Sunday afternoon, Gloria received a phone call from the police. *"Votre fille est tombée sur son dos. On l'amène à l'hôpital."* With her limited French, Gloria understood it as, *Votre fille est tombée dans l'eau.* Your daughter has fallen in the water. And the French word for *hospital*.

My parents took a taxi to the closest hospital, the Hôtel Dieu, just across the bridge on the Île de la Cité. They learned from the reception desk that indeed a child had fallen in the Seine and drowned. In a moment, a policeman would escort them to identify the corpse in the basement morgue. Gloria's legs gave way, and she fell in a faint on the tile floor. Once she'd recovered, she told Jim she couldn't do it, so he went downstairs alone. The drowned child was a little boy, perhaps eight years old. He was dark haired and his lips were blue. My father went back upstairs.

"It's not her," he managed to say.

Phone calls were made, and they finally got Kitty Hayden on the phone at the Hôpital Necker, a children's hospital in the fifteenth arrondissement. Kitty explained that I had been running and fell through a plastic skylight on the roof of the barge and landed on my back, seven feet below. It turned out, after the X-rays, that I had fractured a lumbar vertebra. The doctors said I would have to lie flat in bed for four weeks.

It was a wonderful convalescence, even though my back hurt. In that four-week period, Gloria read me *Pride and Prejudice* and *Wuthering Heights*. I was an avid reader of comic books, but I resisted novels as long as I could. I can still hear my mother's expressive, slightly hoarse voice as she brought to life those nineteenth-century ladies and gentlemen, all for my amusement, her captive audience.

"If that dead child had been you," Gloria would say at the end of her story in a matter-of-fact tone, "I would've killed myself."

CHAPTER EIGHT

⇥ The Brink ⇤

ON MAY 1, 1991, I went with my mother to the opening of the Broadway musical *The Will Rogers Follies*. Her friend Peter Stone had written the book, and the lyrics were by two of her closest friends, Betty Comden and Adolph Green.

I picked up Gloria at Cecile and Buddy's apartment, where she stayed, now that she'd given up her job at Doubleday, and consequently, her place in the Delmonico. In the taxi, she informed me that she'd sold my father's Beauford Delaney paintings.

"What?" I almost jumped out of the seat. "How could you do such a thing without telling us?"

"Why do I need to tell you anything? They're mine. I got thirty thousand for them."

"In ten years they'll be worth more than thirty thousand each. That was a stupid thing to do." She didn't say anything, but I knew I'd pay for those words.

Apparently a Frenchman who owned a gallery in SoHo came to the house to look at them. They were oil paintings from the sixties and early seventies, several portraits and abstracts in yellow tones. The art dealer offered her a check right then, and she felt the offer was too good to pass up. Over the years, she'd sold off almost everything of value my father had collected, and that was her right. Yet I'd always hoped to keep one or two of these oil paintings, because when I was a little girl, Beauford Delaney had been a good friend of mine.

On lazy afternoons in Paris, when I was little, I'd hear the doorbell from my room downstairs, and after Judite let the guest in, I'd wander up to the living room to see if someone interesting had arrived. Sometimes Beauford, an African-American painter who was also living in Paris, would be sitting there on the couch, immobile, elegant, in an old, dark suit, his French beret on his knees.

"Beauford!" I'd shout, running to him and giving him a big hug and a kiss. He smelled to me of wet dust and turpentine, a little like the cabinet under the kitchen sink.

My father once told me that Beauford had tried to kill himself by jumping off an ocean liner, and he had been rescued by fishermen. Why? I wanted to know. Why did he do that? Because he was unhappy, my father explained. He added that it wasn't easy in America for black people, because there was so much racism. What is that? I wanted to know. It's when you don't like someone because of what they look like.

Ridiculous! I exclaimed, a new word for me, and my father cracked a small, mysterious smile.

At one time in the early sixties, Beauford had been so poor he didn't have money to buy supplies, and he made a canvas out of an old beige raincoat. My father had bought the painting, which hung for years in our living room. On the back, you could still see one of the pockets. This was the painting I loved the most.

When Beauford came over, I liked to play hostess. "Do you want something to drink, Beauford?"

"I'm just fine, baby girl."

I knew he'd have a drink with my father in a few minutes. While we waited for him to come down from his office, Beauford asked me how school was going. We talked about this and that, but he was most interested in the art projects I was doing. Once,

I did a portrait of him in watercolor on a large, good piece of art paper from the art supply store and wrote at the bottom: "For Beauford Love Kaylie." I had to ask my parents how to spell his name, which sounded to me like *Booford*. He smiled delightedly when I presented it to him. I was reciprocating, for he'd given me two beautiful abstract watercolors, one for my third birthday and one for Christmas the following year. I still have those.

Sitting in the cab on the way to the theater, I felt as if my mother had kicked me in the stomach. We arrived in a black cloud of unaired resentments, and I made my way to the bar and ordered a glass of white wine. Still reeling, I drank it down as fast as I could and ordered another, which I intended to drink and another after that, before the curtain went up.

The Will Rogers Follies might have been divine, but I was in no shape to appreciate it. Airy and light, each number seemed to feature feathers and sparkles aplenty as I continued my downward slide into self-hatred and despair, with no idea what was wrong or how to go about fixing it.

At the after-party I drank as much as I could as fast as I could, and eventually found myself standing at the edge of a dark and empty dance floor with a disco ball spinning around, among a small group of people talking to the actor Timothy Hutton. He was tall, thin, and wore a serene and contemplative air. He listened intently but didn't say a word.

My mother appeared at my side out of nowhere and in a loud voice said to Timothy Hutton, "You want to fuck my daughter? You can have her for free." She looked up at him with that wild, gleaming defiance in her eyes. I realized then that she was seriously lit, even more than I was. Perhaps she'd meant this as a joke.

"She's joking," I managed to say. "She doesn't mean it."

"I'm not joking, she'll fuck you for nothing," said my mother, staring up at him belligerently. He gazed down at her in penetrating silence, expressionless. Perhaps as a famous person, he was used to being confronted, assaulted, or adulated by strangers. Suddenly she turned and lurched off with the strange, stiff-backed gait of someone with a distended stomach. What was happening to her? What was happening to me?

"I'm sorry," I said to Timothy Hutton. "I'm so sorry. She's drunk."

He looked at me with a small smile and still didn't say a word. I drifted away, feeling physically sick and weak in the knees, as if I'd been assaulted and had my clothes torn off in public.

Everyone was anxiously awaiting the *New York Times* and the all-important theater review. I wanted to leave, go home to the small one-bedroom apartment I'd found the May after Andrew left, which was almost exactly a year ago. How was it, I now considered, that absolutely nothing had changed, progressed, in a year?

I approached the table where my mother was sitting alone to tell her I was leaving. It was a strange, eerie sight, Gloria, maven of entertainment and hilarity, sitting alone at a gloomy little round table covered with a stained white cloth. Had she frightened everyone away? It was entirely possible. I saw now that she was holding the *Times* review.

"They're screwed," my mother said, and chuckled humorlessly. "Poor Betty." I picked up the paper. Frank Rich's review was less than kind.

"I'm leaving now, Mom," I said, my whole body feeling like a tree trunk. Even my voice sounded stiff to my own ear. "You can catch a ride with someone else."

"Just a minute." She pushed herself to her feet, grabbed her jacket and purse from a nearby chair. What would happen, I thought vaguely, if I just kept walking and left her to fend for herself? She'd probably never forgive me, never speak to me again. The thought scared me so much I couldn't even seriously contemplate it.

As we moved toward the exit, she passed a tall, bald man in glasses, standing by himself at the edge of the empty dance floor.

"Ha-ha, you dumb son of a bitch," she said to him in that horrible, teasing voice I remembered so well from my childhood. "You're gonna lose your shirt." She followed this with her How-Do-You-Like-That? look, her lips pressed tight and twisted in a ghoulish distortion of a smile, her chin jutting forward, as if expecting a punch. And then she lurched off toward the exit. Stupefied, I followed her out.

As we waited for the elevator, swaying in our evening clothes as though it were Gala Night on a fancy ocean liner out in the middle of the Atlantic, she said, "That was the producer. I never liked him, the arrogant bastard."

The Will Rogers Follies ran for more than two years, despite Frank Rich's bad review. The producer, whoever he was, didn't end up losing his shirt, and I am glad for him. I hope to God he isn't Italian and doesn't hold grudges the way my mother did.

After I dropped Gloria at Cecile and Buddy's, I came to a horrifying realization: I hated my mother. And if I didn't watch out, I was going to end up exactly like her—alone, drunk, lashing out at the world. But I would be worse because I'd never had her health: I was much more like my father, who while physically strong, had a much weaker constitution.

Okay, I thought. Time to seriously cut back. I'll drink, say, once a month.

I held on to my need to drink, my right to drink, to the bitter end.

Sometime in June, perhaps six weeks later, on a Saturday night I was on my fifth or sixth margarita sitting at the crowded bar in a Mexican restaurant on Amsterdam Avenue with Sally—an old friend from the Columbia writing program who drank the way I used to and was therefore safe to drink with—when she told me that she'd heard Dennis was back in New York and living somewhere nearby. I hadn't seen him in three years and three months, since I'd left him in the New Orleans airport. In a moment of total emotional mushiness, I went to the pay phone in the back and dialed information. His number was listed. I remembered the digits, and dialed—no small feat given the number of margaritas I'd consumed. It was 1:00 A.M., and I got his answering machine—no surprise. I left a message telling him where I was and hung up. Twenty minutes later, he walked into the bar. I saw him moving purposefully through the crowd toward us, and my heart started beating faster. Sidling in between Sally and me sitting on barstools, he ordered a club soda and lime. Something about him was different, his eyes were bright and clear, and there was a sharpness to his features that had never been there before.

"You're not drinking?" I asked tentatively.

Dennis told me that he hadn't had a drink in close to a year. He looked me right in the eyes and said, "I'm an alcoholic."

I was absolutely stunned. "You? An *alcoholic*? You really think so?" But then, I thought, I was a lightweight compared with Dennis. When we'd driven down to New Orleans for a short vacation in 1986, he'd had a cooler full of beer behind the driver's seat and drank the whole way down. *I* never drank in the car. Never.

Sally soon went home, and Dennis and I left the bar and walked around for a while so I could sober up. We went back to his apartment and talked for hours, and as gray light began to bring the room into focus, I broke down and wept over my ridiculous marriage and the state of my life. He made me strong coffee and began talking in general terms about alcoholism and its dynamics. He said, and I'll never forget this as long as I live, "Alcoholics are like cockroaches. You find one, you know there's a nest nearby."

He went to a bookshelf and returned with two books, which

he placed on the coffee table in front of me. One was by Alice Miller, *Prisoners of Childhood: The Drama of the Gifted Child and the Search for the True Self*; the other by Janet Woititz, *Adult Children of Alcoholics*.

"Dennis," I said, dead serious all at once. "You know my mother pretty well. Do you think she's an alcoholic?"

For a second I thought he was going to laugh, but he didn't. He made a huffing sound and gazed back at me intently. "Your mother is definitely an alcoholic," he said in a quiet, neutral voice.

I tried to process this. If I agreed with him, then what did that say about my father? What did that say about my family? All of us? About the way we lived our lives? I felt like Rosemary in *Rosemary's Baby* when she puts the anagram together with the Scrabble pieces and realizes she is surrounded by liars.

It was almost too much to absorb, and I pushed the thought away, deciding that Dennis was exaggerating—he'd become one of those recovered lunatics who in their self-righteous zeal saw an alcoholic in every drinker they knew.

Then he kissed me, and the familiarity of his lips, the smell of his skin and hair, made me feel as if I'd finally reached the safety of a cool and shady oasis after a long, arduous journey.

Despite my mother's insensitivity about my father's paintings, she did see that I was unraveling and felt compelled to help in whatever way she could. Through a friend of hers, we'd found a psychiatrist, and since I didn't have health insurance, my mother was helping me pay for the sessions.

Dr. Ellen was tall and thin and wore her thick, dark hair down around her face, and her short-skirted suits were pastel and form-fitting. She liked to eat those natural chips made from root vegetables, which she shared during our sessions. For some reason that gesture made me feel relaxed and at home. On her desk was the only personal object in an otherwise sterile, beige-toned room: a smiling picture of herself and her husband in scuba diving gear.

I told Dr. Ellen the absolutely stunning news that Dennis thought he was an alcoholic. But even more startling, I'd asked him if he thought my mother was an alcoholic, and he'd said yes.

"What do you think about that?" Dr. Ellen wanted to know.

And here it finally is, I thought vaguely. I couldn't cross this important boundary lightly. If I admitted to Dr. Ellen or to myself or to anyone else that my mother was an alcoholic, that would be a betrayal of everything I'd ever believed or been taught by my parents about life. That would be tantamount to abandoning the Jones fortress forever. I wasn't prepared to do that.

"An *alcoholic* . . . ," I repeated under my breath, practically speechless with shock. Could this be? It wasn't possible. But, yes . . . all evidence pointed in that direction. "I don't know," I said helplessly.

Then Dr. Ellen asked, quite matter-of-factly, "How much do you drink?"

"How much do I drink? Oh, every three weeks or so I might have a couple of glasses of wine." For the most part, this was true. I had cut back substantially. Now, even though I might drink only every three weeks, I could suffer a complete blackout on two or three glasses of wine. Once I started I had no control over the outcome. But, you couldn't say two or three glasses of wine every three or so weeks was a lot. It's not that much at all. Naturally, I did not share these thoughts with Dr. Ellen.

Dr. Ellen nodded and then asked me, "And how do you feel when you drink?"

"I feel . . ." I thought about this for a while, wanting desperately to be honest, wanting truly to fix whatever was wrong. "Brave," I finally said. "And not so alone."

Dr. Ellen nodded again, then asked me to describe my mother's drinking. I told her about our night at *The Will Rogers Follies*. I even told her about Timothy Hutton. Then I felt my face burning up, and my breathing becoming strained.

"I think your mother is an alcoholic," Dr. Ellen said gently, as if she'd thought this for a long time and had just been waiting for the right occasion to say it.

But *she* was the one who said it—not me. I started to feel the need to defend my mother, to stand up for her, but I stopped myself. I trusted Dr. Ellen as I had trusted few people in my life.

I began to try to wrap my mind around this absolutely horrifying possibility.

My mother's ears must have been ringing that afternoon. I'd always believed, as my father did also, that my mother had an unusually powerful sixth sense, even though she tried to suppress it. Nevertheless, she could feel when certain people were in turmoil, and she would pick up the phone and call them, as she called me later the same afternoon.

I admitted to my mother that I'd seen Dennis again. I told her he'd stopped drinking and was really getting his life together.

"You're an asshole, you know that?" she said, disgusted. "You just can't stop fucking up your life."

Suddenly I felt something explode in my chest, something volcanic and out of control, and bitter words erupted from my mouth. "You know *why* I'm so fucked up? You know why? Because you're an *alcoholic*, that's why I'm so fucked up." I started looking around for a cigarette. I knew there was a pack of Marlboro Lights somewhere around here. . . .

"*I'm* an alcoholic?" she shouted, furious. "Well what about *you*? *You*'re the one who should watch it, you know."

Now I brought in the cavalry, the expert words of the professional: "Well, Dr. Ellen says you're an alcoholic." My voice sounded so wrong, so stiff, so unbending to my own ear. Why couldn't I have a normal conversation with my mother without feeling like this?

I could hear my mother lighting a cigarette, then exhaling loudly into the mouthpiece. "I'll tell you what, you go tell that Dr. Ellen that I'm not going to help pay for those fucking sessions anymore. How's that?"

She hung up. And I decided not to call her back. I wanted to see how long the silence would last. And boy, was it a loud silence. I could feel the shock waves of her rage coursing through me and bouncing off the walls, and I heard every word she was saying to my brother, right now, over the phone. I even dialed his number, and indeed, the line was busy. Next she'd call my godmother Cecile, and anyone else who would listen. I shrank into a corner as if in an earthquake. While Jamie and Cecile would try to remain neutral, my mother had no shortage of sycophants and allies who'd tell her I was evil. That of course she shouldn't have to put up with such treatment from her daughter—so spoiled, that kid—and the guilt, the shame, the self-hatred that engulfed me seemed a prison of collapsing bricks from which I would never escape.

My phone started ringing. I let the answering machine take the calls. First, Jamie; then, naturally, Cecile.

Finally, the next day, I called Cecile back.

"Your mother is very upset."

"I told her she's an alcoholic," I said. "She didn't want to hear it."

"She has been drinking more heavily since your father died, but she seems to have it under control."

I started to feel that volcanic rage building up again in my chest, and with my voice shaking told Cecile I had to go.

My birthday in August came and went—no call from my mother. But Jamie did call and tried once again to reason with me to patch things up with her.

"Oh, Jamie," I said, my voice breaking, "Mom's an alcoholic, and she's in real trouble."

"Well," he said equably, "I don't know about that. She's a heavy social drinker, that's for sure. But an *alcoholic*? That's a bit extreme."

Dr. Ellen did not cut me off, even though I no longer could afford to pay her regular fee. She allowed me to continue with her at a reduced rate, for which I will be forever grateful.

With my mother and me not speaking to each other in the summer of 1991, I couldn't go home to Long Island and instead went to the beach in New Jersey with Sally from Columbia. Once I went to East Hampton to visit my best friend from high school, and once, Dennis and I visited his mother on the North Shore of Long Island. I wanted to see Dennis more, but he wouldn't oblige. He was trying to teach me about boundaries. "You need to respect my boundaries," he would say. I responded, "What's a boundary?"

Our relationship, which was more than a friendship because we slept together, but less than a romance, because we'd totally exhausted each other in that department, was vague and unclear. But he would not clarify it for me.

One weekend morning, Dennis called and told me to watch a John Bradshaw six-hour lecture on PBS that afternoon. Coming from Dennis, the cynic of cynics who found Louis-Ferdinand Céline's writing amusing, this was so stunning and bizarre a suggestion that I grudgingly complied.

For about six hours I listened to this weird ex-seminarian and recovering alcoholic talk about societal myths and family myths. He said the bigger the myth around which a society or family bases its beliefs and cultural biases, the thicker and higher will the wall be that they build to protect the myth from scrutiny. He used two examples that nearly blew me right off my futon. The first was the obsessive deification of money and the pursuit of it in our society; the other was the prevalence of alcoholism, and our inability to confront it.

He said that in an alcoholic family, the members inevitably circle the wagons around the alcoholic, then, to protect the myth of normalcy, build walls—a veritable fortress so impenetrable no projectile of truth can penetrate.

Like Tolstoy's Prince Andrej trying with all his might to keep the door closed on death, I tried with all my strength and resolve and logic and intellect to keep the door closed on the truth. And when the truth became too powerful and began to press in upon me, making me feel sad, angry, and panicked all at once, I did the only thing I knew that would quiet the emotions, anesthetize them, and that was to drink. I had to rely on Valium quite a bit to get any sleep at all.

I took to controlling my alcohol intake with an iron-fisted resolve. I spent so much time figuring out what to drink and when to drink and how much to drink and making sure that I would not have to talk to Dennis on the phone if I did drink, that the last six months of my drinking are a blur of self-obsessed worry and fear.

I discovered the term "narcissistic disturbance" in Alice Miller's book *Prisoners of Childhood*. When I came across the following passage, it was as if a light had been turned on in a completely dark room: "We cathect an object narcissistically . . . when we experience it not as the center of its own activity but as a part of ourselves. If the object does not behave as we expect or wish, we may at times be immeasurably disappointed or offended."

In my mind, I could hear my mother saying, *How can you listen to such shit? You have no taste in music, you know that?*

On another occasion: *You wear the ugliest clothes I've ever seen. You have stupid taste.* Perhaps what she meant was, *I wish you were more like me; I wish you liked the same things I like.* My mother could never say, for example, *I don't like strawberries*. For her, it was always, *How could you eat strawberries? They are the most disgusting fruit in the world.*

A parent suffering from a narcissistic disturbance sees her child only as a mirror image of herself. My mother always maintained that she hated her own mother, the Dread Gertrude, and that Gertrude hated her and had taken every opportunity to humiliate her. Gloria fought back with everything she had. One of her greatest weapons had been her father, who adored Gloria above all his other children and taught her the very defiance she used against her mother. "The child, an only one or often the first-born, was the narcissistically cathected object. What these mothers had once failed to find in their own mothers they were able to find in their children: someone at their disposal who can be used as an echo, who can be controlled, is completely centered on them, will never desert them, and offers full attention and admiration."

But, of course, a child cannot help but be a child. A child grows fussy, sometimes rejecting, sometimes demanding, easily exhausted, and exhausting. My mother had no patience for any of this. She adored me—as she was quick to announce—but she could only tolerate my presence in very small doses.

Alice Miller writes that the extreme forms of narcissistic disturbance are depression and grandiosity. That "in fact, grandiosity is the defense against depression, and depression is the defense against the deep pain over the loss of the self."

While children raised by parents with a narcissistic disturbance will most often be allowed to grow and develop intellectually, they are often squashed in the emotional realm. "There are those with great gifts, often precisely the most gifted, who suffer from severe depression. One is free from depression when self-esteem is based on the authenticity of one's own feelings and not on the possession of certain qualities."

Alice Miller describes the secretive nature of this relationship. The parent cannot let anyone else know about this manipulation of the child; and so, the rest of the world remains oblivious, while the child immediately believes the problem is within him or her. And, most strangely, "the mother often loves her child as her self-object, passionately, but not in the way he needs to be loved."

Perhaps my mother did truly love me, or believe she loved me, in any case.

I listlessly began riffling through Janet Woititz's *Adult Children of Alcoholics*, holding it at arm's length, as if the distance could protect me from what was inside. By chance I came upon the "laundry list" of characteristics of ACOAs. The first one, "Adult children of alcoholics guess at what normal behavior is," made me crumple into a ball on my bed. If my view of reality was so skewed that I couldn't rely on what my own eyes were telling me, how was I ever going to tell truth from lie?

I vacillated wildly between enormous relief at having found a plausible explanation for my mother's behavior toward me, and horror at the possibility that it might be true and I might be the only person on the planet who would ever know.

I wondered how a man as wise, intelligent, liberated, and experienced as my father could not have seen any of it. But, then, he'd not had the sanest relationships with women before he'd met my mother. He'd not been looking for a housewife and a mother for his children, after all, but for a lifelong companion who would support his work and his creative process, and, of course, his strong sexual desires, and his heavy drinking.

My mother did not call me for four months. Finally, toward the end of October, she left a message saying she wanted me to come home for Thanksgiving. "Let's just put it all behind us," she said into the answering machine. And just like that, my calling her an alcoholic, her hanging up on me (twice), and my exile were erased from the annals of Jones history.

After that brutal summer of exile, I ran into my old friend Gianna, who had been at Poets & Writers when I'd worked there in the mideighties. She said she'd just been looking at an apartment around the corner, having decided to move back to the City from Sag Harbor. Gianna and I have the same ethnic background—Italian, German, Irish, Welsh—and our features and coloring are so similar that people often mistake us for sisters. Around ten years my senior, she is, and someone I've always loved and admired.

Back when we'd worked together, she would invite me home for dinner, and her partner Bea would cook. The only problem was that Bea would take three hours to get dinner ready, and meanwhile Gianna and I would sit in the living room polishing off two or three bottles of wine. After dinner, restless, Gianna would tell Bea we were taking Toto, Bea's little gray poodle, for a walk, and we'd hit a bar on Second Avenue, leaving Toto tied to a meter just outside, where we could watch him through the window. Bea would chase us down and holler at us for being disgusting lushes, and I'd cower into a cab while Gianna went home.

Gianna had given up drinking about a year before I met Andrew. She had been a guest at our wedding, probably one of three sober individuals out of the 250 at the reception. Not too much later, she asked me out to dinner, and told me about quitting drinking and how she'd left Bea and found herself, and how wonderful her life had become since. I remember thinking, Poor Gianna, what a horrible way to live. Thank God *I* don't have to stop drinking!

I wanted to ask her now, *Are you still not drinking, Gianna?* But I couldn't say it. I realized she probably wanted to ask me a similar question, *Are you still drinking, Kaylie?*

"Are you doing okay?" she finally asked, gingerly reaching out a hand and placing it on my shoulder.

"I'm doing fine. I'm really good," I said bravely. "I've been reading Alice Miller and *Children of Alcoholics*."

"Ah." Gianna nodded meaningfully.

Several months later she told me she'd understood in that instant that I was on the brink, almost ready to leap across that terrifying chasm. But I wasn't quite there yet. She also told me that for the next few months, she fervently, daily, prayed on my behalf.

We exchanged phone numbers, and promised to get together. We hugged, then went our separate ways.

One of the main reasons writing teachers recommend James Joyce's *Dubliners* to students is its epiphanic moments. Nothing is harder to write than those moments of grace, where truth suddenly comes barging in through the darkness and a character is offered a chance to change. I often go back to those moments in Joyce's stories, like the scene at the end of "The Dead" when the self-satisfied, pompous Gabriel realizes he has been misguided his entire life, and has lived with a concept of himself that has nothing to do with the truth. Or the scene at the end of "A Painful Case," when the morally superior aging gentleman realizes his moral superiority has been nothing but a cover for his fear of life and love, and that it is now too late and he will live out the rest of his days alone.

Hemingway had a different method—which is to simply write the facts surrounding the moment of epiphany, and let the reader fill in the gaps. Most modern readers miss the point, though, if it's not spelled out clearly enough for them.

So what was different about the Monday I decided to give up drinking?

Absolutely nothing. I've been considering that day for years and still cannot find a reason why, on that particular morning, my deflector shields were so profoundly weakened that the truth was able to slam into me full blast.

Sunday evening I was invited to a Super Bowl party at my friend Dave's apartment. Dave was the only close friend from Wesleyan I still had in New York. He was a banker and lived in a one-bedroom penthouse. He was a cultivator and studier of roses, and played classical piano, two traits that had always surprised and inspired me, because Dave had been an ace science student in college, as well as a brawler who never backed down from a good fight. He was the best drinking buddy I'd ever had, because when I was with Dave, no one in his right mind would try to bother me.

I spent that afternoon deciding whether I should go. Last time I had gotten drunk was on January 6, when I had drunk several glasses of cheap red wine and awakened with a massive headache and absolutely no recollection of anything that was said during the evening. Today was January 26, and I had vowed to drink not more than once every twenty-one days. If I didn't wait another day I'd be breaking my vow, and that meant I had a problem.

The day before, Dennis and I had had an argument about the unclear state of our relationship. I'd hinted that I thought he was seeing someone else. He dismissed my concerns and cut me off, but I knew he was an excellent liar. I pushed him, saying he had no commitment to me and it was okay, I just wanted him to be honest. He simply refused to discuss it, which made me more suspicious and angry. Instead he said he couldn't commit himself to me because I had a drinking problem and was not facing it. I called him a liar and a zealot, adding for good measure that he was a judgmental son of a bitch who saw an alcoholic everywhere he looked.

He pulled out of a bedside drawer a Twenty Questions pamphlet that urged the person taking the test to seek help if he or she answered *one or more* questions in the affirmative. Dennis sat at the edge of his bed and looked the pamphlet over in silence. I knew what was coming. I was in a fury, but I lay back on his pillows, pretending to be relaxed and perfectly calm and not in the least offended.

"Have you ever felt remorse after drinking?"

"Who wouldn't, with someone like you watching over their shoulder every minute?" I laughed dryly but he didn't even crack a smile.

"Have you ever had a complete loss of memory as a result of drinking?"

"Not anymore." In truth, the last six months were something of a blackout—or gray-out, more precisely—from the effort of controlling when and how much to drink, but I wasn't going to share this with him, the judgmental bastard. This shit-head knows me too well, that's the problem, I thought. Dennis seemed to be growing annoyed as well. His face and neck had turned a deep shade of red, though he tried to maintain his calm composure.

"There's no such thing as *not anymore* with alcoholism," he said, attempting to keep his voice equable and calm. "Pickles can't turn back into cucumbers."

"Pickles? Cucumbers? What the fuck are you talking about? You know what, Dennis? Fuck you." I stormed out and hadn't spoken to him since, and today was Super Bowl Sunday and Dave's party.

So, feeling lonely and misunderstood, I took a Valium so I would not be tempted to drink, and walked the eleven blocks to Dave's apartment.

Unfortunately for me, the old Wesleyan crowd would not accommodate me by being moderate, and Dave's other best friend, Ethan, now a gastroenterologist, had brought half a case of Veuve

Clicquot champagne to celebrate the occasion. Okay, I thought, what's one glass of Veuve Clicquot? And who in their right mind would turn down free French champagne?

Next thing I knew the game was on, blasting away on the television, the Buffalo Bills against . . . I have no idea. I remember snow falling over the field and steam rising from the players' mouths, but that could have been my impaired vision.

Ethan and I polished off the six bottles of Veuve Clicquot and then, as he held the last bottle upside down over my glass and the last few drops trickled out, he suggested we switch to white wine, as the two went perfectly well together. He lit up a fat spliff, and at that point, I thought, What's the difference? So I smoked that too and at least a pack of Marlboro Lights. By the time the wine was gone, the game was over and I had no idea who won.

Late the next morning, I woke up shaking and sick. I felt like a burned-out house with the windows broken and the wind howling through. How long could I go on like this? And what were Dennis and I doing back exactly where we'd started almost ten years ago? What the fuck was going on? I tried to think of a good and certain way of killing myself that would not look like suicide. I certainly didn't want anyone to think I'd killed myself. An accident would be much better. How about a bus? I could walk out in front of a bus. But the goddamn New York City buses were so slow. That's all I needed was to wake up a quadriplegic or something. And without health insurance, no less. My ground-floor apartment was so dark it could have been the middle of the night. I was groping my way toward the medicine cabinet when the phone rang. Normally, in my condition, I never would have picked it up, but for some reason, I did. My hand was shaking terribly and I felt I wasn't getting enough air.

"How're you doing, hon?" It was Gianna.

In an unusual burst of honesty, I told her I was having some kind of nervous breakdown. I told her my mother was slowly drinking herself to death; I told her Dennis was a liar who couldn't even be called a boyfriend because he couldn't commit to a serious relationship and was most certainly seeing someone else; my voice warbled as my throat constricted, and I told her sometimes I wished I had the courage to walk out in front of a bus. I must have sounded horribly hungover, thick with cigarette smoke and alcohol.

"I used to feel that way, too," Gianna said in a tone devoid of judgment.

"Shit," I said. "I'm sorry."

After a moment's silence, she said, "Are you ready, Kaylie?"

I took a deep breath, and before I could consider what I was saying, I blurted out, "Gianna, I've *got* to stop drinking. Help me."

"I'll pick you up in an hour," she said, and hung up before I could backpedal. I realized it was almost 11 A.M., and I was going to have to really work hard to pull myself together in an hour.

Fifty-five minutes later, bathed, clothed, brushed, I stood two feet from my front door, hand reaching for the knob, suddenly petrified. I had the feeling some other part of me was floating up by the ceiling, watching the scene with cold detachment. That part of me looking down from the ceiling knew that if I walked out the door now, and followed Gianna wherever she would take me, my life as I knew it would be changed forever, and there would be no turning back. The buzzer rang. I opened the door and stepped out into the lighted hallway.

"What Money?"

I don't know if my mother ever told this story to anyone other than my father, my cousin Kate, Jamie, and me. She didn't share this one at cocktail or dinner parties.

➤➤   ◄◄

When Tony Mosolino, Gloria's father, died on New Year's Eve in 1947, Gloria was home from Syracuse University for the Christmas holidays. That night she was out dancing at a party at the country club. Her father had recently acquired the second-biggest mansion on the fanciest street in Pottsville, where the heirs to the Yuengling Brewery and the owners of the coal mines lived. The house on Mahantongo Street was done up with no expense spared—Venetian crystal chandeliers on the staircase landings; vases of Napoleonic battles; bronze winged victories from the French Revolution; heavily carved Chinese Colonial desks and side tables; and silver galore. After a sumptuous New Year's Eve feast with the relatives, Tony Mosolino said he had indigestion and sat down in an armchair in the living room. He closed his eyes, and died.

Gloria was phoned at the country club and rushed home. In early childhood, she had lost two siblings to a virulent strain of polio—her eight-year-old sister, Kitty, whom Gloria, at four years old, worshipped and adored; and a two-year-old baby boy, the first Mark. Gloria was not close to Gertrude, her mother.

Gloria even believed that Gertrude hated her and was jealous of Gloria's relationship with her father.

A few days after Tony's funeral, the FBI showed up at the door. Not one agent or two, but a slew of men. Gertrude was upstairs in the master bedroom, and she called frantically to Gloria, who came running. A huge stack of government bonds lay on the bed. Gertrude instructed Gloria to wrap the bonds around her body, under her clothes, as Gertrude was doing herself, sliding them under her girdle.

The FBI agent in charge asked Gertrude where Tony Mosolino's money was hidden. Gertrude said, "What money?" and acted completely stupid, the housewife without a clue as to what her husband was up to when he wasn't home. She batted her eyelids and offered the agent something to drink. He refused and ordered a search of the house. The house and property were turned upside down, top to bottom. The grass was dug up and the garage emptied. No money could be found.

In 1954, when Gloria was a struggling actress in New York City—which Gertrude disapproved of mightily, constantly urging her daughter to return home and marry the nice doctor's son she'd dated in high school—she was up for the part of Marlon Brando's love interest in the movie *On the Waterfront*. Her screen test had gone quite well—better than Eva Marie Saint's, according to Gloria—and Elia Kazan, the director, told Gloria the part was hers, *if* she got her buckteeth fixed.

She took the bus home to Pottsville to ask Gertrude for the money. As she described this scene to me, I imagined it taking place in the elegant front entryway, below the wide, gently curving staircase and Venetian crystal chandelier; however, this would mean that Gloria wouldn't even have bothered to enter the living room before putting forth her request to her mother. Gloria had never been one for small talk.

"I need money to get my teeth fixed," she told her mother.

"I don't have any money," Gertrude said flatly.

"What do you mean, you don't have any money? What about all those bonds we wrapped around ourselves when the FBI came looking? That was at least a hundred and fifty thousand dollars!"

Gertrude said, "You must have dreamed it. You always had a wild imagination. I don't know what you're talking about."

Gloria punched Gertrude in the mouth and fled back to New York City. Without the money to get her teeth fixed, she told me, she lost the part to Eva Marie Saint. Gertrude cut her off completely, and Gloria's uncle John Mosolino, cousins Joanie and Kate's father, gave her money every month until she married my father.

Gloria never forgave her mother and saw her fewer than a dozen times over the next forty years.

CHAPTER NINE

⤜ Grace ⤛

ANY RECOVERING ALCOHOLIC WHO HAS found the way to sobriety can help lead a fellow sufferer toward relief from this hopeless condition, just as Gianna led me. But attempting to explain to someone who has never been exposed to alcoholism how recovery could possibly work seems only slightly less difficult than trying to convince an alcoholic in denial that death, slow or fast, is around the corner. Many courageous thinkers have tried—doctors, therapists, sober alcoholics—and yet, only a person who has experienced grace can understand the mystery of how a destroyed life can be turned around.

In this country, even if we know better, for the most part we still think of alcoholism as a moral weakness. Only recently has the notion that alcoholism is a disease caught on in the social zeitgeist, and most educated people will now at least pay lip service to this concept. And yet, on an unconscious and primal level, the majority of us still feel that having an alcoholic in the family is a *shanda*. This is why the relatives continue to circle the wagons and try to hide the alcoholic's drinking—and protect the family from public scrutiny and judgment.

Medical research has revealed that in about one-tenth of the population, the liver processes alcohol differently, releasing a chemical messenger that creates the craving for another drink; once that second drink is taken, the desire is doubled. But the real problem of the alcoholic is actually centered in the mind, because we can't remember why it was such a bad idea to pick up that first drink. Once we start, we can't stop; and when we stop, we can't remember why we shouldn't start again. It is a form of mental illness, like a manic-depressive who, after being stabilized on medication for a while, suddenly decides she is fine and no longer needs her pills.

For me, the hardest part of giving up drinking was not *giving up drinking*—but getting my family to accept that I was an *alcoholic*, a terrible word that was still only whispered in my mother's house. My mother and father and their friends used to "go on the wagon" quite often. "Going on the wagon" always implied that they would soon step *off* the wagon, as if this were a necessary, if unpleasant, rest period everyone had to take. But it was only a rest period, not an end to drinking forever. Admitting to my mother that I was an *alcoholic* was saying out loud that I had to stop drinking completely. And that, in the Jones fortress, was considered a fate worse than death.

My first few months sober were terrifying, but they were also filled with adventure and fun. I felt as though I were stumbling through a foggy landscape of new and befuddling emotions, but each day, out of the gloom stepped helpers—complete strangers, but also people I had known before in my drinking life, and lost—who appeared out of the mist as if by magic and walked with me for a few paces before disappearing again. I still see their faces and honor them all, whether they stayed sober, or not.

One of the people who walked with me for a while was an unemployed executive assistant exactly my age named Michele. Recently, while they'd been drinking, her husband had held a loaded pistol to her head, which compelled her to run away from him and seek help for her drinking problem. With three weeks sober each, we were very much in the same state of mind. We began spending

Friday evenings watching animated films—*Bambi, Snow White, Sleeping Beauty, The Secret of NIMH,* and my all-time favorite, *101 Dalmatians.* We cried our eyes out at the fantastic bravery of those wonderful dogs. What a metaphor for early sobriety! We bought the most extravagant desserts we could find —Napoleons, sundaes topped with whipped cream, disgustingly rich Ben & Jerry's mixes, and éclairs—oh, éclairs, how I love you still!

While I had trouble recognizing my internal landscape, the world outside by contrast looked sharp and new, and each day felt like an epic adventure. Without the anesthetic, my senses were totally overwhelmed. Acts as simple as choosing a toothpaste in the drugstore baffled me. I had never considered what kind of toothpaste I liked but had always bought whatever toothpaste the man I was with liked. I had no one around to tell me what to do. What did *I* like? I had no idea. I bought a different, tiny tube each time, to try out all of them. I settled on Aim. "Do you know that Aim is an excellent toothpaste?" I would tell people, and they would look at me with mild concern.

When I went to the grocery store, I didn't know what to buy. I felt like I hadn't eaten a normal meal in years and didn't even know what I liked to eat. Had I ever shopped for food on a regular basis? I couldn't remember. It occurred to me as I was walking down the aisles one day that I could eat anything I wanted, because *I* would be the one deciding. And I could plan a few days in advance. What a revelation.

I found out very quickly that I had a passion for fresh-brewed French roast coffee. I went to bed every night with my mouth watering at the thought of that first cup in the morning, creamy with half-and-half. If I met a friend for dinner, as I was getting ready to leave, I would rub my hands together briskly and say, "I'm off to get my coffee ready for tomorrow morning!"

And there was something else to look forward to when I got home: I'd discovered that right before bed, a cup of warmed milk sprinkled with honey and nutmeg, accompanied by reruns of *Miami Vice*, quieted my overanxious mind and put me tenderly to sleep.

All in all, I felt more hopeful, and more youthful, than I had in years. Every day except Sunday I went to Gilda Marx's bodybuilding class, which kept me not only fit and trim, but also from wanting to jump out the window when the phone rang and it was someone who could, with just one word spoken into my answering machine, stir up all the darkness and terror and self-annihilating impulses from the muddy depths of my being. Emotions such as anger, fear, and sadness would sneak up from behind and hold me paralyzed in their grasp. I remember hearing my mother's voice for the first time on my answering machine; I'd just come home at nightfall from Gilda Marx. Gloria sounded slightly drunk and wanted me to meet her at Elaine's for dinner. Suddenly my skin felt prickly hot, and my breath caught in my throat. I had to sit down. Was this anger? Or fear? I had no idea, but didn't like it. There was no way I could meet my mother for dinner in my raw condition. I could pretend I never got the message . . . but that would be dishonest. Part of my new way of living was to be rigorously honest. I called Gianna. She told me I most definitely did *not* have to go out to dinner with my mother. She told me something incredible, totally staggering in its simplicity: "*No* is a sentence with a period at the end of it."

Not with Gloria, it wasn't.

I called my mother, punching in the number with a trembling hand, and told her I couldn't meet her for dinner. She wanted to know why not. I immediately began making up excuses. Too much work. Too tired. Feeling lousy. I realized someone had probably canceled on her, which was why she'd called me so late. None of these excuses appeased her in the least. "You're a pain in the ass, you know that?" she said, and hung up.

I felt sick with guilt, like a thirteen-year-old who's done something wrong, the age I'd been, in fact, when these powerful feelings had first overwhelmed me, and I began to anesthetize them.

Dennis, it turned out, was indeed seeing someone else, a co-worker of ours from the Writer's Voice, where he was now also teaching a beginning fiction workshop—a position for which I had recommended him. When I saw Dennis coming down the hall with his new girlfriend the poet at his side, I felt my skin was made of glass and everything I was thinking and feeling was visible to him. Going to work was such an ordeal I almost quit.

It was Gianna who told me that going to the North Pole to avoid someone living at the South Pole was not learning to accept things as they are, but continuing to react to circumstances beyond my control. She promised me that if I stayed in the moment, continued to pray and ask for help, and didn't project into the unknown future, things would get better. I had never prayed a day in my life and wasn't about to start praying now, but I didn't tell Gianna this.

"*When*'s it going to get better?" I asked her belligerently. But she remained calm and serene and asked me if I'd had a drink today. "NO!" I shouted into the phone, outraged at the suggestion.

"Then it's been a good day," she said simply. When I didn't answer, she added, "You're in the hallway and it feels scary right now but just keep going. There's another door, and you're going to find it. And then the whole world is going to open up to you."

"Whatever," I muttered gloomily. But, for the moment, her words had to be enough.

On one of that year's warm March mornings, I walked out of my apartment and saw a tree beginning to bud. I stood there and stared at it for a long time, dumbfounded. The sky above was a deep, ringing blue, and the bright green, almost neon green of the tiny buds stood out sharply against it. I felt as if I'd never before

seen such a miraculous display of life. Is that God's work? I wondered. The next day, the temperature dropped radically and several inches of snow fell, and I went outside to check on the tree.
I was worried. What happened to buds when a frost hits so late
in the year? I asked a few of my new sober friends—ladies who
lunched—but being New Yorkers, they had never pondered the
question. For several weeks, I watched the tree, and then one day,
seemingly all at once, it burst into white blooms. I stood there and
wept like a fool, because I thought it was the most beautiful thing
I'd ever seen, and I'd lived on that block for almost three years
and had never noticed it before.

That same week, sitting on the crosstown bus on the way to
teach my writing class, I looked up and saw a poem on a poster
in the advertising space above the windows. Part of the Poetry in
Motion series, it was by Langston Hughes:

LUCK
Sometimes a crumb falls
From the tables of joy,
Sometimes a bone
Is flung.

To some people
Love is given,
To others
Only heaven.

I was engulfed by such a wave of grief that for a few moments
I couldn't breathe. I folded in over myself, started to cry. I missed
my stop and had to walk three blocks back to the Y.

I hadn't seen my mother since I'd stopped drinking, but I went
home for Easter weekend. I'd finally admitted to her over the

phone sometime in March that I thought "I might be an alcoholic." Her response was, "Don't be ridiculous."

Apparently as soon as we hung up, she called Cecile and said, "Kaylie's joined the Moonies."

That first evening the dinner table was filled with the usual suspects, her aging buddies from around the neighborhood, assembled for a Friday-night meal. She poured me a glass of red wine, and the prickly smell went right up my nose and into my mouth, making my taste buds spring to life. I took the glass to the sink. Her sixth sense and stress radar were functioning perfectly, and she looked right at me and muttered, "Look at Carry Nation over here."

I didn't answer. There was a big silence at the table. After an excruciating hour, I went into my room and called Gianna, who was at her house in Sag Harbor for the weekend, and asked if I could stay there that night.

I returned to the living room to tell my mother I was going over to Gianna's. She replied, without a hint of humor, "What, you've gone gay too?"

No one cracked a smile—except for Gianna, who fifteen minutes later was positively howling with laughter.

With the extended Memorial Day weekend coming up, I decided that going back out there for another dose was more than I could bear in my fragile state.

James Ivory and Ismail Merchant had optioned *A Soldier's Daughter Never Cries* the year before, in the spring of 1991, and that option money along with my teaching commitments had so far kept me from having to find a real job. I'd just gotten a check from Merchant Ivory, renewing their option for another year. They had two film projects lined up for production in France before *A Soldier's Daughter Never Cries*—*Jefferson in Paris* and *Surviving Picasso*. It was still uncertain if the film would ever get

made, but along with my check I'd gotten a phone call from Jim
Ivory reassuring me that they still intended to go forward with
the project, but that it would take some time.

Also, Terrence Malick, the brilliant and famously private film
director, had recently announced he was coming out of a twenty-
year hiatus to direct his own adaptation of *The Thin Red Line*, my
father's second novel in the war trilogy that had started with *From
Here to Eternity*. I'd just gotten option money for that project too,
and for the first time in years, I was flush. At least I could stop
agonizing for a while.

I decided to take a two-week trip to Key West with a neighbor, Jennifer, who wanted to learn to scuba dive. I had heard that
Key West was teeming with sober individuals who would be more
than happy to reach out to a neophyte like myself.

When I told my mother I wasn't coming out for Memorial
Day, she did her silent number, followed by her vague refrain, "I
don't care, do what you want," and hung up on me.

I was dismayed to find, when we arrived in Key West and took
our first walk, that Duval Street, which leads to Mallory Square
and the waterfront, is a gauntlet of open bars with neon signs
advertising colorful, half-price happy-hour drinks named after
Hemingway characters. It didn't help that Jennifer, who had no
idea what I was going through, thought the bars looked like a
lot of fun and wanted to stop in. Jimmy Buffet's "Margaritaville"
blasted forth from outdoor speakers, and all the people drinking
inside looked like there was nothing in the world they'd rather
be doing. It occurred to me that the reason there were so many
sober people in Key West was that there were so many drunks. I
was sorely reminded of the French Quarter in New Orleans and
I wanted to go home to New York and my safe, daily routine and
support system. I resolved not to pass by this street again, but
all the streets in Key West seemed to lead there. I felt alone and

afraid, and guilty for having once again so intensely displeased my mother.

I resented the happy drinkers in the bars and wanted to be them instead of me.

I toured Hemingway's house, and there were about a hundred cats living on the grounds, direct descendants of Hemingway's original cats. Hemingway had installed a drinking fountain for them in the garden, the base of which was a finely detailed tile urinal from his favorite bar, where every afternoon he used to drink himself into a stupor. His writing studio had been left intact, his old typewriter still on the desk. It looked so much like my father's office that I felt a knot in my throat. Had I betrayed my father? Had I betrayed them all by accepting that I was an alcoholic?

I remembered my father telling me when I was a little girl, "Guilt is just bullshit. Don't ever let anyone make you feel guilty."

But how did one learn to stop feeling guilty?

I joined a fitness club for the time we were there and went to two classes a day, but the grinding anxiety I felt just being on vacation sober for the first time in my life—the overpowering itch to move, to do, to run—was not quieted. I went scuba diving twice a day as well while Jennifer took the training course. Even diving, which I had so enjoyed in the past, did not make me feel calmer, or more serene.

One evening, at twilight, while Jennifer was napping, I went for a bike ride alone, pedaling furiously and randomly down the labyrinthine streets. I found myself once again back on Mallory Square, where a concrete pier demarcates the sudden end of the United States. At the far side of the square stood the gauntlet of open bars that called to me like sirens from a rocky shoal. In the back of my mind a voice said, Why not? Pedal over there, step into any one of those bars, order a Brett Ashley, or a Robert

Jordan, or an Old Man and the Sea, or whatever the hell they're drinking—and all your worries will vanish in an orgy of booze and boys on vacation.

But what would Gianna think? And anyway, all my worries would be back tomorrow morning, having grown during my drunken stupor into a clamoring barbarian horde.

The sun was about to set, and a small crowd had gathered on the quay. I had stopped my bike some distance away, and now put my foot on the curb and watched as the red sun touched the water and began its downward slide into the waves, the bank of clouds on the horizon exploding into a diorama of pink and red mountain ranges. For the first time in my life, 112 days away from a drink, I earnestly prayed.

God, if you're there, help me.

The sun disappeared into the waves and a dark blue curtain fell slowly over sky and water. I waited for a while as the people drifted away and the bars continued to blast their party music out into the street, but I felt nothing. Resigned, I pushed my bike forward and pedaled away.

I went back to New York convinced I would never be able to travel again. I felt like a person on dialysis; leaving home was no longer an option. Gianna insisted it would get better, but I did not believe her.

I reread Bill Styron's *Darkness Visible* and was once again seized by the brilliant, totally illuminating thought that I was not an alcoholic, only clinically depressed. The next time I saw Gianna, I mentioned this to her. "William Styron says in *Darkness Visible* that alcohol is good for him. It was only when his body rejected alcohol that he sank into depression. You know, Gianna, I don't think I can write without it."

Gianna did something I'd never seen her do before: she snorted derisively through her nose. After she'd regained her

Zen-like composure, she said, "That book should be used in every alcohol and drug rehab center as a classic, textbook case of denial."

I didn't know how to respond to that, so I remained silent.

I continued to think my life had reached a dead end. But I never failed to call Gianna, sometimes two or three times a day, trying to explain that I didn't think I was going to make it. She told me to pray, to just accept *her* faith in me, and that everything would be all right.

For years, I'd wanted to start a writing fellowship in my father's name. In November 1992, a group of college professors and childhood friends of James Jones were getting together in Robinson, Illinois, to found the James Jones Literary Society, and it was my opportunity to try to put my wish into action. Kurt Vonnegut had once mentioned to me that he hoped one day there would be a James Jones fellowship for struggling writers, so I decided to call him to ask his advice. He was my mother's neighbor in Sagaponack, and we'd become friendly over the years. Kurt, while brusque, was one of the kindest and most generous writers I've ever known. He had given me a jacket blurb for my first novel and told me quite strenuously, whenever he got the chance, that I was an excellent writer and should not live in my father's shadow. "You're just as good as he was," he'd tell me. I did not believe him.

My parents had met Kurt in Paris back in the early seventies. Kurt and his wife, Jill Krementz, had had a terrible fight, and she had taken off with all his cash and credit cards and he was wandering around the streets, penniless and depressed. He somehow found out where my father lived and came and rang the doorbell. It must have been late in the afternoon, because my dad opened the door himself. There stood a tall, wild-haired, slightly stooped man.

"Hi, I'm Kurt Vonnegut," he said. "I'm a science fiction writer—"

My dad was an avid science fiction reader and cried out, "Kurt Vonnegut, by God, I love your books!" And he invited him in and they proceeded to get stinko, sitting around the pulpit bar. My dad got the whole sad story of how Kurt had been wandering around Paris without a cent, and he loaned him money so Kurt could pay his hotel bills and get home to the States.

I was always afraid to call Kurt because I felt I was disturbing a genius at work. But this was important enough that I picked up the phone. He answered, grumpy and annoyed, a genius at work who had been disturbed, so without further ado I reminded him of what he'd said years ago, and put forth my plan to try to start a first novel fellowship in my father's name.

"A fellowship?" he said. "Forget it. You need an endowment. There's no way in hell you'll find a hundred fifty, two hundred thousand to get the thing started. Nice thought, though."

But at the gathering in Robinson, Don Sackrider, a retired commercial pilot who now lived in Miami, put up the first $5,000—seed money for the fellowship. Don had been raised in Robinson and, at seventeen, had been the youngest member of the Handy Colony in Marshall. He felt the Colony had given his life direction, and he wanted to offer the kind of help to struggling writers that he'd received when he'd shown up on the Colony's doorstep as an aimless young man.

A few weeks later, I met Kevin at a Writer's Voice reception. In the crowded, echoing room, he ambled over to me and introduced himself. He said he knew I was a teacher there and that he'd heard wonderful things about my class. In his early thirties, he had a stoic, angular face and a thin slit of a mouth, but his eyes were large and expressive, a tawny color, with long black lashes, and when he gazed at me they seemed so gentle and vulnerable

I felt scared. He wore an old black cotton long-sleeved T-shirt and faded blue jeans, and carried slung over his shoulder a thin, black nylon windbreaker that was surely no protection against the late-November cold. For some reason a poem by Rimbaud, "Ma Bohème"—"Je m'en allais, les poings dans mes poches crevées . . ."—about the poet's happy-go-lucky homeless travels, passed through my mind.

A crazed poet, I thought. Run!

We started talking about books and writing, and I sensed immediately he'd lost someone close to him. Perhaps it was a familiar shadow I saw lurking behind his eyes. I knew I had that look too, and he probably sensed I was also a member of that unenviable club. He said he'd recently moved to New York from North Carolina because of his job, but his true love was writing. He'd been a freelance journalist and screenwriter and had an idea for a novel. By the end of the evening, I gave him my phone number.

A couple of weeks later, we had our first date—which wasn't really a date because Kevin had called and asked me for writing advice. It was a Sunday morning in mid-December, at a loud and trendy art deco diner on Second Avenue. Concerned that he'd think I was overly interested in him, I arrived straight from my Gilda Marx bodybuilding class in my sweats, and that seemed to convince him immediately that whatever interest I had in him, it wasn't romantic.

Before the food even arrived, I told him I hadn't had a drink in eleven months and felt completely unprepared for life. I figured if this was going to scare him off, better to know right away. He responded evenly that his parents drank heavily but never considered the possibility they were alcoholic. His father had died of a heart attack when Kevin was twenty-six, on New Year's Day, while watching football on TV. Better to know you're an alcoholic than not, Kevin said.

After a short lull, I asked him what he did when he wasn't writing.

Kevin worked for an airline, and he could fly standby, for free, anywhere in the world and his idea of weekend fun was going to the ticket counter at the airport and checking which flights were lightly booked, and getting on a plane bound for South America, or Europe, or California. He just packed an extra sweatshirt and a pair of thick socks, in case the flight was bound for Reykjavík in January.

He smiled happily, and I shuddered at the thought. Having just taken my second sober flight, I had no intention of ever getting on a plane again.

I told him that in the old days, when I was drinking, I handled air travel with two or three vodkas and a Valium, passing out and coming to when the plane landed. Now, I explained with a mirth-less laugh, I would *never* fly anywhere unless it was absolutely necessary. His expression went from hopeful to crestfallen. It hadn't occurred to me until that moment that he was considering asking me on a romantic air travel date.

He tried to pay the bill with a credit card, but the place only took cash. Now he looked sick to his stomach with embarrass-ment, his face turning ashen. I felt so bad for him I didn't know what to do, so I smiled, reached for my handbag, and said he could get the next one. This didn't seem to help him feel better, so I started belittling myself by telling him I'd never been on a "date" in my entire life and wouldn't recognize one if it fell on my head from the sky.

When we walked outside I noticed he was still wearing that skimpy nylon windbreaker, even though it was freezing cold, and I had the urge to take him shopping for a coat.

We read *All the Pretty Horses* at the same time, having sepa-rately bought the book. Sitting in a coffee shop near the Writer's Voice late one dark afternoon just before Christmas, I told him I thought it was a beautifully written book, but such crazy notions of romance were for teenagers. At our age, such careless foolishness was no longer possible.

"Why not?" he said. "I just turned down a promotion in Washington, D.C., because of you."

We hadn't even slept together yet, and he turned down a promotion? I was suddenly terrified of him. But this was the most romantic thing anyone had ever done for me. He reached across the Formica tabletop and placed his hand over mine. His palm was warm and dry, several degrees warmer than mine, comforting. He told me he'd done the long-distance relationship thing and he would never do it again.

"I think you're the one," he said solemnly. "Maybe you're not, and that's fine. But I want to know, and I'm not going to find out by moving to Washington, D.C."

A month later, on January 27, 1993, one year to the day after I stopped drinking, my mother was scheduled for hip replacement surgery at Lenox Hill Hospital. A month before her operation, her surgeon, Dr. Brenner, a renowned sports medicine specialist, asked Gloria and me from behind his wide, imposing desk if he should know anything about Gloria before he operated. My mother told him she was in perfect health. That settled, we all stood up; I hung back and let her limp out into the waiting room ahead of me. As Dr. Brenner stood by the door waiting for me to pass, I turned to him and told him point-blank that my mother had a very serious drinking problem, and I was worried about the anesthesia, how it would affect her if she was full of alcohol.

"Don't worry, I'll take care of it," he murmured, and patted my shoulder.

The day of her surgery, I woke up angry and resentful. It was my one-year anniversary of sobriety and fuck her anyway. As Kevin got up and dressed in his suit and freshly laundered shirt for work, I was cold and silent. When he left, I didn't say good-bye. At 7:00 A.M. I picked my mother up at Cecile and Buddy's and took her by cab to the hospital. After we'd waited for three hours, a nurse marched us into a room, asked my mother to step behind a curtain, and told her to undress. Two or three other people in white lab coats came in, and when the nurse slid open the curtain, I saw a small, fragile old lady, gripping a flimsy hospital gown in one tight fist over her chest, her knuckles white with tension. Her eyes were wide with fright as she glanced around at all these strangers, and I suddenly felt frightened myself.

"Mrs. Jones," said the first nurse, clipboard in hand, "how many drinks do you have a day?"

My mother seemed to give this some thought. "Six," she said with finality, looking the nurse straight in the eye.

Six? I thought. Six? My God, she has six before lunch. Don't believe her, I wanted to shout. As if six drinks a day—as opposed to twelve, or twenty, or thirty—weren't cause enough for concern.

The last thing they did before rolling her off to surgery was ask her to take out her dentures. With tremulous fingers my mother reached into her mouth and took out her upper teeth, then handed them to a nurse, who swiftly rinsed them and put them in a plastic container. Suddenly my mother's whole face caved into her mouth, and she looked exactly like my grandmother Gertrude; my breath caught in my throat. I went back to the waiting room on shaky legs and collapsed into a chair, stunned into a kind of emotional paralysis, unable to read any of the three books I'd brought along to pass the time.

I wanted to call Kevin and apologize for my behavior that morning, but I didn't know where he was—probably somewhere in Midtown, visiting clients.

In the early evening, when she'd awakened in her private room, grumpy and in pain, Dr. Brenner arrived, checked out everything, and then asked me to step out into the hallway. There, he squeezed my arm and said, "I'm going to talk to your mother about her drinking." I felt flushed with gratitude: finally someone was going to face her down.

Dr. Brenner led the way back into the room.

"Mrs. Jones," he said, "after you go home, you must get control of your drinking. You should only have one drink a day, preferably red wine."

Had he never taken a course, not even a two-hour seminar, on alcoholism, in his seven years of medical school? Didn't he know that alcoholics can't drink *at all*? Didn't he understand that with one drink, the obsession is triggered? He was giving her permission to continue drinking, just as she had always drunk.

I walked out into the shiny, brightly lit hall, blood pulsing behind my eyes. Down by the elevators, a familiar figure in a pinstriped suit stepped out from behind a pair of sliding doors, then stopped and looked around. It was Kevin. I hadn't expected him—or asked him—to come. He saw me, raised his hand, and began walking briskly in my direction, his arms outstretched. My heart suddenly felt light as air and began to flutter wildly in my chest.

As a result of my having told Dr. Brenner about my mother's drinking problem, every time they brought her meal tray, they brought her a shot of bourbon in a plastic pill cup. I gather their greatest concern was that she not go into withdrawal on their watch. Her drinking problem, however, appeared to be none of their concern.

"Why are they doing this?" she asked me accusingly. "They think I'm an *alcoholic* or something. I don't need this." She pushed away the tray and the offending shot of bourbon.

While I was around, she didn't touch the booze. I started to wonder if I wasn't completely insane. Perhaps she wasn't an alcoholic after all. Perhaps, unlike me, she *could* control her drinking. Suddenly I had the liberating thought, Yes, she's really all right.

On her third day in the hospital, Kevin and I walked into her room in the late afternoon to find my mother holding out her water glass and her old friend Ed Trzcinski—a renowned drunk—pouring scotch into it from a silver flask, his hand shaking so badly the metal rattled alarmingly against the glass. Addie Herder, the collagist, was there as well; and Cecile, who stood off to the side, looking annoyed but smiling nervously at her old friend's antics.

My mother turned her head toward us with a dismissive glance, then took a demure sip from her glass.

"The fun's over, folks," she said. "Carry Nation has arrived."

I felt everything inside me drop, as if I were standing in a fast-moving elevator. She had metamorphosed back into her old self, the Red Queen holding court.

Triz, as he was known, threw me a contemptuous look. "Amazing how two people who were always so much fun could raise such a wet blanket!" he said with a barking laugh.

I felt Kevin's warm hand move protectively to the center of my back. I gazed at Triz stonily, which clearly annoyed him and that was fine with me, because I had never liked him, not even as a child. He had been my mother's lover long before she'd met my father, and Triz never let anyone forget it. My father had tolerated Triz's presence, in small doses, the way one might tolerate a good friend's loudmouthed kid.

Ed Trzcinski had cowritten one successful play in the early fifties, *Stalag 17,* based on his experiences in a German POW camp during World War II. He'd had this one big Broadway hit, followed by a Hollywood film, and then spent twenty years embroiled in a lawsuit against the producers of the TV show *Hogan's Heroes,* who'd stolen his idea and not paid him a cent. He never finished another play. Behind his back, my mother called him The Playwrote.

I glanced at Kevin and saw such a pale, drawn look of dismay on his face, I could feel a big attack of rage simmering in my chest.

Kevin murmured, "Let's go," and we slipped out into the hall without another word, leaving them to their revelry. We could hear them talking and laughing all the way down the hall.

Kevin refused to give up his flying habit, so I had to go back to therapy to learn to stay calm on planes. Within a year—but not without a few anxiety attacks in airport bathrooms—we'd traveled to Mexico, Belize, Paris, and California, and down to North Carolina to visit his mother.

Just before Christmas 1994, we flew down to Miami for a long weekend to visit Don Sackrider, to discuss the future of the James Jones Literary Society First Novel Fellowship. Don lived in a beachfront condo on Key Biscayne. The weather was unusually warm for December, low eighties and clear skies. Don knew we were avid scuba divers and drove us down to Pennekamp State Park on Key Largo, about an hour and a half from Miami, to explore their protected reefs. After our dive, Don suggested going farther down the causeway to Marathon Key, and stopping there for lunch at an outdoor restaurant he liked.

After lunch we kept driving west along the causeway, cerulean green water stretching into aqua blue to the rounded horizon on either side. We followed the declining arc of the sun until we reached Bahia Honda, a state park shaded by enormous coconut palms.

"Why don't we drive to Key West for dinner?" Don suggested. "It's only forty minutes from here. If you guys share the driving on the way back, it won't be so bad. We can make it back to Miami by midnight."

Don had spent a good deal of his life traveling, and being adventurous, in his opinion, is what makes travel interesting. We readily agreed and got back into his big, comfortable Lincoln Continental with cream-colored leather seats.

In Key West, Don parked the car at the edge of Old Town, and we got out and stretched. We found ourselves in the midst of some weird mass exodus, people of every age walking slowly and joyfully down the street.

"I wonder what's going on?" Don mused. "Shall we?" He opened his arm, and we stepped into pace with the crowd. The shop windows and palm trees along the street were bedecked with Christmas lights, a strange sight, with everyone suntanned and in shorts and T-shirts and summer frocks. One toy store window had a train set, complete with a snowy alpine village, "Jingle Bells" playing, and a miniature Santa hanging from a nylon string, flying round and round on his sled. When the street came to an end, I realized with a sudden jolt that we were standing at the far end of Mallory Square, and the crowd was gathering to observe the sunset, excited as children waiting to enter a circus tent.

It was much more crowded than the last time I'd been here. Jugglers, acrobats, and tourist kiosks on wheels dotted the square. From the neon-lit open bars at the corner of Duvall Street came Jimmy Buffett's voice, still wasting away in Margaritaville.

"It's Sackrider luck," Don said delightedly.

The sun's red glow outshone the bar's neon lights, the ocean spread out below it like a wrinkled blue silk sheet sprinkled with rubies. An awed silence descended over the square as all faces turned toward the horizon. We weaved our way to the edge of the concrete pier for a better view. Kevin stood behind me, and I could feel his solid chest against the back of my head and shoulder blades. Just as the sun touched the waves, two bagpipers began to play the first chords of "Amazing Grace," the hope-filled, mournful notes skirling out over the crowd, dissipating as they touched the water, brave and unapologetic and resonant as only a song about grace can be.

Two and a half years ago I had stood on this square, straddling my rented bicycle, and stared at this setting sun and asked

God for help. At once the past and present seemed to fold over each other, and I was my old self, standing here, alone and afraid, believing I was broken and unfixable; but I was also myself, here, now, no longer the person who stood outside of the circle of human experience, jealously looking in. My life suddenly seemed filled with possibility. The sun was sinking so fast I could feel the roundness of Earth and its quiet rotation beneath our feet, and the planet's tiny fraction of space in the vast universe, and for the first time in my life, I felt the true nature of something immense and indefinable, but immeasurably tender and forgiving, holding me in the palm of its gigantic hand.

You see, it seemed to whisper, *I've been here all along.* All I'd needed was time, but time was never something I'd been willing to let pass slowly, at its own pace.

My breath was knocked out of me and my knees buckled and I dropped to the ground and sobbed, folded in two as the bagpipers continued to play. I felt Kevin's hands grip my shoulders and his knees pressing into my back.

Long after the sun had set and darkness fallen, I sat there, trying to pull myself together, to breathe, swallowing hard. I riffled through my handbag for twenty dollars to give the bagpipers. I stood on shaky legs, looking up at Kevin. He silently took the money from my hand and turned to find the musicians.

Kevin came back, gazed at me for a long time, and his lips turned into a tentative half-smile. Don, standing a little ways back, came forward and placed his hand gently on my shoulder. I began to babble, to try to explain, but words simply couldn't do justice to the enormity of what had just happened to me. In all my years of drinking and experiencing moments of ecstatic communion with humanity—feelings of such warmth and overpowering love that I thought myself one with the universe—never, never once, had I experienced anything close to this, and I was stone-cold sober.

"I Wasn't on the List"

After I'd stabilized and gained some sober time, it was not quite as difficult for me to be around my mother, and once in a while, on the nights I taught my class in the MFA Program at Southampton College, I would sleep in my old bedroom in the Sagaponack house.

On this particular late-winter night, my mother had set the table elegantly, with wineglasses and her good silver, and waited for me to come home. It was around nine when I walked in, exhausted from the long day. As she sautéed shad roe, I picked up the *New York Times* TV guide from the top of the television, folded to today's date. She'd checked off certain programs in ink. I turned the pages and saw that she'd done the same for every night of the week, almost like an appointment book, and I suddenly noticed how quiet and empty the house felt around us.

She'd prepared steamed broccoli and boiled new potatoes smothered in salt, pepper, and olive oil. She sat at her usual place at the head of the long antique table, with me on her immediate left, the same table that had made the journey from Paris some twenty years ago. I didn't know what to talk about. I never knew what to talk about with her. Dinners at this table seemed to me more like a hostage negotiation than a time for relaxing conversation.

My mother, sipping inexpensive white wine poured from one of those magnum bottles, launched into the latest news. At least now she'd stopped pouring me wine. A famous writer friend, she told me, was "back in the booby hatch."

"What kind of booby hatch?" I wanted to know, because with Gloria, this could mean anything.

"I don't know what kind of booby hatch," she said, exasperated. She was never a detail person. She said that the writer had developed an addiction to sleeping pills.

He had been calling my mother weekly from the place to update her on his progress—why he called her, she had no idea, but she thought maybe it was because she could still make him laugh. Last week he told her he'd thrown the finger paints at the finger-painting therapist. "Don't you know who I am?" he'd shouted at her.

Most recently he had called Gloria to tell her that his doctor had talked him into making an amends list, and on a piece of paper, he'd written down the names of all the women he had slept with. He then presented this to his long-suffering wife, when she came to visit on Family Day.

"What a stupid thing to do," my mother said with dismay. "Now she's furious at me." She knocked back her wine and refilled her glass.

"You slept with *him*?" I cried, aghast.

"No, you dope. She's mad at me because now she thinks I've got something over her. I'm the only one of all her friends who wasn't on the list."

CHAPTER TEN

✈ Legacy ✈

KEVIN AND I MOVED INTO a railroad flat apartment in March 1994. For the first few months I felt like I did as a little girl when my best friend Lee Esterling used to sleep over on a Saturday night and I felt so happy it was like a national holiday. But with those sleepovers, I knew it would end on Sunday afternoon, a dark cloud on the horizon.

"Now we can have a sleepover every night!" I said to Kevin. Every morning upon waking, it still seemed a perfect miracle to me that he was still there. But Kevin was not free from the effects of his own childhood traumas. We had bizarre communication problems.

"Shit. I forgot to buy half-and-half," I might say late at night. Kevin would sigh and get up off the couch, heading for his coat. "Where are you going?" I'd ask, perplexed.

"Didn't you just ask me to go buy half-and-half?"

After we'd been living together for a few months, his taciturn moods became more pronounced, staying with him for days, and he had trouble sleeping. When I tried to coax him into talking about it, he shut himself up in the far end of the apartment, the room we'd turned into his study, at times staying there all night. I had trouble sleeping without him and paced the bedroom in a fury, feeling rejected and victimized, watching the thin strip of yellow light under the closed door. He had newspaper clippings, magazines, papers, and books spread out across the floor, as if he were desperately searching for something.

Panic set in. I was certain he was planning to leave me. I had no idea what was wrong. When talking calmly didn't work, I started shouting at him, insulting him, as if that would help, but he remained distant and silent. The more I hollered, the more he withdrew, to the point where I felt like hitting him. I told a sober friend I wanted to kill myself, and she urged me quite vehemently to call the Caron Foundation in Pennsylvania, which had a reha- bilitation program for children of alcoholics.

The lady who answered the phone asked me if I was suicidal, which freaked me out. Absolutely not, I told her. She explained the program was a six-day intensive during which I would have no communication whatsoever with the outside world. Also, she recommended I not talk to any Caron "alumni," because know- ing what was coming would decrease the effect. There was an opening in two weeks, and she made me pay the entire fee, almost $2,000, by credit card over the phone. "Why can't I pay when I get there?" I asked.

"Because we've learned from experience that unless people pay up front, they cancel, or don't show up. It's insurance." She chuckled, but I did not see the humor.

Later that day, when Kevin got home from work, his face ashen with exhaustion and tension, I told him I'd called the Caron Foundation and would be going in two weeks to their ACOA workshop, then burst into tears. He came toward me and held me. "I have to get help too," he said. "I don't know how to live with anyone. Don't worry, we'll work this out. When you come back, we'll go shopping for an engagement ring."

I woke up the next morning, cured. I immediately wanted to call the Caron lady back and cancel, but since I'd already paid the money—which I could hardly afford—I knew I had to go. Now I understood why she'd laughed.

The six-day workshop at the Caron Foundation was the most intense and painful experience I've ever gone through in my life. It was the gateway to a lifelong journey of dealing with my anger and my terror of abandonment.

Kevin and I got married in August 1995, a week after my thirty-fifth birthday. Peter Matthiessen, an ordained Buddhist priest, married us in the garden of his zendo in Sagaponack. Kevin's brothers, Joe and Jon Heisler, stood as his best men, along with Jamie. We were a little worried about how Kevin's two staunchly Catholic, elderly aunts would react to the Buddhist ceremony; they were greatly reassured when my mother introduced her old friend Pat Kennedy Lawford to them as "the sister of the president."

A few weeks later, as we were walking up Second Avenue, we passed a children's furniture store, and I stopped to look in the window at the beautiful, shining white cribs and brightly colored bedding. "Oh, look how pretty!" I said, turning to him with a smile, but he had fled to the end of the block and was standing there innocently, waiting for the light.

By February 1997, Kevin's fear of fatherhood had diminished somewhat, and I wanted a baby desperately. We had been trying to conceive for eighteen months and were getting ready to start infertility treatments. On one of my Southampton teaching nights, exhausted from stress, too tired to drive back to the city, I decided to stay at my mother's. I was sitting at the kitchen table, eating a slice of apple pie when my mother came in from a dinner party. She was shivering, in a flimsy black knitted coat.

"Do you realize what today is?" she asked me. I had no idea. "Today is February twenty-seventh, Jim's and my fortieth anniversary. Can you believe we've been married for forty years?"

This seemed a strange way to put it. "That's amazing," I responded.

Still shivering, she poured herself a big glass of scotch. She said, "I really need to get myself a good winter coat. I have nothing to wear out."

"What about your mink?" I asked, surprised.

She seemed startled for a moment, and then annoyed. Apparently she realized too late that she'd backed herself into a corner. "I gave it to Cousin Anne," she said abruptly, dismissively, then puckered up her lips and stuck out her jaw petulantly, as if she expected me to say something judgmental or nasty. Remember, I told myself, restraint of pen and tongue . . . Keeping my voice steady and devoid of sarcasm, I said, "Wow. How did that happen?"

During the Christmas holidays, she told me, she'd been invited to a party at John and Julienne Scanlon's house in Sag Harbor. John Scanlon was the public relations guru who'd made a fortune fixing the tainted reputations of such giants as not only a major tobacco conglomerate but also the Catholic Church, and a cardinal who'd been caught having an affair. John and Julienne Scanlon were friendly with my mother, but not close friends. All I knew about Julienne was that she'd been married to James Earl Jones. Once, at some cocktail party, I was sitting on a couch next to my mother and Julienne Scanlon, when my mother said to her, "How was it, being married to James Earl Jones? I'd like to ask him to marry me, that way I wouldn't have to change my stationery."

My mother continued her story: "Their house was done up all Martha Stewart." There were candles flickering in all the windows and an enormous Christmas tree in the foyer. It was a very cold evening, but the Scanlons' enormous, opulent house was warm and filled with music and laughter, and the crème de la crème of Hamptons society.

Gloria arrived in her full-length, ebony-colored mink with a shimmery chocolate brown satin lining—a gift from Walker. The mink was the only trace of Walker remaining, much like Clementis's fur hat in Kundera's *The Book of Laughter and Forgetting*. I tried to recall exactly the novel's opening: the Czech Communist leader stands bareheaded on a balcony overlooking a victory parade with his number two man, Clementis, beside him. It's so cold that the solicitous Clementis takes off his own fur hat and places it on the leader's head. Photographs are taken. But within a year, Clementis is accused of treason and executed, and quickly airbrushed from the photo. The only thing left is his hat.

My mother was telling me the names of all the rich and famous people arriving at the party, but I was thinking about *The Book of Laughter and Forgetting* and can't remember what she said. Nevertheless, Gloria, standing in the brightly lit foyer of the Scanlons' house, was surprised to find her own niece, Anne Mosolino, in a maid's uniform, greeting guests and taking their coats as they entered. Anne had married a local boy, a builder like her older brother Max, and during the busy summer months and winter holidays, Anne picked up extra money by waitressing for different catering companies.

"Hi, Aunt Gloria," she said, and reached out to take Gloria's mink coat.

For a few hours, my mother drank and watched gloomily as her niece played servant to the rich and famous, carrying around trays stacked with fancy hors d'oeuvres and drinks. "It just pissed me off," she told me. "That's all. I felt sorry for her."

As Gloria was getting ready to leave, Anne approached, buried under a pile of coats, including my mother's mink.

"Take it. It's yours," Gloria said, pushing the mink coat back into Anne's arms.

And my mother went home coatless in the icy night.

"She just took it? That seems a bit strange," I now said, thinking, How could she take a fur coat from a drunken old lady on a freezing cold night?

"Why shouldn't she take it?"

I was assailed by the weird image of Anne, only around five feet tall, in my mother's long mink coat. She'd look like a child playing dress-up. This whole story perturbed me.

"You're just mad because you wanted me to give it to *you*," my mother said. "Because you'll never have a man rich enough to buy you a ten-thousand-dollar mink coat."

First of all, if I'd wanted a mink coat, Kevin most certainly would have gone out of his way to buy me one. We were getting ready to try in vitro fertilization at $10,000 a pop, and insurance would only cover the first attempt. But I'd never had a fondness for mink coats or any other coats made of animal fur. This was probably a result of seeing a *Life* magazine article when I was six or seven that showed horrifying pictures of baby seals being clubbed to death and skinned. Also there is no fucking way Walker spent $10,000 on a mink coat. Maybe two or three thousand.

I could no longer restrain myself. "You're completely out of your mind," I said, my tone brittle with contempt.

"And you're an asshole," she said with finality, and lit a cigarette.

"And you're a woman without a mink coat."

After a while, since she didn't say anything, I said, "I'm going to bed. Good night."

I could feel her eyes boring into my back as I made my way across the long kitchen, toward my room.

A few weeks later, I learned I was pregnant. And then everything happened at once.

James Ivory, the film director, called and told me they had gotten the money together and were starting preproduction on *A Soldier's Daughter Never Cries*. "We're going to start shooting in Paris in October," he told me. I could tell by his tone that he was delighted.

Jim Ivory and his producing partner, Ismail Merchant, had first optioned *A Soldier's Daughter Never Cries* in 1991, and that option money kept me from having to find a real job for the last six years.

"I have some news too, Jim," I told him now. "I'm going to have a baby at the end of October."

"Well, that's inconvenient." He didn't sound quite so delighted. But we both laughed, and there was a silence, after which he said, "You'll just have to bring the baby with you down to North Carolina for the second half of the shooting."

A week or so later, the director Terrence Malick announced that he was starting production on his own adaptation of *The Thin Red Line,* the second novel in my father's war trilogy that had started with *From Here to Eternity.* Then, not long after that, my fourth novel, *Celeste Ascending,* was bought by HarperCollins. It seemed to me that, as the Georgians of the Caucasus say, "God stumbled over the mountains and dropped the horn of plenty upon our land."

Terrence Malick invited Kevin and me to visit the set of *The Thin Red Line* in Queensland, Australia, over the summer. But mine was a "high risk" pregnancy, and there was no way I could fly that distance at six or seven months pregnant. My mother went, traveling with her close friends Barbara Hearst and Betty Comden.

Upon their return, Barbara Hearst called me, terribly upset. According to her, my mother had drunk continuously, from the moment she got into the limousine that picked her up at her door, all through the plane ride, during the visit to the set, and during the return trip. There had not been a moment when my mother wasn't incapacitated from drink.

Barbara said she'd had no idea the problem had gotten that bad. "Did you know Gloria was that bad?" she asked me. Of course I knew. She'd been this way for a solid decade; she'd just been able to hide it. But now, instead of feeling righteous, I felt guilty, because the implication seemed to be that I should have done something to stop my mother.

Barbara told me she was organizing an intervention. I had looked into this option several years earlier and discussed it with experts in the field. What I'd learned was not encouraging. For an intervention to work, the entire family, friends, and anyone else directly involved with the problem drinker have to be in agreement, and present a cohesive, united front. I did not know the man Barbara had hired to plan the intervention, although he was a professional with a good reputation, but I knew already that Barbara would not be able to convince my cousins and my brother and many of my mother's friends to go along with it, and I told her so. Jamie did not know Barbara well and certainly would not trust her to organize something as personal and emotionally difficult as an intervention. I told Barbara she had no idea what she was getting into and the plan was bound to backfire.

Nevertheless, Barbara called our cousin, Max Mosolino, to elicit his help. As soon as they hung up, he called Gloria and told her what Barbara was planning. No doubt Max felt he was being loyal, but just as I had feared, Gloria did not wait to hear Barbara's point of view. She simply shouted, "Off with her head!" and exiled Barbara from her inner circle. Of course Gloria could not afford to lose some of her closer friends, who were perhaps only peripherally involved, like Betty Comden, so she simply decided that Barbara was the only one to blame.

When she called to voice her outrage at Barbara, I told her exactly what I thought. "You absolutely have to stop drinking, Mom. That's not the issue. But I told Barbara an intervention wasn't the way to go."

"You're a good, loyal girl."

"No, that's not it. I just didn't think it would work."

"Well, you're still a good, loyal girl to stick up for your mother." She'd heard what she wanted to hear. And all I heard was the gratitude and approval in her voice, and it made my heart leap with joy. At thirty-six, I was no more advanced than one of Pavlov's dogs, whose tail starts to wag the minute the feeding buzzer goes off. I made my own self sick with loathing.

Still, this moment in her good graces did not prevent me from getting caught in her temper tantrums. In August, when I was six months pregnant, she threw me out of her house again. I can't remember what I said on this particular afternoon that set her off, or if I'd said anything at all, only that I was standing, enormous and vulnerable, between the antique dining table and the butcher-block-covered cabinets, when she shouted at me to get the hell out of her house and never come back.

I said, "Mom, for God's sake. I'm pregnant."

"I don't care," she said, "get out of my house."

No matter what I might have said or done, I knew this was wrong. I did not deserve this, and I no longer felt that earth-shattering guilt and remorse and shame coursing through me, but I still felt rage at the injustice and couldn't stop myself from trying to interpret, or understand, what had triggered this explosion. Then I tried to stop myself from trying to figure it out. When that didn't work, I tried to count the number of times she'd thrown me out or exiled me: four. Versus the number of times I'd told her I hated her: once (when she threw Kevin and me out on Christmas Day). Versus the number of times she'd told me she didn't like me and never had: at least ten. Versus the number of times I'd kept my mouth shut and capitulated: countless.

What is the definition of insanity?

Doing the same thing over and over again, expecting different results.

I quietly turned away, went into my room, and packed my bag. I went out through my room's back door to avoid further confrontation, got into my car, and drove off. At around exit 44 on the expressway, I had to brake suddenly when traffic came to a halt, and I started to feel severe cramping in my abdomen.

We had known for a month that the baby was a girl. At first, the news had stunned me. A *girl*! I had always expected a boy. At least I'd know how to deal with a boy. But God had given me a girl. What kind of mother was I going to be to a baby girl, with my baggage? Would my baby hate me? I had been so worried, and yet now, I felt overwhelmed with love. *Oh, please, God, let her be all right.*

I kept repeating the two prayers I knew by heart, like a mantra, all the way home.

That afternoon, my obstetrician sent me to the hospital for tests. I had a sonogram, and an EKG of the baby's heart. The EKG was normal, but the sonogram showed some kind of unusual shadow on the uterine wall. The obstetrician did not seem too concerned about it, or at least he let me go home, recommending a sonogram every week for the next several months. He told me not to get too excited, to stay home and relax, which was exactly what I did. I was very good at denial myself. When my mother was out of sight, I could almost entirely block her from my mind. For the rest of the summer, Kevin and I sat in our air-conditioned apartment and read, or watched TV, and it was very peaceful indeed.

Cecile must have told my mother about my visit to the hospital, because a week later, Gloria relented and called to invite us out for Labor Day weekend. I thanked her, but said I was going to stay put, my tone distant and removed.

"You'd be much better off out here, in the country." She sounded offended.

"I need to stay really quiet right now," I told her.

"Well, this is the quietest place in the world."

It was as if she'd never thrown me out, yelled at me, or done anything to disturb my peace of mind. Most probably she'd convinced herself that I'd stalked off in a huff, lacking a sense of humor, or, even worse, being *such a moody neurotic*. I started once again to doubt my own sanity. I couldn't even talk to her on the phone without getting upset.

I went into labor on Saturday evening, November 8, a half hour after we'd finished eating Mexican takeout. Kevin hasn't eaten Mexican food since. I spent a pretty bad night waiting for things to progress the way the Lamaze people had told us they would, but right from the start the contractions did not follow the normal pattern, and I began losing a lot of blood. We went to the hospital at 5:00 A.M. and the intake nurses laughed at us. They told us all first-time mothers showed up at the hospital way too early, looking completely horrified at the pain they were experiencing, as if they'd expected a walk in the park. I'll never know if the pain was normal or not because I've never had another baby, but with this baby, I was suffering from a placental abruption—a serious tear in the uterine wall that fifty years ago would have cost both of us our lives.

Some twelve hours later, on Sunday afternoon, I had a hemorrhage, and there was still no sign of the baby coming, so the doctor recommended an emergency C-section.

I asked Kevin to go call my mother again. She had come into town that morning and was at Cecile's apartment. Kevin came back and said that Cecile had picked up the phone and told him Gloria had been drinking since she'd arrived, and was now incoherent. I understood that. She was nervous and upset and scared that I was going to die, and couldn't face what she was feeling, so she drank, which was what she always did when confronted by any blip whatsoever on the emotional Richter scale.

I was awake through the procedure, although they hung a blue sheet over my chest like a curtain so I couldn't see what they were doing. My teeth were chattering, the operating room was so cold. I felt some tugging and pulling, and then heard the baby's first cry. A few moments later, Kevin came around the sheet with the baby in his arms and tears streaming down his face, though he was smiling. I lifted my head to kiss her. She looked me right in the eyes, then her lips latched onto mine, and I kissed her over and over, crying out, "She kissed me! My baby kissed me!" The nurse, whose name was Ada, said, "No, honey, she's just looking for your breast."

"I'm going to give you something to put you to sleep now," said the anesthesiologist, and I felt a strange, wonderful warmth coursing rapidly up my arm and through my system. I had time to think, Ah, Peace. This must be what death feels like, before the world went completely black—a deep, soft, warm, silent cocoon of darkness.

I regained consciousness in a post-op room with Kevin standing beside the bed, holding my hand. He told me the baby was fine and everything was all right. I asked for water. The vigilant post-op nurse said no, I'd throw it up. I asked for ice chips, and again she said no. As soon as she walked away, Kevin sneaked off and got me a cupful anyway. I loved this about him; he wasn't afraid of authority the way I was. I sucked gratefully and slowly on the ice, and didn't even feel sick to my stomach.

I was moved to a room with a wall-to-wall window overlooking the East River and Roosevelt Island. It was very late, and the armchair Kevin was sitting in by the window looked miserably uncomfortable. I told him he should go home and get some sleep. He stood up, practically staggering, and shuffled his feet by the door for another five minutes. I urged him to go, and he promised to return first thing in the morning.

All night long I heard bassinet wheels squeaking down the hall from the nursery and crying newborns passing by my door. My heart would start to palpitate, for I felt I was about to meet the most important person I would ever meet in my life. Finally, in the blue-tinted predawn light, they brought her to me, a perfect baby who already seemed able to focus on her surroundings.

"Best baby in the nursery," the nurse said, "never cried all night."

Someone had arranged her Mohawk of fine hair into one long finger curl, a little wave cresting on the top of her head. Her eyes, bright and clear, were gray, with a blue rim around the irises. The nurse left us, and the baby and I peered at each other for a long moment, in the stillness and silence of early morning.

I know you, I thought. And I can see you already know me. I brought her to my breast, and she latched on immediately with a greediness that stunned me. A moment later a tiny sliver of sun peeked above the flat rooftops of Roosevelt Island across the river and bathed the room in an eerie orange glow, which grew in intensity until the shiny linoleum floor and all the metal contraptions in the room turned the color of lava.

Thank you, thank you, thank you, God. I know I don't deserve this gift. I swear I'll be the best guide I can be and I'll always try to recognize the difference between my ego and hers, and I'll be there when she needs me, every time she needs me, as long as I live. Tears of gratitude streamed from my eyes and dripped onto the baby's head.

When Kevin arrived about an hour later, I told him about the incredible sunrise. Every morning for the next four days, he arrived in time to see it, but the sky was overcast and the rising sun did not show itself again.

That first morning of Eyrna's life, I basked in the afterglow of that sunrise, happier and more serene than I'd ever felt in my life. James Ivory called from Paris to congratulate us, and told me the filming was going very well. Once a week or so he'd been calling and sending FedEx packages of photographs of the set and the actors, asking for specific details concerning certain French expressions, and offering amusing anecdotes. Lying there in the hospital bed, I did not even mind the burn of the cesarian incision. I had some kind of anesthetic drip that went straight into my spine, and every now and then a nurse would appear and give me a shot of Demerol, and I asked repeatedly, "Is it okay for me to nurse her with these drugs?" and she'd respond, "Yes, yes, it's fine . . ." and I had my baby, and my life seemed to lack nothing except parents.

A bouquet arrived, two dozen of the largest, most perfectly shaped, glorious pink roses I'd ever seen in my life. They were from Dave, my dearest friend, who'd poured me into a cab on my last night of drinking on Super Bowl Sunday, 1992. The roses were the size of linebackers' fists and their scent filled the room with a light, airy perfume.

My new sober friend Nora came by, and she looked beautiful in the sunny room, her long red hair curling around her pale face and her green eyes bright. I felt so happy. I admitted to her I was afraid because I was enjoying the drugs too much.

"Relax, honey," she said, laughing. "This one's a freebie."

She looked into the baby's eyes and said, "An ancient soul, this one." Nora deftly lifted the little bundle into her arms, as if she'd spent her whole life lifting and rocking babies. "Yes, you've been here a few times already, haven't you?" she murmured to Eyrna. How strange, I thought, to hear someone else say it, for that is exactly the feeling I had when Eyrna and I first looked into each other's eyes.

Around noon, my mother arrived, reeking of stale smoke and alcohol, her face and stomach so swollen she looked like an inflated effigy of herself. She didn't say hello but went right to the bassinet at the foot of my bed and peered down at the sleeping baby.

"She's not beautiful," she said hollowly. "She doesn't look like anybody."

Kevin, who was sitting across the room in the armchair by the enormous window, gazed at me helplessly. "Do you want to sit down, Gloria?" he asked, rising.

"No. I'm only going to stay a minute."

It was clear to me that she was furious. She was practically bristling with rage. But why? I'd scared her, I guessed. She did not like being scared.

"What's the name again?" she now asked.

"Eyrna Holland Heisler," Kevin said slowly, pronouncing her name *Air-na*. Eyrna was the name of Kevin's ninety-three-year-old maternal grandmother, a Dane who'd come to the United States in the twenties to find a better life. Now she was very frail and sinking fast. When she'd been told the baby's name on the phone early this morning, she'd cried. Holland was for my mother's and my great friend, Irma Holland Wolstein, who had died of cancer two years before. Her husband, Ben, was the analyst who had helped me so much during the nadir of my first marriage, and Kevin and I still met him for dinner around once a month. Holland was also the name of the town in Ohio where Kevin's grandparents had settled.

"That's the ugliest name I ever heard in my life. It sounds like a German maid's name," my mother stated. Kevin slowly sat back down in the armchair. He didn't say a word. I could see by the stoic expression on his face that he was going to wait this one out.

"I can't imagine why you'd pick such an ugly name," my mother continued. If she was spoiling for a fight, she wasn't going to get one here. Not today. She was met with complete silence.

But I knew why she was really saying this. She'd told me she wanted me to name the baby Catherine, for her sister Kitty who had died of polio at eight. I did not want to name my baby Catherine. I had on so many previous occasions folded under my mother's will, I just plain decided that this time, it was my baby, and I was going to name her what I wanted. One thing was certain—no matter what name we picked, if it wasn't Catherine, or Gloria, she would have said it was a terrible name, the worst name she ever heard.

After another minute of weighty silence, my mother took a pack of Marlboros and a lighter out of her purse and just as she stuck a cigarette in her mouth and brought the flame up to it, Kevin stood up and calmly but firmly said, "You can't smoke in here, Gloria. That's a newborn baby."

Without another word, my mother turned on her heels and walked out the door.

I stared at Kevin across the room, my eyes and mouth wide with shock, wanting to say something bitter and angry.

"Don't," he said gently.

As soon as we returned home from the hospital, Jamie and his wife, Beth, came up from Washington with their one-year-old, Isabel Kaylie Jones. Beth's parents brought Isabel's white wicker newborn bassinet down from Westchester for Eyrna, all festooned with pink and blue ribbons. I found this positively astounding— that Beth's mother would have spent hours threading ribbon through a bassinet for her daughter, much less for me. I thanked them profusely, and they just shrugged it off, as though it were nothing, as though this was what grandparents were supposed to do.

Three weeks before Christmas, when Eyrna was five weeks old, Kevin, Nora, and I flew with Eyrna down to Wilmington, North Carolina, to be on the set of *A Soldier's Daughter Never Cries*. Most people don't even leave the house with a five-week-old baby, and here we were on a plane. There was so much luggage we looked like Fitzgerald's Dick and Nicole Diver—we had the stroller, the diaper bag, the portable crib, my industrial-size breast pump, the little igloo for preserving breast milk, the baby clothes and two-way radio, the BabyBjörn, and sundry feeding and cleaning paraphernalia.

When we visited the set for the first time, I felt as though I'd walked through a *Star Trek*–like rip in the space-time continuum. Electric cables, television monitors, lighting and sound parapher-nalia crowded the front hallway of the two-story saltbox house. Gingerly stepping over the wires, we crossed the foyer—and it was as if we were standing in my mother's Sagaponack house.

The novel closely parallels my childhood in Paris and then our move to the States, and Jim Ivory had warned me that I might be disappointed if his aesthetics did not reflect "reality." I asked Jim which reality did he mean—his vision? My novel? My family's memories? Or mine?

On the walls hung three luxuriant Paul Jenkins paintings, on loan from the artist, a lifelong friend. In the living room stood a replica of our eighteenth-century wooden pulpit bar. My father loved that irreverent grandstand so much that when we moved to Sagaponack, he had to take out a wall to get it into the house. Standing in this miraculous reconstruction, I felt like a visitor from the future, beamed by transporter back into the past. I had a panicky feeling—the urge to tell someone this story was not going to turn out well at all. My mother had gotten to the point now where she was unable to go two hours, night or day, without a drink.

Above the landing hung the Alexander Calder mobile the artist had given to my father in the early 1960s. They had been friends, and my father had written a moving essay about Calder's work. But wait! My mother had sold the mobile years ago. It was a look-alike, of course, but for a moment it fooled me. Upstairs, on the wall in the boy's room was a sand-and-glue map of the United States, as crooked as the one Jamie had made as a school-boy. In the girl's room was the watercolor alphabet my parents' friend Addie Herder made for my third birthday. *A* is for Ace, in a family of card players. *L* is for Laughing, and all the faces of my parents' friends stare at me from behind the glass. *K*, in the original, was for Kaylie, and *J* for Jones.

Not here. *C* was for Channe, and *W* for Willis—the characters in my book. Poor girl, I thought, she has no idea what's coming.

I went to the window and looked out over a blue marsh leading to the Atlantic, visible on the horizon. The sun was setting, leaving streaks of pink and purple over the water, and there were tall reeds swaying in the wind, reminding me of Sagg Pond. Eyrna, in Kevin's arms, began to fuss, so we went back to the minivan so I could nurse her.

When we got out of the van, a tall man was approaching us with long strides across the brown, winter lawn. It was Kris Kristofferson. He shook my hand and lifted the baby into the air, an expert, with six small ones of his own. "You wrote so beautifully about your father," he said. "He must have been a wonderful man as well as a wonderful writer."

I looked up at him, suddenly choked up. He had eyes just like my father's.

In a little while, James Ivory filmed the scene of the father's first trip to the hospital. Nora took Eyrna for a walk, and Kevin and I watched the shooting from inside the house. Kris Kristofferson, sitting in his office, behind his typewriter with papers piled everywhere, breathed exactly as my father had in his last few weeks, as if he couldn't catch his breath, as if he were drowning. I started to tremble, overtaken with fear. I was witnessing the whole thing all over again. I felt like shouting, "No! No! We can fix this! We have to fix this, before it's too late!"

A few days later, Jim filmed the scene in which the mother lies on the couch, her ubiquitous bottle of scotch within reach, utterly paralyzed by her grief. I watched Barbara Hershey on the monitor, then I went outside and walked down to the water's edge and breathed in and out, slowly, for a solid five minutes. Barbara came out to find me. She had gone to Sagaponack to spend a day with my mother, to acquaint herself with the person on whom her character was based. I never asked Barbara how that went, but the look in her dark eyes as she now approached me said it all. She hugged me, and I started crying on her shoulder. "I hope this film will bring you some peace," she said gently. "I hope it will bring you closure."

How could this have happened to us? I thought. How did we get to the point that we've grown to expect nothing from each other but pain?

When it was time for me to start teaching again that spring semester at Southampton College, I decided to try to bring Eyrna with me to my mother's house, against Kevin's better judgment. Reexperiencing the past on the set had given me insight, and I felt a new compassion for my mother. She did not *have* to be alone, and I could surely be more understanding and kind. But I was not quite brave enough to leave a three-month-old baby alone with someone who was drinking, so I asked my friend Alice, an old friend from high school who was sober now also, and living in East Hampton, to come over and watch Eyrna at my mother's while I was gone for three hours to teach my first class.

When I got home, I could hear Eyrna screaming all the way from the kitchen, and I ran to my room, panic-stricken. I found her lying in her own excrement on a towel on the bed, her face red and contorted as a shriveled apple, and Phyllis Newman, my mother's old buddy, sitting in a chair across from Gloria at the side of the bed, trying to calm her down by making jokes about how they'd never been the kind of mothers who changed diapers. But the look on my face silenced Phyllis immediately, and before

I could say anything, my mother said, "I threw that Alice out. I can't stand her. She's an asshole."

Alice had not called me, not wanting to disturb me, so she drove off and left fourteen-week-old Eyrna alone with my mother. Apparently Eyrna had started howling and wouldn't stop, so Gloria had called Phyllis and begged her to come. Between the two of them, they managed to get the dirty diaper off, but neither knew how to, or wanted to, clean her up or put on a new diaper. Neither knew how to fill a bottle with frozen breast milk and heat it, and perhaps they were too afraid to try.

I swiftly lifted Eyrna into my arms. The minute she recognized me she stopped howling. I was too upset to speak. I cleaned her up, changed her, and put her into clean footie pajamas. She reached up and started grabbing for my breast. When she latched on, she let out a sigh of relief that reminded me of how I used to feel after my first shot of vodka at the close of a very long day. When she was sated, she pulled back and gasped, her head lolling to the side, her eyes rolling back in her head as though she were completely drunk.

I picked up the phone and called Nora in New York. Nora listened to my gruesome tale and then said, "It's not just about you anymore. My aunt Maureen dropped her little Johnny on his head when she'd had a few too many cocktails, and he's spent the rest of his life in diapers, drooling in a wheelchair."

Nora's words hit home: my mother's house was not physically safe. It was no longer about me being kind, or trying to help her contain her drinking problem. I could not be the alcohol police and the mother of a newborn at the same time. I had to make a choice. I had put my child in danger; I had relied on my friend Alice, who had not done the right thing. What if my mother *hadn't* called Phyllis? What if she'd dropped Eyrna?

I called Kevin and told him I was coming home. He asked me to wait until morning, because I was too upset to drive. He was right, I realized, so I went out into the kitchen and told my mother I was exhausted and needed to go to bed. She didn't say a word.

First thing in the morning, I packed us up and left.

Later that day, I called her from the city and told her, as calmly and as gently as I could, that I wouldn't be staying with her anymore. It was too much stress for her and for the baby. For once she was not angry but heaved a great sigh of relief.

I hired a babysitter to stay with Eyrna in New York on Thursday afternoons, while I drove out to Southampton College and back. I carried a state-of-the-art, industrial-size breast pump with me to work, along with a little Igloo cooler, and collected so many little plastic containers of breast milk that Kevin said I could have fed an entire orphanage of newborns.

For the next five months, we did not see my mother. When she called, perhaps every three weeks to see how everything was going, I told her we were fine, but tired.

"I don't understand why all you mothers with babies are so tired all the time. *I* was never tired when I had you."

I didn't bother to point out that she had not been the one to get up and feed me or change me in the middle of the night. Nor during the day, for that matter. What was the point of going into it?

I was finally, after six years without a drink, learning to keep my mouth shut.

The premiere screening of *A Soldier's Daughter Never Cries* took place in East Hampton in July. Ismail Merchant invited all the great American literary lions who'd been my father's friends to attend a lunch in my mother's garden, preceding the evening screening. It was a catered event with a big tent and tablecloth-covered tables, and all the writers showed up. Norris Church and Norman Mailer and Rose and Bill Styron flew over from Massachusetts. Inge Morath and Arthur Miller came from Connecticut; Kurt Vonnegut and Jill Krementz, and Maria and Peter Matthiessen drove the half mile down Sagg Main Street; E. L. Doctorow and his wife, Helen, came from Sag Harbor. There were our good friend Joe Heller and his wife, Valerie, who lived in Amagansett; and Shana Alexander, who lived on the beach in Wainscott.

Kris Kristofferson arrived in a limousine from New York, with Ismail, Jim, and Ruth Prawer Jhabvala—the novelist and screenwriter who'd won two Oscars for her Merchant-Ivory adaptations.

We seated Kris Kristofferson next to my mother, because I knew she'd like him, and if she was going to act up, he'd be able to handle it.

"My God," he said to her during the appetizer, "if they dropped a bomb on this tent they'd wipe out half the canon of American letters in one swoop!"

She liked that a lot.

After lunch, as we stood in the garden and Kris bounced Eyrna up and down in his arms, he told me my mother had asked him to spend the night with her.

"She asked you to spend the night with her?" I repeated, incredulous.

Yes, he told me. Apparently my mother had said, "I like you, you remind me of my husband. Why don't you stay and spend the night with me?"

"And may I ask you what your response was?" I said, trying to make light of it.

Kris told me that after some thought, he'd said, "Well, I'm honored. But this is kind of a business trip. I think I'll have to take a rain check."

Stunned, I complimented him on his gentlemanly behavior and quick thinking.

That night, Ismail Merchant escorted Gloria down the red carpet and into the East Hampton Cinema as the cameras flashed.

My mother was extremely nearsighted but would never wear her glasses at public events. Ismail walked off for a moment, and meanwhile the writer Salman Rushdie approached through the crowd and was now standing beside Gloria. Unable to see, she mistook him for Ismail. "It must be wonderful, traveling all over the world, hanging out with so many interesting people," she said, making conversation. "Do you get back to your homeland much?"

Rushdie, who'd been hiding for several years from an Islamist fatwa, gaped at her in silence.

The only thing she said to me all day was in the limo on the way to the post-screening party. "That was a terrible movie. They miscast everyone except for Kris Kristofferson. It was boring and dreary. Our life was much more interesting than that. You don't get me at all and you never will. I'm much too complicated for you."

"He Called Me Lucky"

Gloria loved to tell the story of the summer in the early seventies when they were "dead broke," and for the last two weeks of August, she and my father borrowed a damp little apartment in Trouville from a friend of theirs named Johnny Romero, who owned a nightclub in Paris. Trouville is the hilly coastal village across the inlet and over the bridge from her much fancier sister, Deauville. They sent us kids off to the beach on rented bicycles, or to horseback riding lessons, or to tennis lessons, or to the Deauville pool, and at night we were left with a babysitter, while they got all dressed up in black-tie attire and hit the Deauville casino.

My father had decided to try to alleviate his money troubles by playing chemin de fer baccarat, which is like blackjack, but the highest number you can achieve to win is nine, and you can't go over and bust, because the tens digit is ignored, so tens and face cards are worth zero. *Baccarat* means zero, the worst hand in the game.

On this particular night, Jim had lost several thousand dollars and was getting ready to quit. Gloria had been watching him intermittently, playing a little roulette across the room. Out of nowhere, she hit three wins in a row—low-paying (one to one), easy wins on red, or black, odd or even. She bet again, and won again.

"*Mesdames et messieurs, faites vos jeux,*" called the croupier. Place your bets.

Knowing Jim was in trouble, and with the all-or-nothing

recklessness she was renowned for, Gloria placed her winnings, five hundred francs—a hundred dollars—on zero.

"*Rien ne va plus . . . ,*" said the croupier, calling an end to betting. She closed her eyes and began to mumble a Hail Mary, her favorite foxhole prayer.

"*Zéro, mesdames et messieurs. Zéro.*" She couldn't believe her ears. The croupier deftly began to slide her 17,500 francs' worth of chips toward her.

She felt a tingling sensation, the charge of electricity buzzing down through her fingertips and through her feet to the floor. She could feel people murmuring, watching with sudden interest. Knowing it was sheer folly but unable to resist, she pushed the entire hill of chips over to Black. Double or nothing.

"*Rien ne va plus,*" said the croupier.

She watched him spin the wheel and drop the little ivory ball. She held her breath. *Click, click, click,* around it went, then it fell to the thin circle of numbers, and landed. The wheel slowed, and she saw that the number was black.

She had just won 35,000F—$7,000. Her audience clapped and cheered. She gave the croupier his tip, then inelegantly shoveled as many chips as would fit into her elegant little evening purse, and pressed the rest to her chest.

"Excuse me, please. *Pardon, s'il vous plaît.* Excuse me." She dodged her way through the black-tie-and-evening-gown-clad crowd to the chemin de fer table, where Jim sat stoically, his chiseled face unmoving and unreadable to anyone but her.

Without saying a word, she bent over and dumped her chestload of chips and then the ones in her purse onto the green felt table before him. He looked up at her, his countenance suddenly straightening, his eyes glowing with relief.

"Lucky," he said to her, with a twitch of his thin lips. He'd always thought of her as extremely lucky and even named her Lucky in *Go to the Widow-Maker,* his love song to her. On the next hand, he became the banker and held the bank for several hours, winning every hand.

By the time he turned the bank over to the next player, he'd won 100,000F, or $20,000, enough money at the time to pay for a brand-new Peugeot station wagon and one year's tuition for Jamie's expensive private American school.

CHAPTER ELEVEN

⇢ Chicken or Egg ⇠

IN LATE OCTOBER 1998, I had lunch with my mother at Bobby Van's in Bridgehampton. This was the new, brightly lit, upscale Bobby Van's, not the old, dark tavern where my dad and his writer buddies used to drink. That place was now a fancy continental-style restaurant.

By this time, though she was only seventy, Gloria's memory was failing badly, but she managed to hide it well. The friends she still had must have only seen her at her best, when she pulled herself together to meet them for lunch, or dinner. When she was in public, she could still be amusing, even hilarious; and clearly, she was not cruel or biting to others the way she was to me.

I did not particularly feel like having lunch with her, but I steeled myself for the occasion. I put on my best face, and my lightest voice. As I ate my salad and my mother pushed hers around her plate, for some reason, she wanted to know what kind of credit card I used that I could draw money out of machines, so I took out my wallet to show her.

"That's a nice wallet," she said. It was a black calfskin wallet that unfolded into three sections, one for cards, one for bills, and a change purse on the side.

"Thanks."

"How much did it cost?" she wanted to know.

"About eighty-five dollars," I said. I'd gotten it on sale.

"Eighty-five dollars! Are you out of your mind, spending that kind of money on a wallet?" She took out her own wallet, a beige cloth purse. "I got this at T.J. Maxx for ten dollars."

I didn't respond; it seemed utterly pointless to argue. I suddenly felt unbearably uncomfortable. She waved to the waiter to bring her another glass of white wine. She'd had a Bloody Mary and a glass of wine already—for her, maintenance drinking. I asked for a refill on my coffee.

"No really, that's just ridiculous to blow money like that!"

She sipped her wine and I drank my coffee. Why, I thought, is it almost impossible for us to get through even an hour without a disagreement? When she made me angry, my whole body still went completely stiff, as if I were being embalmed. Now, at least, I was aware that it was anger—repressed and turned inward, so that it ate away at my insides like poison. I looked at my watch. I told her woodenly that I had to go, I had to teach my class. I started to push back my chair. She made a petulant face, puckering her lips. I didn't get up. I didn't like this face; it made me feel like a bad child.

What was I doing here? Did I even miss her anymore? I missed an idealized version of her. I missed the carefree, shining summer days of my late teens and early twenties, when her house and garden were filled with fragrant flowers and music and laughter and the clinking of ice in lovely glasses. We used to have so much fun, and everyone wanted to stay with us.

I did not like the person she had become. She said terrible things about her friends behind their backs. She, who had been a great liberal, now made horribly racist comments. She complained constantly about her health and refused all help. I realized now that she had become someone who, under normal circumstances, I would have run from as fast as I could. Was it possible to fall out of love with your own parents?

She asked the waiter for the bill. I offered to split it with her, looking down as she made her tip calculations. The total was $84.52—the same as my wallet. Suddenly I started laughing. I expected a riposte, but she looked at me questioningly, her eyes vague. She hadn't caught the irony. Clearly, in her view, lunch was an opportunity for civilized drinking—a necessity that could not be avoided, while buying a marginally expensive wallet was not.

My mother had her first major bout of cirrhosis seven months later. Incontinent, unable to recognize her surroundings, she lay for several days on a urine-stained love seat in the TV room. Mary, the housekeeper, finally couldn't stand it anymore and phoned Michael Mosolino, who immediately called his brother Max, and then Jamie, who called me, and the four of us dropped everything and rushed out to Sagaponack. When we arrived en force, Mary was wandering around the kitchen in tears, wringing her hands.

Gloria did not even look human, lying there bloated and grunting like some kind of phocine beast. Jamie and Max lifted her to her feet and carried her, staggering and protesting, out to the car and to the Southampton Hospital Emergency Room. She tried to wave us off, furious that we were interfering, but she could not formulate a coherent phrase, could no longer walk on her own, and could barely control the movements of her arms or legs.

At the hospital, she kept repeating, "I've been kidnapped," and told the nurses and doctors she wanted to go home.

They took ultrasounds of her liver; they ran blood tests; and they gave her psychological tests. Gloria was profoundly malnourished and dehydrated and had cirrhosis, and Korsakoff's syndrome—extreme memory loss and confusion caused by a deficiency of vitamin B to the brain—and alcoholic neuropathy in her arms and legs, a painful form of nerve damage.

And yet the young doctor who came out to meet us in the

waiting room said he could not keep her against her will. She refused to stay, and legally, they could not force her to do so. They wheeled her out, and she stared at us with abject fury, as if we'd committed some horrendous crime by bringing her here, which made us all feel guilty and ashamed and doubt our resolve.

I told the doctor, my voice tight with rage, "So what you're saying is that if she'd drunk arsenic, for example, then you could keep her, because that would constitute a danger to herself, but since it's only alcohol, it's not considered suicidal behavior? I swear, if she goes home and dies, I'm going to sue this hospital for everything it's worth."

The young doctor stared at me blankly, as if to say he didn't make the rules. Then he said, "You'd need two separate psychiatric evaluations and a court order to have her committed against her will. That can't happen overnight, and meanwhile, we can't keep her."

I find it absolutely astonishing that hospitals don't consider alcoholics in the advanced stages of the disease "a danger to themselves or others." What could be more dangerous than this level of intoxication? The doctor prescribed Librium and sent us home.

The hospital was so concerned that Gloria was going to die, the same doctor called me at the house a few hours after her release with the number of an excellent private nursing service. I hired an R.N. named Linda, who came right over and stayed for six weeks. At night we hired nurses' aides to sit by my mother's bedside. We immediately put Eyrna's baby gate around Gloria's bed so she couldn't roll out. She couldn't stand up, much less walk to get booze for herself, although she certainly tried. Nurse Linda pumped her full of Librium, and we held vigil, day and night, waiting for her heart or her liver or her kidneys to give out.

We spent hours trying to get my mother to swallow vitamin B–enriched protein shakes, but her entire system had shut down, and the neurological damage was such that for the first two weeks, she couldn't swallow without great concentrated effort. Her legs swelled to three times their normal size and turned brown.

After my brother and cousins went home, back to their lives and jobs, I stayed, along with Eyrna, who was nineteen months old and already walking and talking in full, cohesive sentences. Cecile, who in the summer lived half a mile down the street, stopped in three or four times a day.

People I hardly knew came by constantly and gave me unsolicited advice. One old friend of my mother's suggested we find Gloria a job, that this whole "episode" had been brought on by boredom. I called Gianna, who'd recently moved to Sag Harbor to raise her adopted daughter, Nina. They both came over at sunset, and Gianna ran interference for me while Nina entertained Eyrna. Everyone had a doctor who was better than my mother's doctor, whom they wanted to bring over. Finally, an old friend whose opinion I trusted told me about a Dr. Stephen Goldfarb, who had admitting privileges at Southampton Hospital.

Gianna and I sat in the kitchen, waiting for Dr. Goldfarb to arrive.

"She's in very, very bad shape. You understand she might not make it," Gianna said quietly, her eyes serious.

"Yes," I said.

Dr. Goldfarb walked in, carrying his old-fashioned black doctor's case. He had a sweet, round face, blond hair, and intelligent blue eyes. I took him upstairs to evaluate my mother. A while later, he and Nurse Linda came downstairs, looking none too optimistic. "It's hard to tell right now," said Dr. Goldfarb. "It's touch and go. It'll depend entirely on how strong she is."

"Oh, she's strong," said Gianna. "Anyone else would have died a long time ago."

He prescribed diuretics, and Wellbutrin, an antidepressant, which he explained would help with her anxiety and cravings.

"Most people who have an addiction to alcohol or drugs suffer from some form of depression," he said. "So they self-medicate. Problem is, alcohol is a depressant, so ultimately, it just exacerbates the condition. It's a chicken-or-egg situation."

Finally! A doctor who has a clue! I had been convinced for years that my mother suffered from depression and anxiety, which she medicated with alcohol. I felt like throwing myself into his arms.

After three weeks of painful detoxing, my mother sat up in bed one morning and looked out at the world with the terrified eyes of a small child. She slowly, tentatively, pushed herself up to a sitting position and hoisted her fragile legs over the side of the bed.

"I'm going downstairs," she said.

"Darling, that's not a good idea, you're still very weak," Cecile pointed out.

"I'm going downstairs," my mother said. The child was also willful and stubborn.

Thirty pounds lighter, she stood on her stick-thin legs and took a few shaky steps, stumbling, gripping the furniture and walls. Having emptied the house completely of alcohol, even the vanilla extract and rubbing alcohol, we helped her downstairs, and for a few hours she sat in the library/TV room, gazing at the furniture and books, as if she'd never seen them before. Her hands would get ahold of an object and endlessly pat it, rub it, worry it.

After a while I went in to check on her. She was sitting in one of the two high-backed Louis Treize red velvet chairs, her fingers circling the rounded grooves at the end of the carved armrests.

She looked up at me and said, "Hello, Mother," her voice formal and alien.

"I'm not your mother, I'm Kaylie. I'm your daughter, Kaylie."

"Why are you holding me prisoner, Mother?"

"This is your house, Mom," I said, my voice trembling. "This is *your* house."

"Yes, Mother. But what have you done to your house?" I'd never heard her speak as politely and distantly to anyone except the Dread Gertrude.

Eyrna came running in from her swim in the pool. "Gammy, Gammy!" she cried, and threw herself into my mother's legs. Gloria winced from the pain but ran a shaky hand over Eyrna's damp curls.

"And there's little Kaylie," she said in a sweet, fragile voice, looking up at me. "She's a beautiful baby, isn't she, Mother? We all love her so much. She's a little high-strung, just like I was, but you'll learn to love her too, when you get to know her."

I asked Dr. Goldfarb on his next visit if my mother's memory would return. He said he didn't know. It would depend on many factors, not the least of which was how strong her will was.

One of her friends, upon seeing the Wellbutrin by her bedside, told her it was an antidepressant. Gloria, horrified, had the friend throw out the bottle.

"You're trying to drug me!" she shouted at me when I came upstairs. "I'm not nuts, Mother, I don't need any crazy-people pills! And I don't like that doctor anyway. I want you to fire him, he doesn't know what he's talking about."

Of course she wouldn't like Dr. Goldfarb; the man had spelled it out for her, clear as day. You drink, you die. Take this pill, it will help. But my mother would not even take an Advil because she was so terrified of drugs. For any ailment—menstrual cramps, upset stomach, flu, toothache—a shot of alcohol had always been the cure.

I considered mashing up the pills and putting them in her protein shakes, but what was I, the alcohol police? How long could that last? Must I give up my life and move in with her permanently to keep track of what she ate and drank and get her to take her pills, as if she were a recalcitrant child? Some people did that kind of thing, but I would not. Kevin called every day, wanting me to come home. "Let someone else take the brunt of this," he said. "Why does it have to be you?"

"Because there's no one else," I told him, my voice hollow.

The same month my mother was teetering between life and death, the James Jones Literary Society symposium, planned a year in advance, was to be held at Southampton College, hosted by the MFA program of Long Island University. The speakers were Norman Mailer, William Styron, Budd Schulberg, Peter Matthiessen, Joseph Heller, and Betty Comden. There was no way to cancel now, and the day before the event on the last Saturday in June, the entire James Jones Literary Society descended upon us. I made a big pasta dinner and salad on Friday night, and invited everyone to my mother's house. I was on edge, uncertain still if she would survive, but my friends from the Society were kind and generous and asked nothing of me, and offered to help in any way they could.

The Society rented a small private plane to fly Norman Mailer and William Styron in from Cape Cod and Martha's Vineyard. I was amazed to find, when I arrived at the college, that the 250-seat Duke Auditorium in the college's brand-new Chancellor's Hall was completely packed, with people standing three deep in the back, leaning against the railings near the exit doors, and sitting on the steps leading down to the podium at the front of the sloping hall. Larry Heinemann, the National Book Award– winning Vietnam veteran, to my delight, had driven down from Boston to attend, with several other veteran writers, including the poet Bruce Weigl.

The aging literary giants got up one by one and spoke about my father and his place in American letters, and their personal relationships with him. They all spoke of his war novels, feeling strongly that they would endure.

Bill Styron read the eulogy he'd written for my father's funeral service in 1977. It was a beautiful piece of writing, condemning the critics for their lack of foresight and their pettiness. Budd Schulberg told of meeting my father as a young man in New York, just after *From Here to Eternity* was published. But to Budd, Jim still seemed like a lost and lonely country boy, and Budd told the funny story of how early one morning, my father described the kind of woman he was looking for. "I need a girl, but not for tonight. I need a partner for life. But she has to be beautiful. It would be nice if she looked a little like Marilyn Monroe—but she has to be smart, and she has to understand writers." Budd instantly thought of his friend Gloria Mosolino, who had been Marilyn's stand-in on *The Seven Year Itch,* and had just written a novel herself.

My mother once told me that while they were dating, my father read her book, which was about her father the Italian gangster in Pottsville, Pennsylvania. My father told her the book needed massive revisions. She put it away and never wrote fiction again.

Norman Mailer talked about his reaction to reading *From Here to Eternity* for the first time. "I truly suffered," he said, "because it was too damn good." He added that when he first met James Jones, he felt he'd met an extremely honest and simple man who "had the wisdom of an elegant redneck," probably the finest oxymoron I'd ever heard. Larry Heinemann, sitting on the steps leading into the front of the room, howled with laughter at that one.

I was so pleased that Norman Mailer had come to offer such kind and generous words. Especially because he and my father had such a terrible falling-out in the early sixties that my father went ballistic whenever Norman was mentioned. It had apparently been over a nasty comment Bill Styron had made about my father's writing, which Norman reported to my father. Bill had apparently apologized profusely to my father, explaining that they'd been drunk at the time. My father had taken Bill's side in the matter, and Norman, taking offense, wrote very nasty stuff about both of them in his book *Advertisements for Myself.*

The first time I ever spoke to Mailer was at a cocktail party at Jean Stein's Central Park West apartment ten years earlier. The dining table had been pushed back to make a bar, and I was standing in the overcrowded room with my mother when Norman walked in with his wife, Norris Church.

"Shit, there's Norman," my mother muttered. "Run!" But we couldn't run, we were hemmed in by the crowd trying to get to the bar. Norman approached us, and I steeled myself for some sort of confrontation between him and Gloria.

"Hello, Gloria. I'm glad to see you," he said with a warm smile, holding out his hand.

"Hello, Norman," my mother replied stiffly, taking it. "This is our daughter, Kaylie."

He turned to me and said simply, "I loved your father. He was the best friend I ever had, and I've missed him every day of my life. Losing him was one of the worst things that ever happened to me."

This was the tough-talking, wheedling, arrogant son of a bitch my father was so angry at all through my childhood? I couldn't believe it. Norman introduced me to Norris, and we shook hands. Her smile was kind and wide open in her beautiful face. She towered over us and had long, thick auburn hair, the kind of hair and creamy pale skin you read about in romantic nineteenth-century novels.

They stood with us in the crowded room for a long time, much longer than one ever expects at a cocktail party packed with luminaries. Norman told me that the thing he regretted most was the last exchange he had with my father. They'd run into each other at Elaine's, sometime in 1977, which must have been, Norman supposed, just before Jim died. My father was sitting at the bar, and Norman, feeling brawny, walked up to him and said, "Let's settle this thing once and for all, Jim. Let's go outside and fight it out."

"I can't, Norman," my father said, "I'm sick. I've got a bum heart."

Norman said it was the way he said it that had struck him so. There was no bravado, no self-pity, no anger in his words. Just a fact, and the total exhaustion in his eyes. Norman had not known his old friend was sick, and hadn't known what to say. So he said something foolish, like, "Well, then maybe next time."

And that was the last time Norman had seen my father.

Now he said to me, "I'd like to make it up to you. I want to be your friend."

"You can make it up to her right now," my mother interrupted, "you can give her a quote for her new book about Russia."

"Send it to me tomorrow," he said, and searched through his pockets for a piece of paper to write down his address and phone number.

"If you give her a quote for her novel," my mother persisted, "I swear, Norman, I'll . . . I'll . . . give you a blow job."

Norris burst out laughing, throwing her head back, and Norman chuckled delightedly as blood rushed to my face. I started laughing too, out of nerves. When we finally parted company, I murmured to my mother, "Are you crazy? And anyway, you always said you're terrible at blow jobs."

"Yeah, but he doesn't know that. And anyway, they know I'm outrageous and full of bluster. He knows I'm never going to give him a blow job. Look"—she pointed with her chin across the room—"Norris is still laughing."

After the symposium, I was having a big garden dinner party at my mother's, catered by cousin Michael, and paid for by the Society.

Kevin and I reached home only a half hour before the guests

and hurriedly changed our clothes and walked around, making sure the house was presentable. Michael's staff was still setting up the bar and the round tables, covered in white tablecloths. Just as cars began to arrive, it hit me. *My mother* was the hostess, the one everyone turned to for amusing anecdotes and irreverent humor. But she was upstairs, lying in bed, a blank slate, with no notion of what was going on around her. I began to shake and hyperventilate. What was I going to do? For a few minutes, I felt what it would truly be like without her, and I was petrified. I had to go stand by the tall lilac bushes by myself and take deep, calming breaths. The grounds were beginning to look run-down, even though purple and white phlox and bright orange poppies bloomed all around among the weeds. Gianna found me standing there, and I could see the concern and compassion etched in the lines of her face.

"I don't know what I'm going to do," I said helplessly.

"You're going to do just fine," she said, and she went to find Kevin, who came quickly. He said I didn't have to do a thing, the party would take care of itself.

"The lilacs need cutting," I told him helplessly.

"Don't worry about the lilacs. I'll cut them back tomorrow," he said.

When Larry Heinemann arrived, he took me aside and asked if he could meet my mother, and I led him quietly through the bustling kitchen and empty living room.

Since the publication of his novel *Paco's Story* in 1986, my mother had kept a hardcover first edition of the book on her living room coffee table, a place of honor reserved for very few books. The publisher had sent it with a "compliments of the author" card. Larry saw the book lying there and asked if I'd put it out just for him.

"No way," I said. "It's been lying there since your publisher sent it to my mother in 1984." I could tell by the look in his huge, armor-piercing blue eyes that he didn't believe me.

Paco, the eponymous narrator, tells his Vietnam tale of woe to "James," his tone bitter and angry and full of reluctant admiration. I asked Larry what I'd always wanted to know—if the "James" to whom Paco speaks is James Jones.

"Yes," Larry told me. "Yes, it is. But," Larry added, "in Vietnam, the soldiers called to each other, 'Hey, Jack!' Soon, with the war going from bad to worse, this was elevated, with exquisite irony, to 'Hey, James!' So, 'James' is James Jones, the quintessential World War Two writer who'd been a grunt himself, but it's also every single filthy, hard-core, buck-ass private who ever fought a war for his country."

"God, my dad would have loved that," I told Larry.

We climbed the steep stairs and entered my mother's room to find her sitting up in bed, all washed and brushed and looking beautiful in a pale green Indian-style caftan. She kept smoothing down the flowery blue comforter that covered her legs, a repetitive, strangely unnerving motion. Her dark blue eyes, the same color as the comforter, looked up at us expectantly, uncertain of where she was or what we might want from her.

"Hello, Mother," she said to me in a sweet, innocent, formal, little-girl voice that chilled me to the bone.

I said, "Mom, this is Larry Heinemann, the writer. You remember *Paco's Story*? He wanted to meet you. You loved his book. You have it downstairs on the coffee table."

Larry kneeled by her bedside and took her hand. "Gloria, I'm Larry Heinemann. I loved your husband. His work—" He took a deep breath, and suddenly choked on his words. Tears began to fall from his eyes. As his face contorted, he dropped his head, and his shoulders began to shake. I felt like I couldn't stand up and went and braced myself against the wall.

The only other man I'd ever seen cry like this was my father.

I could still picture him in our Paris living room, down on one knee, reading from his own manuscript, as tears dripped down his cheeks. And the time he showed us the poor Japanese soldier's wallet. And once, listening to a recording of Robert E. Lee's great-grandson reading the great general's surrender at Appomattox, my father sat down, hands on his knees, and began to shake, his face contorted, tears streaming, just like Larry.

I slid down to the floor, knees to my chest, and sat there with my back against the wall, unable to speak. My mother looked toward me, her eyes afraid, questioning. What is it you expect me to do? her expression seemed to say. The three of us remained like that, not speaking, for what seemed like a long time.

"Well, then . . . ," Gloria said lightly, her hands continuing to stroke the blue comforter. "Well, well, well . . ." Her downcast eyes seemed to have discovered some new and fantastically interesting pattern in the weave.

A moment later, Nurse Linda walked in. Larry stood up, breathed deeply, ran his hand roughly over his face, and I slowly got back on my feet. Downstairs, Larry led me straight to the garden bar under an ancient hops hornbeam tree and ordered a bourbon on the rocks. "What'll it be?" he asked me.

"I can't drink," I said. "I'm a drunk. If I drink, I'll end up just like my mother, but much faster."

"Well then I'll drink for both of us," he said, and asked the bartender to make it a double. The smell of bourbon—a liquor I'd never liked—wafted up my nose and ignited my taste buds, and I suddenly wanted a drink very badly. The white wine the bartender was pouring suddenly looked very crisp and appealing. Maybe just one glass . . . But who the hell was I kidding? I wanted a whole fucking bottle of vodka, not one nice, crisp glass of white wine.

My mouth went suddenly dry, and I didn't know what to do with my hands. Then I heard Eyrna's high-pitched laughter reverberate off the big, leafy hops hornbeam tree behind the bar; I turned toward that lighthouse of sound, and like a person navigating through a dense fog, made my way toward the new swing set in the back garden. As I came around the house corner, I saw Kevin pushing Eyrna in her bright yellow sundress and pantaloons and matching canvas sneakers, high up into the darkening air alight with fireflies.

After a while, my mother was drawn downstairs by the tinkle of ice in glasses and the general commotion. She floated out to the porch and sat next to Joe Heller on the swing that hung by thick chains, and he held her hand, patting it gently, as if she were a child. I was reminded of an evening many years before, when Joe Heller had tried to fix my mother up with his close friend, Mario Puzo, who had recently been widowed as well. "You're both Italian, he's a writer—what could be better?" said Joe, and he set up their date, even accompanying them on it.

I came home late from an evening at a local bar and found the three of them in the living room. My mother, sitting regally in a hard, tall-backed Spanish chair of carved, dark wood, was holding Mario Puzo's hand, who sat at the very edge of the couch, as if he were about to fall off. My mother was crying (which meant she was completely plotzed, for she never cried), and Joe Heller, their silent chaperon, sat at the other end of the room, sadly shaking his head.

"You're very sweet and charming," my mother said to Mario Puzo, "but I still love my husband, you see. And he was a much better writer than you."

Now, pale and luminous, she looked around at her oldest and dearest friends, and seemed slightly calmed and comforted by the familiarity of their faces. Yet, she was strangely disconnected from her surroundings, as if she were a ghost wafting through her own house. Joe Heller continued to gently pat her hand, calmingly, as if he understood exactly what she needed. It occurred to me for the first time that they were all silver-haired now, their beautiful, intelligent faces lined by hard-earned experience and the ravages of time.

Some weeks after the party, Gloria suddenly came to, sitting on the low wicker couch on the porch, and there, before her, was a curly-headed baby face peering up at her.

"Eat, Gammy, eat!" Eyrna had taken the chewed piece of chicken nugget out of her own mouth and was pressing it to her grandmother's lips.

My mother's eyes snapped into focus, as if some switch had been flicked on. "Okay." She took the soft morsel into her mouth and made an effort to chew and swallow, looking into the golden eyes of Eyrna.

Nurse Linda said, "That's good, Eyrna. See, you're the only one who can make your grandmother eat."

Kevin, just a few feet beyond the porch, who had been trying to rescue the 150-year-old lilac bushes from an invasion of fast-growing, choking weed trees, overheard this and came bounding up the porch steps. "Don't ever say that to her," he said to Linda, his voice trembling with anger. "It's not her responsibility to make her grandmother eat. She's twenty months old, for God's sake."

I'd never seen him this angry. At six or seven, Kevin had been the "hero child" in his family, the one who quietly went downstairs in the very early morning, after his parents' drinking binges, and turned off the oven that held the blackened and abandoned meal; he emptied the overflowing ashtrays; he searched for cigarettes smoldering in the corners of the couch and under the table; he washed the martini glasses and the shaker and poured whatever booze was left, if there was any left, down the sink. By the time his two brothers and his parents awakened, the house looked normal. Nothing weird going on here. Then, that night, they would start the whole chaotic, sordid dance all over again.

After she'd eaten a bit, my mother stood up on shaky legs, said she was tired and wanted to go back upstairs. Nurse Linda jumped up to help. "I'm fine, I'm fine," my mother said, shrugging Linda off. She grabbed both sides of the door frame and slowly, deliberately, lifted one leg, then the other. She staggered a few steps, then grasped the stairway's wooden rail with a trembling hand and tried to pull herself up the steep stairs to her bedroom. We all had rushed to encircle her, to hold her if she fell, but it was Eyrna who stepped in behind her grandmother, placed her dimpled hands flat on Gloria's bottom, and pushed. "Me help, Gammy, me help you up stairs! Me push!"

When, a few months later, Gloria was once again able to drive, she relearned the topography of her neighborhood, inch by inch, mile by mile. She memorized the roads, her friends' names, their phone numbers. She taught herself to write all over again. She never let on that she didn't remember; she never asked a single question; she never asked for help.

"Why Is This Shit Always Happening to Me?"

This was one of my mother's favorite Willie Morris stories.

→→   ←←

Willie Morris, the onetime editor of *Harper's* and best-selling author of the memoir *North Toward Home* had moved out to Bridge-hampton after he'd left the literary life in New York. One of the main reasons my parents chose Bridgehampton as a place to settle was that Willie had made it his home.

On our first day in our new rental, the Vreeland house farther south toward the beach on Sagg Main Street, Willie, who was a renowned practical joker, decided to play a trick on Gloria. The phone rang, and Gloria picked up.

Disguising his voice and putting on an excellent local Bon-acker accent which he'd perfected over the last few years, Willie said, "Hello, this here's Bob Wznyzfski of the Southampton Highway Department. We'll be arriving tomorra at, oh, three o'clock with the bulldoza and the wrecking crew."

"What bulldozer? What wrecking crew?" my mother shouted, suddenly furious.

"Well, everything's in orda on this end—the papers all been signed for the new highway extension. It's only going to clip about, oh, ten feet off yer kitchen, nothing much—"

"What? Highway—what are you talking about? I just got here! I just rented this house!"

"Well, the ownas already been told all about—"

"Oh, why is this shit always happening to me? You can just go fuck yourself, Mr. Whatever-the-hell-your-name-is, that's all."

And she hung up.

I had been sitting at the round, pockmarked wooden kitchen table, looking at the cartoons in a *New Yorker* magazine, listening to her side of this peculiar exchange. It was mid-June and a dense fog rolled in over the brilliant green landscape. Leading right up to the Vreelands' lawn lay an enormous, rich brown field with row upon row of young, bright green potato plants, stretching as far as the eye could see.

"Who was that?" I asked my mother, curious.

"Ah, no one. Some asshole from the Highway Department had the wrong number."

Two minutes later, when Willie called back, howling with laughter, she realized she'd fallen prey to one of his infamous pranks.

"Well, goddamn you, Willie, you had me going," she said, laughing with relief, a hand pressed to her heart.

CHAPTER TWELVE

-⯈- Death of a Writer -⯇-

ON AUGUST 2, 1999, THE summer of my mother's cirrhotic collapse, Willie Morris died in Jackson, Mississippi, from a heart attack brought on by advanced congestive heart failure, the disease that had killed my father. Willie was only sixty-four years old and had also struggled with alcohol abuse for many years.

When I went upstairs to tell my mother, she stared at me blankly and said in a dreamy voice, "That's such a shame," as if she knew this was the appropriate response but had absolutely no idea what I was talking about. At that moment, my mother's loss of memory seemed a blessing, for if she'd been herself, the news of her dear friend's demise would have sent her on a bender the likes of which I didn't even want to consider.

While I did not remember ever meeting Willie before our return to the States in 1974, he'd come down to Miami to visit us during our first winter back from Europe, and had within two days become the uncle Jamie and I never had. It seemed to us we had always known him, and he'd always been a part of our family. He was a sweet, modest, jovial teddy bear of a guy, quite a few years younger than our parents, with unkempt hair, in wrinkled extra-large Lacoste polo shirts, and rumpled khakis sliding off his hips. A natural storyteller, he had us rolling on the floor with stories of his childhood dog, Skip, and his great-aunt who'd survived the Civil War but had found no one to marry because all the boys from her hometown of Yazoo, Mississippi, had been killed fighting. He imitated his maiden aunt's high, warbling voice as she used to call to him from the window at four o'clock in the afternoon, "Willie, tahm fa beyed! Come on eein an' hayave a wahrm cup o milk, nahw!"

During that visit he talked my parents into moving to Bridgehampton. Many of my parents' writer friends had already made the move to the area, and the idea appealed to them both. They would be close enough to New York for my mother, and far enough away for my father.

It was hard for Jamie and me to believe that this sweet, unkempt, easygoing man had been, during the sixties, one of the most important, artistic, and innovative editors on the New York literary scene. He had been appointed, in 1967, the youngest editor in chief of *Harper's* magazine. At that time of great civil unrest, he published the works of some of America's most creative liberal thinkers, causing an uproar. He printed Norman Mailer's *Armies of the Night* in its entirety, without break. He published a big chunk of William Styron's hugely controversial novel *The Confessions of Nat Turner*, and helped launch David Halberstam's career as one of America's preeminent journalists. Willie stood opposed to the war in Vietnam, believed strongly in civil rights, and took a left-wing attitude to the other hot issues of the day. Eventually, he caused too much upset for the magazine's conservative owners and was fired from *Harper's* in 1971. Around that time he published *North Toward Home*, a best-selling memoir about his childhood in Mississippi, his education, and his move north. Nowadays, though, Willie Morris is best known as the author of *My Dog Skip*, a young adult novel about his childhood pet, which was a national bestseller and made into a Hollywood film in 2000.

There is a large, framed black-and-white photograph by Jill Krementz that still hangs over the bar of Bobby Van's restaurant in

Bridgehampton. In it, standing in front of the old Bobby Van's across the street, are Truman Capote, James Jones, John Knowles (author of the literary classic *A Separate Peace*), and Willie Morris. I used to love looking at that photo, but now it only upsets me, because the loud, echoing, overpriced new Bobby Van's has nothing to do with the quiet hangout the writers were drawn to in the seventies and early eighties. Once, while I was standing near the bar, waiting for a lunch table, I heard a woman ask, "Who're they?" pointing up at the picture. And a fellow beside her answered, "Oh, just some old writers that used to live around here a long time ago."

During our first summer in the Hamptons, when I was about to turn fifteen, my dad gave me a copy of *In Cold Blood,* and I read it, gripped and horrified by every page. I became fascinated with the book's author. What I really wanted to know, and asked my father, was how Truman Capote knew so much about these people, not just the victims, but the murderers too? My father explained that Capote had gone to Kansas and spent a long time researching the book and had gotten deeply involved in the players' lives.

"I know him," my father said. "He lives around here. He hangs out with Willie in Bobby Van's."

"You guys *know* him?" I practically shouted, as if we were talking about Mick Jagger. This made my dad laugh. After a moment, he added, in case I had plans to marry Truman Capote, "He's a homosexual." Over the years, I'd announced my desire to marry Keir Dullea, who'd been in the first film of *The Thin Red Line* and spent a great deal of time in our apartment when I was three; then I'd transferred my affections to Johnny Hallyday, the French pop star who rode a black motorcycle; and most recently, I'd announced my intention to marry Willie Morris in about ten years.

My father proceeded to tell me a strange tale of Truman's relationship with the murderers. Truman, my father said, had fallen in love with weaker, subservient Perry Smith, and that after Truman witnessed Perry's execution by hanging, he had a nervous breakdown from which he never fully recovered. My dad also told me that Perry Smith had slit Mr. Clutter's throat because he'd been dared to do it by his dominant lover, Dick Hickock, the tougher and meaner of the two thieves. Perry didn't want to come off as a wimp in front of Dick, who constantly teased him for being a *girl*. My father believed—as Truman apparently did—that Dick had shot Mrs. Clutter and her daughter Nancy, who were bound and lying in their beds upstairs, though Dick denied this to the end.

"How do you know this?" I asked, mystified.

"Well, Truman talked to me about it. And he talks a lot to Willie. I'll introduce you to Truman, if you want," my dad concluded mildly.

A few days later, I walked across the street to meet my dad in Bobby Van's. My father said, "There's Truman." He was alone, sitting in the very back of the now empty restaurant, knocking back martinis. My dad stood up and walked me over to the table.

"Hi, Truman. This is my daughter, Kaylie. She just read *In Cold Blood* and wanted to meet you."

Truman looked up from his martini and said, "Hi, Jimmy! Why, darling girl, how *sweet!*" in the highest, most effeminate voice I'd ever heard in a man. We shook hands; his was limp and damp and I was struck speechless. I couldn't believe this funny-looking, boiled shrimp of a guy was responsible for the massive, macho book I'd just read. Despite Truman's strange voice and effeminate demeanor, my father treated him with extreme deference and respect, which for some reason impressed me.

On the way home, I asked my dad what he would do if two guys broke into our house like the guys did in the book.

"First of all, I'd never let them tie me up. Very calmly, I'd say, Look, kill me if you're going to, but I ain't lettin' you tie me up." He turned his eyes toward me. "Never let anyone tie you up," he said. "Never. If they're gonna kill you, they'll kill you anyway. If there's a chance they're vacillating, you're better off untied. Show 'em you're not scared. If someone was going to hurt my family, that's the only reason I'd kill anybody anymore. I'd kill 'em first chance I got." He said this so simply, so serenely, that I felt a chill run up my spine. I was so glad he was my father.

Willie had been my father's closest friend in the last two years of his life. And like some kind of modern-day Pied Piper, he was a man to whom children and animals were naturally drawn, and they adored him absolutely and blindly. But showing up consistently had never been one of Willie's fortes, though his heart was filled with kindness; at times, he'd disappear for weeks, refusing to answer the phone. Then he'd amble into Bobby Van's and find his crew sitting there at the bar or at a quiet corner table, knocking back the booze.

My father once told me, while he was teaching me to drive, speaking in the same quiet and measured voice he'd used to describe his own father's troubles with booze, that Willie was an *alcoholic*. He said Willie was trying these days to stick to white wine because he couldn't handle the hard stuff at all anymore.

One dreary winter night in 1977, I wrote up a proclamation naming Willie as my godfather. My father, Willie, and I solemnly signed it, at first as an amusing joke. But as my father's illness progressed, Willie seemed to take his responsibilities more seriously. My father, at the end of his life, really needed Willie, and Willie came through for his old friend, a real trouper. I was a senior in high school that winter, and Willie took my mother and me to visit colleges, because my father was too sick to go.

Only weeks after my father died, I had my senior prom and was graduated from high school. At that time I could have asked Willie for anything, and he would have done his best to give it to me. My fabulous twelfth-grade English teacher, Ms. Weaver, didn't have a date to the prom, and he escorted her—because I asked him. He came to my graduation and practically held my mother up through the ceremony. The valedictorian, a boy named Andrew Fisher, mentioned my father in his speech, and I sat like a statue on the stage among my classmates, stony eyed.

Willie took the tapes my father had recorded in the hospital in his last weeks and finished *Whistle* for him. But the tragedy of my father's untimely death sent Willie over the edge, and in his grief, he gave up the white wine and went back to the bourbon he'd been trying so hard to avoid the last several years.

Willie fell into a deep depression after my father died, and a few years later, while I was still in college, he left Long Island for good and returned to Mississippi.

Four years passed, and when I was a senior at Wesleyan, I called to tell him I'd made Phi Beta Kappa, and that I'd won the hundred-dollar promise he'd set forth on the day I'd left for college. Willie had been Phi Beta Kappa, as well as a Rhodes Scholar. He sent me a hundred-dollar check the next day. I learned later that he was flat broke, and this was a huge amount of money for him, and I felt guilty for holding him to his promise.

I had to go to his funeral, so Kevin booked us tickets on a flight to Jackson, Mississippi, with two layovers each way because that was all that was available on such short notice, and we packed Eyrna up for the long, hot, arduous trip.

Willie's casket would lie in state under the dome of the old state capitol in Jackson, with the service and funeral following in Yazoo City, his hometown, on August 5, my thirty-ninth birthday.

We left our bags at the motel and drove our rented car straight to the old capitol building. The wet heat in Jackson felt like a clawing, angry presence. Willie's close friend Dean Faulkner Wells, the niece of William Faulkner, was standing outside on the steps, smoking. She was with several people I didn't know. I'd met her numerous times, with Willie, so we went over and said hello. It took her a moment to place me; then, her eyes tearing, she said Willie had left life exactly the same way he left parties. With a cigarette smoldering in her shaking hand, she reminded us of how, late in the evening, when a few last friends were gathered around talking, Willie would simply sneak away, retire quietly, without saying good-bye to anyone. This was true, and I suddenly felt the great chasm of the last decade, and of being cheated of a last opportunity to say good-bye.

We found Willie's wife, JoAnne, and I hugged her stiffly, formally. She seemed immobilized, struck numb by grief. I told her my mother was too sick to come. She looked at me with her dark, velvety eyes and asked me what was wrong with Gloria. Tired of the bullshit, the pretenses, I said she had cirrhosis and Korsakoff's syndrome and had almost died. I told her Gloria had completely lost her memory.

"My mother was an alcoholic. She died of cirrhosis at thirty-six," JoAnne said. "I know exactly what you're talking about."

And suddenly her marriage to Willie no longer seemed such a mystery.

Under the large, echoing dome of the state capitol, Eyrna played on the white marble floor with Willie's twenty-two-month-old step-grandson, while towering above their heads, illustrious persons, including politicians and Hollywood producers, arrived from all over the country, forming a line to pay their respects. David Halberstam, William Styron, Pat Conroy, Richard Ford, Ellen Gilchrist, Winston Groom, and John Grisham were among those present. I saw my childhood friend David Rae Morris, Willie's only son, whom I hadn't seen since my last visit to Mississippi, in May 1986. It was the spring when Dennis and I decided to drive down to New Orleans. We'd stopped to see Willie in Oxford, Mississippi, where he was then writer in residence at Ole Miss.

By 1986, Willie's drinking had progressed to such an extent that he was barely functioning, and I had trouble imagining how he conducted his classes. He pulled himself together and took us on a day trip through the cotton fields of the Delta, his old black Lab Pete, a stray he'd picked up in Bridgehampton, panting and drooling in the backseat. Willie sipped Scope the whole time from a bottle he kept between the front seats, and smoked Viceroys nonstop, so his car was cloudy with smoke.

On our last night, we went to dinner at Dean Faulkner and Larry Wells's house, and met her nineteen-year-old son, John-Mallard, known as J-Bird. We drank and drank and drank and finally, around midnight, we all—except for Larry Wells, who begged off—piled into Dennis's car and drove to the old Oxford cemetery to visit William Faulkner.

Half the family was buried on one side of the path with FALKNER engraved on their headstones; on the other side lay the ones who'd gone along with *Pappy* and changed their names to FAULKNER. It was Pappy who'd added the *u*, Willie now told us as he poured a hefty shot of bourbon from his bottle onto the grass-covered grave. Old Pappy thought *Faulkner* was more elegant, Willie explained, and chuckled merrily at the great writer's antics.

Through the dense fog of my drunkenness, this *u* made me feel uneasy, for it seemed phony and vain, not something I would ever expect from the genius who'd written *The Sound and the Fury*. I was still, at twenty-five, under the delusion that to be a truly great writer, you had to be a truly exceptional human being. And part of that, I supposed, was accepting oneself as one really was.

After a while we staggered back to Willie's modest ranch house and stayed up until sunrise, and continued to drink unrestrainedly until I was so drunk I became perfectly lucid, speedy with clarity. I felt as if I'd been plugged into a wall socket and could hear a sharp electric buzzing in my head. I was way past being able to sleep and was probably closer to alcohol poisoning

James Jones, circa 1936—I love this funny picture of my father at about age fifteen. He looks like a nerd!

James Jones publicity shot, 1951—My father is barely thirty years old in this photograph, which was used on the back cover of the first edition of *From Here to Eternity*.

James Jones at work at the Handys' home, Robinson, Illinois, circa 1948—The Handys built an addition onto their ranch house, just for him, a twenty-seven-year-old veteran with a desire to become a novelist. A wall of glass bricks separated him from the rest of the house.

Gloria and James Jones the day after their wedding, Haiti, February 1957—They look so happy here, a shining, golden couple.

My mother with me at three months, Paris, 1960— This was from a series taken by a *Life* magazine photographer.

Gloria and James Jones on the Quai aux Fleurs, Paris, 1959—My mother is pregnant with me in this photo. Shortly after, she was bedridden for the duration of the pregnancy.

Gloria Jones, circa 1958—She was an image of perfect glamour, with her satin dress, painted nails, a cigarette, and a martini. I couldn't wait to grow up and be just like her!

Bill Styron and James Jones playing harmonica—This photo was taken in Biarritz, France, in the summer of 1965. We often took vacations with the Styrons.

Norman Mailer, Adele Mailer, Gloria, and James Jones, circa 1958—This is the only photo I have of Norman and my father together. Soon after it was taken, they got into an argument and did not speak for close to twenty years.

James Jones, Sylvia Beach, Thornton Wilder, and Alice B. Toklas, Paris, circa 1958.

James Jones with Montgomery Clift, circa 1953—They met during the filming of *From Here to Eternity* and became good friends. My father taught Clift how to play the bugle and how to box.

James Jones and Lowney Handy, about 1955—Behind them is the house he built for himself with the money he made from *From Here to Eternity*. None of Lowney's charisma and attractiveness can be seen in this picture. She was around fifteen years older than my father, her star writing pupil.

James Jones and Peter Lawford, Normandy, 1961—My father was hired as a consultant on the movie *The Longest Day*. Here he and Peter Lawford are checking out a rifle.

Frank Sinatra, Deborah Kerr, Burt Lancaster, James Jones, and Fred Zinnemann—This is a publicity shot of their arrival on Oahu to begin filming *From Here to Eternity*.

Judite, Jamie, and me in East Hampton, summer 1966—Judite did not usually come with us on summer vacations, but coming to the States was a special treat for her. This was her second visit to the United States.

Me and Jamie at our grandmother's in Pottsville, Pennsylvania, summer 1968—We're playing with our new blond and shining American toys.

Me in Venice, 1961—I caught typhoid fever on our way to Yugoslavia on a scuba-diving expedition and nearly died. This was taken on the beach of the Hotel Excelsior, where I found myself again some thirty-seven years later for the Venice Film Festival screening of *A Soldier's Daughter Never Cries*.

Jamie, our dad, and me, Skiathos, Greece, summer 1967—He read us the entire *Odyssey* sitting right here at this table. It was so dark at night that he had to bring a hurricane lamp to the table so he could see.

Jones family on the lower quai, 1967—We look so elegant and wholesome! It took my mother two slaps on my bottom to get me into this itchy yellow outfit from Belina's, the most expensive kids' store in Paris. It is a knockoff of the real one she is wearing. I wore it once, on this day, for the pictures.

Me and my father, East Hampton, 1966—I love this picture. I look just like him, same expression, same body language.

James and Gloria Jones at the pulpit bar, Paris, circa 1969—I believe this picture is from 1969 or 1970, just before my father was diagnosed with congestive heart failure. He looks extremely bloated and unwell.

Gloria in Spetsai, summer 1972—We stayed with our friends the Woods for three summers in the early 1970s. It is high noon and my mother is carrying the ouzo and ice down to the boat.

Henry Kissinger, me, and my father, fall 1976—This was taken at a publication party in Washington, D.C., for my father's book *WWII*. My dad was stunned by the number of army and government dignitaries who turned out for him.

Bodil Nielsen, Rose Styron, Irwin Shaw, Gloria, Bill Styron, and the corner of my head in the back, at the pulpit bar, Paris, 1973—The ladies were singing The Writer Fucker Club anthem, "Take Him" by Rodgers and Hart.

At the East Hampton High School Senior Prom, June 1977—Photographs are deceiving. My father had died six weeks earlier, and I weighed ninety-seven pounds.

Me and my mother, photographed for a book on women, spring 1979—I don't remember who suggested we pose for this book, but we did. We had fun doing it. My mother was in pretty good shape, working for Doubleday and spending several days a week in New York City.

James Jones Literary Society symposium, 1999—Budd Schulberg, Joseph Heller, Gloria Jones, and Norman Mailer. It was the last time this group of literary lions was together.

Posing after the luncheon, July 1998—Standing: E.L. Doctorow, Kurt Vonnegut, Peter Matthiessen, me, William Styron, Arthur Miller, Ismail Merchant, James Ivory. Seated: Kris Kristofferson, Gloria, Norman Mailer, Ruth Prawer Jhabvala, and Anthony Roth Costanzo, the young actor in the film.

Jamie playing backgammon in Sagaponack, circa 1985—Poker, backgammon, chess—don't be fooled by Jamie's
easygoing, self-effacing demeanor. You'll
lose your shirt.

Kevin's and my wedding day,
August 12, 1995—We always called
this blooming white tree our wedding tree. Only a few hours later, my
mother, in a rage about something or
other, threw us out of her house.

Eyrna, me, and Bill Styron,
July 1998—The day of the garden party before the screening
of *A Soldier's Daughter Never
Cries*.

Eyrna as Dorothy, 2000—Eyrna watched *The Wizard of Oz* at least five hundred times. Kevin bought her this outfit, complete with ruby slippers, Toto, and basket, which she wore every day until it no longer fit.

Eyrna and me in Carl Schurz Park, spring 2002—My student Scott volunteered to take some shots of me for a catalog. I brought Eyrna along and he snapped this wonderful candid shot of us laughing.

Gloria and Eyrna in Sagaponack, July 2002—I believe this is before Gloria started drinking again. She's still very thin and her eyes seem clear and thoughtful to me. I keep looking for clues as to what triggered her relapse. I have no idea.

Gloria, Eyrna, and me, summer 2002—This is the only photo of the three of us I have, taken at a cocktail party at Eleonora and Michael Kennedy's house in Wainscott. We'd been away for a month and my mother was very happy to see us.

Wearing my Black Belt, first time, December 2006—I passed my Taekwondo Black Belt test. The next day, with Mr. Luis Sevilla, holding my Black Belt certificate.

than I've ever been in my life. The buzzing did not abate, and I did not sleep or come down from that drunk for two full days.

Recently, reading Larry L. King's biography, *In Search of Willie Morris,* I learned that around this time, Willie had been arrested for drunk driving, and had punched the cop who'd pulled him over, and spent the night in jail.

Also around this time, Willie met JoAnne Pritchard, and began to come out of his despair, though it apparently never left him completely. Eventually he gave up his position at Ole Miss and moved to Jackson with JoAnne. They were married—to everyone's astonishment—in 1990, and Willie seemed to "turn a corner" in his depression and his drinking.

Willie always helped with the James Jones Literary Society whenever I asked him. He was the keynote speaker at several symposia, including an early one in Robinson. Kevin and I took him to the Jones family plot in the Robinson cemetery. He stood there before the graves in his old windbreaker and sagging khaki trousers, hands stuffed deep in his pockets, for a long time in silence. He admitted to us that he had driven to Robinson before, just to see where my father had grown up, but he hadn't asked anyone for directions to the Jones home or to the cemetery plot. He'd just sort of quietly snooped around, as was his wont.

The last time I saw Willie he'd brought JoAnne up to New York in 1996, for the publication of his young adult novel, *My Dog Skip,* which became a big success. Kevin and I met them and my mother for dinner at Elaine's. JoAnne, who had several grown children of her own, had dark, lustrous hair and eyes and a pale complexion, and a poised demeanor. Willie was still drinking bourbon, but he seemed happy and didn't look as bloated and unkempt.

I could tell my mother was in a mood; her lips were pinched in that unpleasant way. Perhaps she felt threatened by JoAnne and the brand-new life Willie had started that had nothing to do with us. Out of nowhere she said to Willie, "What was that broad's name? The one who kept grabbing your crotch under the table that time at Shelby Foote's house? Did you ever end up fucking her?"

Willie blushed but said not a word. JoAnne, an elegant southern lady to the core, looked down at her plate and busied herself with her food. She held her countenance, and I was glad my mother had not been able to rile her. And if my mother had been expecting a laugh, she certainly didn't get one. Not from them, and not from Kevin or me.

It was no surprise, then, that the Joneses were not included on JoAnne's Christmas card list, or kept up-to-date on Pritchard-Morris family events. I'd hear from friends over the next several years that Willie was doing much better now that he was with JoAnne.

Willie's funeral service at the First United Methodist Church of Yazoo City was packed with mourners. JoAnne asked us to sit with the family, and I was deeply touched by this kindness. To keep twenty-one-month-old Eyrna quiet during the service, we gave her a bag of pistachio nuts in their shells. She busily set to breaking open the shells and munching loudly on the nuts. Willie's coffin, covered with flowers, lay not five feet away, and although some people glanced at us with mystified, perhaps even indignant expressions, I felt sure that Willie would have been delighted to have his old friend's granddaughter present, even if she was eating pistachios, for this scene was exactly the kind that amused him greatly.

Among those who spoke were Willie's fifth-grade English teacher, Josephine Ayres Haxton, and his close friends Bill Styron and David Halberstam, who talked of his brilliance, his extraordinary skills as an editor, his legacy as a writer, his kindness, his generosity of spirit, and his jokester's sense of humor.

This reminded me of our first months in Bridgehampton, when Willie would disguise his voice and pretend to be the highway commissioner coming to tear down a wall, or the dogcatcher about to put our dog to sleep for biting a neighbor. My mother got taken by him every time, and I remembered her on the phone, begging a certain Mr. Steppenkowski the Dogcatcher not to kill her dog. By that fall, when we moved into our new house just down the street, these pranks of Willie's had become so commonplace that my father told the Soviet cultural attaché, who called to invite him to Moscow, to fuck off. The cultural attaché gasped, coughed, stammered, and the line went dead. The attaché tried again five minutes later, and they both pretended the earlier conversation had never taken place.

Several speakers described Willie's involvement in the civil rights movement during the sixties, when he put himself on the line to uphold his most profound desire for equality for southern African-Americans. It was Willie who'd brought to Hollywood the idea of a film based on the murder of the civil rights activist Medgar Evers, which became the critically acclaimed *Ghosts of Mississippi*. Willie had also been a mentor to struggling writers and had been instrumental in encouraging Donna Tartt and John Grisham with their first novels, when they'd been his students at Ole Miss.

In closing, the First United Methodist Choir sang "Abide with Me," Willie's favorite hymn, a beautiful rendition that brought everyone to tears. In the ensuing silence peppered with sniffles, Eyrna yelled out, "More, please!" And people giggled into their handkerchiefs despite themselves.

A Delta blues trio played at the grave site in the steaming Yazoo cemetery, which Willie loved and wrote so passionately about in *North Toward Home, My Dog Skip,* and his last, posthumously published novel, *Taps*. The gravediggers, convicts in striped pants, stood off in the distance, leaning on their shovels, smoking. Our friend Winston Groom said a few kind parting words. Winston, who'd grown up in Mobile, Alabama, had been a Washington reporter when he decided to write a novel about his Vietnam experiences. He moved out to Bridgehampton and wrote *Better Times Than These*, with Irwin Shaw, Willie Morris, and my father as his mentors and champions. Later, he wrote the novel *Forrest Gump*, which was made into the very successful film.

Finally, a group of schoolboys played taps on their bugles. Willie had once been among their number, playing the taps echo at the funerals of soldiers fallen in the Korean War. (This is what his novel *Taps* is about.) While Eyrna, in her bright yellow sundress, romped and skipped among the gravestones chasing butterflies, I thought of Willie trying to track down a regular army bugler to come play taps for my father's service at the Bridgehampton Community House. Buglers, he was told, were no longer enlisted men. A Senior/Sergeant Mastrolio, who'd played taps at the funerals of two presidents, volunteered to play for my dad.

We gathered later that evening at JoAnne and Willie's house, which they'd just recently remodeled to suit both their working needs. There was nothing familiar about the house, nor the crowd, and Kevin and I knew no one, except for JoAnne, David, Bill Styron, and Winston Groom. I wandered over to Bill, who was standing with a glass of white wine in the backyard. The air was hot and close, like a bathroom when you've left the shower running too long. I waited until he was alone and then launched into some questions about the Holocaust research I was doing for a new novel. He talked about the flak he'd taken for writing *Sophie's Choice*, a novel about Auschwitz, when he was not Jewish, and having a character, Sophie, a prisoner at Auschwitz, who also was not Jewish. He told me to disregard everyone and just write what I wanted to write. He felt the Holocaust was a human experience, not a Jewish experience, and that no one had a right to censor any writer's exploration of the subject. Some people I didn't know wandered over, and soon I excused myself and drifted back into the unfamiliar house.

I searched the bookcases but did not find a single copy of my father's books anywhere, nor a photograph, nor any other memento from our shared past. It was as if by moving into his new life, Willie had locked us all away in the attic. I stood alone in the living room and saw his glasses and a few note cards he'd been writing, along with the week's TV guide, lying on the ottoman before his favorite leather armchair, as if he'd just gotten up for a moment, perhaps to get something to drink. I wanted to call out to him—but if his ghost had come traipsing through the doorway, would I have known this man, or would he be someone else entirely?

I climbed the stairs to his study to see if I could find the Willie I knew there, as if he'd perhaps sneaked away from the party. Nothing was familiar in his study either. I felt as though I were visiting the shrine of a beloved stranger, just as I had when I'd stood in Hemingway's study in Key West.

When I'd spent that dreadful semester in Paris during my junior year of college, I accompanied a friend to a party at the apartment of one of Tolstoy's great-great-grandsons. The Tolstoy apartment, which was the boy's parents', was in the elegant, staid, uninspiring sixteenth arrondissement. The young man, whose first name I cannot remember, was tall and stately and looked so much like young Lev Tolstoy that I couldn't help but stare at him. Knowing absolutely no one but my friend, I wandered down the apartment's long hallway and found an entire wall adorned with ancient Tolstoy family photographs. This was so stunning to me that I took a step closer, so that my nose was almost touching one of the frames. Here was my beloved Lev, ancient and white-bearded in his ubiquitous peasant garb, surrounded on all sides by his offspring, and beside him, his wife, Sofia, blunt-faced and wearing a long-suffering expression. As I was standing there, the great-great-grandson glided down the hall and passed me without a backward glance.

"What an amazing display of photographs!" I cried out after him in French, stopping him in his tracks. "I *love* Lev Tolstoy. His writing changed my life! And it's really amazing how much you look like him!"

The aristocratic young man gazed at me with a cold and condescending expression. "I've never read his books," he said.

"Oh but you must!" I said. "That's an incredible legacy to have. You should be very proud!"

"I couldn't care less," he said, "I'm not at all interested in books." And he bowed slightly, and walked away. Jesus, I thought. If a writer's own family doesn't even realize the importance of his work, who will stand up for him? Who will pick up his banner and carry it forward after he falls?

I will, I thought. *I*'ll fight for you, Lev Tolstoy, even if your pansy-assed great-great-grandson won't. And I had the strange sensation that Lev Tolstoy was closer to my blood and to my heart than to his own offspring.

My eyes drifted over the contents of Willie's study—books I did not know and photos of strangers. Never mind, I thought, Willie wrote it all down in his memoirs, and even if the details are romanticized, even if the dates are wrong, the books will endure. And we will always have Bill Styron's books, and Truman Capote's, and Faulkner's, and Tolstoy's books, and my father's books, and those, no matter what else, will always be worth fighting for.

"This Is Not the Palais de Justice!"

This is a story my mother especially liked to tell French people who visited our home in Sagaponack.

→→　←←

Our Paris phone number must have been one digit off from the Palais de Justice's main line. The Palais de Justice was the block of buildings on the Île de la Cité that included the infamous and ancient Conciergerie prison, police headquarters, and all the judicial branches of government, including the courts. During the fourteen years we lived in our apartment, we got at least two calls a day for the Palais de Justice. This was, of course, before the invention of answering machines, voice mail, or caller ID. In France, to this day, it is practically impossible to get the phone company to fix a problem, and equally hard to get your number changed. This was one of the many aspects of French life that drove my father insane.

My parents' French friend Monique taught them how to say in French, "You've dialed the wrong number. This is not the Palais de Justice." *Vous vous trompez de numéro, ce n'est pas le Palais de Justice.*

With Gloria's accent, however, it came off sounding something like, "*No, voo voo trompay la numerow, say nay paw la Palay duh Joostees!*"

The French callers, fearing that some foreigner had been hired to man the lines, would start yelling and insist on being transferred to the appropriate department, while Gloria kept repeating, *"No, no, no, say nay paw la Palay duh Joostees!"* After several attempts at making herself understood, she would say, "Oh, go fuck yourself!" and slam down the receiver with a colossal bang. Good thing those old black rotary phones were as sturdy as Sherman tanks.

A moment later, the poor caller would be trying again.

At this point, my father would say, "Here, give me that phone," and he would launch into his slower, more carefully enunciated, but hardly more comprehensible, version of the same words Monique had taught him, with little embellishments of his own: *"Jeuh m'excuse, mosoor, voo voo trompay leuh numero, ici nay paw leuh Palay de Joostees."*

When I was five or six, I told him that *je m'excuse* had a different meaning than *je suis désolé*. *Je m'excuse* meant the speaker was somehow responsible for the problem, while *je suis désolé* meant it was almost certainly someone else's fault. In any case, the caller would inevitably start shouting, as if that would help, and my father would then tell the person to fuck off, and slam down the phone.

When our Portuguese nanny Judite, or her mother Sylvina, answered such calls, the accent would be quite different, but hardly clearer. *"Nao, boo boo trompe, mossio, ici nao s'est la Palais da Justisa."*

Shirley MacLaine, the actress who'd played Ginnie Morehead in the film of *Some Came Running*, had apparently taken a shine to my father, and for several years, during her visits to Paris, she would call the apartment in an attempt to get together with him.

I remember once, I was standing near my mother when the phone rang.

"Hello?" Her face went from expectant to furious in two seconds flat. She covered the mouthpiece with her hand and whispered, "It's that shitty Shirley MacLaine again!"

Suddenly, she said sweetly into the phone, her voice going up several octaves in an excellent imitation of Judite's and Sylvina's Portuguese accent, *"Nao, nao, madami, mossio nao pas iciʒi!"* No, no, madam, monsieur is not here! And she slammed the receiver back into its cradle, wiping her hands of it, a job well done.

CHAPTER THIRTEEN

⤞ Hope ⤝

IN LATE OCTOBER OF 1999, on a day when the temperature shot up to the mideighties, I drove the extra half hour from Southampton College to Sagaponack to visit my mother and spend a few hours with her. Her eyes were clear and her face relaxed, devoid of the old belligerent, rageful tightness. She looked like a completely different person.

"I'd like to go to the beach," she said. "Do you have time? We could have a picnic."

Stunned, I went to see if I had a bathing suit somewhere in my room. I found one, and my mother packed a lunch of hard-boiled eggs and fresh local tomatoes, sliced and drenched in salt and olive oil, in a plastic Ziploc bag. We had the last peaches of the season, some dark bread, and a good French cheese. She brought Diet Coke, her new drink of choice.

I realized that I hadn't been to the beach with my mother since the summer of 1975, when we'd first moved here.

Now, on this gift of a hot summer day in October, we spread out our towels on the warm sand and sat. Her one-piece flowery bathing suit was so old the elastics had given out and hung limply around her skinny thighs. Her dark blue eyes seemed innocent and amazed. Perhaps it was the sharpness of the world, the edges that were no longer blurred, that surprised her so. I'd felt that way when I stopped drinking almost eight years before, and I felt a strange new kinship with her.

"Do you want to take a walk?" I asked her.

"No, this is nice, just sitting here." She opened the plastic bag of tomatoes and eggs and picked out half an egg with two fingers, then handed it to me. It was marvelous and made me feel as though I'd never tasted an egg before. Suddenly starving, I reached for a tomato and another half an egg.

I watched her eat a slice of tomato and realized I hadn't seen her enjoy food in years. She'd tied her thick, lustrous silver hair back in a little ponytail, and her face, without the bloat and expression of constant outrage and fury, had gone back to being beautiful, with her fine, straight nose, sculpted mouth with slightly protruding teeth, and prominent, rounded cheekbones. I saw glimpses now of the person she had been when she'd met my father, and of the shining, mercurial goddess I had so loved and adulated, and also feared and dreaded, when I was a little girl.

There were so many things I wanted to say to her now, but I had no idea where to begin.

"Remember how we used to dance?" I asked her.

She turned to me, her eyes seeming to search back through her scrambled memory banks. "Yes . . . I was a great dancer," she said, as if by rote, as if her mind were playing a tape. I would never know, over the next seven years, what she remembered, what she was simply repeating, what she'd relearned through sheer will and trial and error, and what had been erased from her mind forever.

Nervous, I changed the subject, and filled her in on Eyrna's latest tricks.

For about a week, Kevin had been leaving for work late almost every day because, invariably, something crucial was missing from his pockets—his Metrocard, keys, billfold, or one of his credit cards. Finally, he'd discovered all these missing objects pushed deep into the toes of his sneakers, boots, and shoes.

"Who's been putting my things in my shoes?" he said in a deep, Big Bear voice.

Eyrna replied with an innocent face, "Mommy did it!"

When I asked her why she hid Daddy's things, she said it was because she wanted him to stay home and play with her and not go to work.

Terri, the nurse from the doctor's office who was supervising Eyrna's development, had recently given her a verbal developmental test, and Eyrna's responses were literally off the chart for her age.

"Hmph," said my mother with a sniff, "I could have told you that."

I told my mother that during a recent drive, Eyrna had said, "Mommy, I have two questions."

"What's that, Baby?"

"Can we stop at McDonald's? And why are we here?"

"Here, you mean, driving home to New York?"

"No, here, right now. *Here.*"

My mother wanted to know how I'd answered. I'd said, "Yes, we can stop at McDonald's. And we're here on Earth because God put us here."

My mother gazed at me for a long time and said, "There is no god."

"Oh, but there is a god, Mommy," I said, feeling something huge pushing against a wall inside me. I'd been standing with my finger plugging that dam for so long, I was frightened of what lay behind it. "Look." I gestured to the sparkling ocean, the sky, the golden beach stretching out before us in both directions, rounding to a fine line at the horizon. "Look at us sitting here. You've got a chance, now, Mom. There is a god."

She continued to gaze at me, but there was no meanness in

her eyes. "Well then, he can go fuck himself," she said, her voice hollow.

I shoveled the last tomato into my mouth, followed by a chunk of bread. I was eating out of nerves now. I swallowed hard and charged bravely on. After that conversation with Eyrna, I told my mother, I had pasted luminescent replicas of all the planets on her ceiling, in an order that made them seem to be circling the overhead light, right above her bed. And we'd memorized them together—Mercury, Venus, Earth, Mars, Jupiter, Saturn, Neptune . . . I told her which one was ours and why it was the only one inhabited—that we knew of, so far.

But Gloria was no longer listening.

After a long silence, I said, tentatively, "You're so much better when you're not drinking, Mom. You're like your old self again."

"Really?"

"Yes."

"I always thought I was so much more fun drunk." After a while, she added, "I don't remember anything, you know . . . about when I was sick . . . Not a thing."

"It was awful," I told her, my voice unnaturally low. Where was my anger now? It had left me, and I felt completely lost. I felt that thing pushing inside me, and tears blocking my throat. "I stayed with you the whole time. I never left your side."

"I know you did. You're the best daughter anyone could have. I don't know what possessed me to drink like that. It was stupid. I'm not an *alcoholic*, I guess I was just bored."

Ah, here it was. Rage, my old friend, my protector—not gone, after all. As it pulsated inside my chest, I could feel the wall getting stronger, the onslaught on the other side of it receding. "It was awful," I said again, my voice going tight and hard. "You hurt a lot of people, not just yourself. You can't drink, Mom. You *can't* drink."

She looked at me, her rain-cloud blue eyes defiant, then afraid, then they skipped away toward the ocean, which continued to glitter calmly in the sunlight.

"Please. Please, don't ever tell me. I don't want to know," she said.

I thought about this for a moment and considered giving her the gruesome details. Perhaps if she knew, she would take responsibility. But I couldn't bring myself to do it. She was still not well, and perhaps with time, she'd see the truth. As long as she didn't drink, there was hope. "We were very scared, Mom," I said slowly, evenly. "You have so many people who love you . . . You have your grandchildren—you have Eyrna—who wants to spend time with you . . ."

"I know," she said. "You're a good girl. And I'm very grateful."

In 1977, after my first semester of college, I drove back to Sagaponack to spend Christmas with my mother and Jamie. It was our first Christmas without my father. He once told Jamie and me that on Guadalcanal, soldiers in his company would shout "Home for Christmas!" as they charged across open fields under heavy Japanese machine-gun fire. It made them feel brave, and I felt anything but that.

The last place I wanted to be that year was home for Christmas, but there was no way around it. I wasn't going to abandon ship now. Our dad's last words to Jamie, who was just sixteen, had been, "Take care of the house. Take care of the house, and everything else will be all right."

The East End landscape was incredibly stark that night as I drove for long stretches on Montauk Highway with no light for company but the distant stars and the two yellow beams of my headlights. Then I'd pass a house with one or two windows glowing warmly in the surrounding darkness. Eight P.M. and I drove through the town of Bridgehampton without hitting the brakes.

Bridgehampton was still the un-chic Hampton, the poor rela-
tion in that fancy family. There were a few dim storefronts, and
private homes with Christmas decorations twinkling in the windows. Garlands of white lights sparkled on the potted evergreens
along Main Street. The town had two restaurants, Bobby Van's
and Billy's Triple Crown, dimly lit and almost empty as I passed.

I turned off the highway onto Sagg Main Street with a heart
so filled with grief there was no space left for other emotions. I
passed the old cemetery where my father is buried, straining my
eyes through the blackness for a sight of his pale new headstone.
Until my father, there had been no new graves in that cemetery
since 1886.

The street was deserted. Our house, which stood atop the only
hill in Sagaponack, was lit up from basement to attic, as welcom-
ing as a passenger ship in the night. The house had been raised
by shipbuilders shortly after the Civil War, according to the real
estate broker who'd shown it to us. My dad bought the house on
sight, although it was in disrepair. What had thrilled him most
was the view of fields in every direction. He said they reminded
him of Illinois.

I entered the house through the kitchen, went on to the living
room, where I saw a Christmas tree still bare and my mother sitting on the couch, staring at it. The boiler in the basement clicked
on and began to hum, breaking the silence.

"I couldn't face doing the tree," she said in a barely audible
murmur, and took a long swig from her scotch glass, the ice
clinking loudly. I could smell it from the entryway—familiar,
pungent, sweet, and cool, it reminded me of her kisses when I was
a little girl.

Jamie, then a senior at East Hampton High School, came
downstairs, and we set about solemnly untangling the Christmas
tree lights brought from Paris, which our dad had picked out with
meticulous care. There were strands of bright red strawberries

nestled among green leaves, and another of darker raspberries, and two strands of clear, beautifully realistic icicles—my favorites. Digging through the ornaments, I pulled out a heavy golden sphere speckled with tiny glass stars; it was a music ball that played a lighthearted, tinny, hopeful rendition of "Silent Night." Our tradition had always been to place this ornament on the tree first and listen to the song while our father untangled and hung the lights. I hooked the musical ball onto a strong inner branch.

The simple, high, hopeful notes echoed through the room.

"Oh, God," my mother said in a small, high voice and buried her face in her hands.

How would we ever pull ourselves together, and go on? My mother was talking about moving into the City. It might be less lonely there. But always there were our dad's words, *Take care of the house . . .*

My mother did end up renting an apartment in the city for several years, but she never permanently moved, and never gave up the house.

By 1999, my mother's first sober year, the Sagaponack house was surrounded by what old-timers refer to as McMansions, at varying stages of construction, on crowded half-acre lots. Hammers and saws buzzed all day long. Cars zoomed by, radios blaring. One day, while walking with Kevin and Eyrna along Third Avenue, we saw a woman in a sweatshirt that read SAGAPONACK.

"The beginning of the end," my husband grumbled, and we laughed uneasily.

The summer before, while Gloria had lain upstairs in her bed in that gray zone between life and death, Eyrna and I had taken a short break from watching her and gone to explore the new paved road behind the house, in what used to be a vast potato field. A woman who'd just moved into one of the new McMansions shouted at us, "This road is private property!"

"Private property!" I shouted back, not at my calmest. "Private property! You have some nerve, lady. My family's been living here for a quarter century. So why don't you try a little neighborly civility?"

On our way out from the City that Christmas, with Eyrna in her car seat and the trunk filled to bursting with Christmas presents, the highway was crammed with cars. Even the ancient cemetery had new graves, including Cecile's husband, Buddy Bazelon, who had died after open-heart surgery in August 1995, ten days before our wedding.

As we drove by the cemetery, I looked for my father's and Buddy's gravestones in the gathering gloom, and I liked to think of them keeping each other company. It seemed a less lonely place.

This Christmas, despite the wild and extreme construction going on all around my mother's house, we had a great deal to celebrate. Gloria had survived her bout with cirrhosis and hadn't had a drink in six months. Jamie and his wife, Beth, and little Isabel Kaylie were driving up from Washington, and Cousin Anne and her husband, Frank, would come from Sag Harbor with little Andreas. Cousin Michael now lived in Watermill with his wife, Julie, and their baby, Andrew. Max and his wife, Jennifer, were driving over from Connecticut with Olivia. And Cecile, of course, would cross the highway from her house a half a mile down Sagg Road.

Eyrna, just over two, had moved into Gloria's bed from her own single in my back room. Sometimes I'd go check on them and find them sound asleep, entwined like our old Christmas tree lights.

That night, as we decorated the tree and the ancient and resilient music ball played its tinkling, hopeful "Silent Night," the music could barely be heard above the joyful din of children, who I hoped would never remember this house any other way.

. . .

Looking for picture books for Eyrna, I came across a book I'd adored as a child, *Are You My Mother?* by P. D. Eastman. I opened it and started reading, feeling as if I'd found an old friend. A mother bird with a little polka-dotted red scarf tied around her head decides to leave her unhatched egg in the nest for a minute, to go find food for the baby bird who's coming soon. While she's gone, the egg hatches and the baby bird finds himself alone in the nest at the top of a tree. He decides to go looking for his mother. He falls out of the tree and starts walking. He finds all kinds of animals—a kitten, a hen, a dog, a cow—and asks them, "Are you my mother?" and they all impassively answer no (with no great concern, I might add, for his well-being). He sees a jet plane and starts shouting up at it, "Here I am, Mother!" until he freaks out, and a great big crane with a digging shovel at the end carries him gently back to his nest. A moment later, his mother returns with a fat worm for them to eat.

Thrilled, I took the book home. I took it out of my bag and said to Eyrna, "This was Mommy's favorite book when she was little. Do you want me to read it to you?"

She sat on my lap on the living room couch and I began to read. By the time the baby bird reached the cow, Eyrna burst into tears. "Stop! Mommy, stop."

"What's the matter?" I was crestfallen.

"It's too scary," she said.

"But he finds his mother at the end," I assured her.

"It's too scary," she repeated, and slowly closed the book, her dimpled hand flat on the cover, a definitive statement.

I'm not one of these Hans Christian Andersen or Grimm's Fairy Tales types, who thinks it's important to let children know at a very tender age that the good guys suffer horrendous tortures and don't always win. They'll learn it soon enough. In second grade, at Christmastime in school in Paris, the teacher played us a record of Hans Christian Andersen's *The Little Match Girl*. The little barefoot girl tries to sell matches in the street during a blizzard and freezes to death in someone's doorway, dreaming of a warm fire and Christmas dinner. I felt sick to my stomach for a week and did not enjoy Christmas that year. I never forgave that self-righteous bitch of a teacher for pulling such a lousy trick on us.

It certainly had not been my intention to upset Eyrna with *Are You My Mother?* I thought about it for the next couple of days, wondering why it had terrified her so, and why I'd liked it so much as a little girl. I realized that Eyrna had never for a second been away from me or wondered if I was coming back; I, as a little girl, anxiously wondered all the time where my mother was and if she'd return to me. The book was a great comfort to me, but for Eyrna, it was a fear she'd never known.

Since Kevin and I didn't have any other children and didn't know anyone with toddlers, other than Jamie and Beth, who lived in Washington, D.C., we read many books on parenting and did our best to muddle through. One Sunday night, driving back from dinner at our cousin Kate's house in Whitestone, Queens, Eyrna, around two and a half, was in her car seat in the back, next to a friend of Kate's who was riding with us back to the city. As we drove past La Guardia Airport on Grand Central Parkway, Eyrna turned to the man sitting beside her and said, "That La Guardia Airport. It's for near places. Faraway places, you go to JFK."

"Really?" the man said.

"Yes. JFK is for Cafornia and Paris. They far away." After a silence, she asked him, "You know the planets? Mercury, Venus, Earth, Mars, Jupiter, Saturn, Neptune, Pluto. Pluto is *far away*. But maybe Pluto *not* a planet, they not sure yet . . ."

Discreetly, he leaned forward between the front seats and murmured, "Have you had your kid's IQ tested? I mean, that's not normal. Babies aren't supposed to know things like that."

We didn't know what normal was because neither of us had ever experienced, in our families, anything that even came close to normal.

A few weeks later I took Eyrna to the Hayden Planetarium in the Rose Center at the Museum of Natural History. I hadn't been there in years and had heard that the new computerized laser representation of the universe was mind-blowing. I explained to Eyrna that we were going to see a show that would let us see where we were, our Planet Earth, in the universe.

We sat down in our comfortable seats and stared up at the dimly lit, vaulted dome above us. The audience sat in a kind of awed silence, as if in a church. Eyrna began an enthusiastic count-down as the lights dimmed, and I joined her. "Ten, nine, eight, seven, six . . . Blastoff!" we shouted.

The first image was of a bird's-eye view of the building where we were, as if we were floating in the sky looking down on Eighty-first Street and Central Park West. Then, the point of view pulled back so we were looking down from space at the Upper West Side of Manhattan. Then, pulling back yet farther, we saw the East Coast of the United States. Then, the entire continent; then the rounded blue globe of the world; and then, Earth shrank to a tiny marble circling the sun, along with all the other planets of our solar system. Then suddenly the solar system shrank into the distance, as if we were traveling rapidly through space, going farther and farther away until our sun and its planets were only a white speck of dust among thousands and thousands of solar systems in the Milky Way galaxy. Then, even the Milky Way galaxy shrank until it was just a swirling, tiny speck among millions of other galaxies. Everyone should be forced to see this, I thought. God is so much bigger than I thought . . .

Eyrna squeezed my hand. "Mommy, it's too far away. Make them take us home!"

. . .

Early the next spring, Kevin and I took Eyrna in her stroller to
the Bronx Zoo to see a brand-new baby giraffe, six feet tall, born
a few weeks earlier. Posters all over the zoo announced the opening of the new gorilla exhibit, so we decided to wait in line.

We stood in the warm sunshine among the strollers and babies
and children and parents and grandparents and cotton candy and
ice cream dripping everywhere and the chatter and laughter and
howling, and I remembered that I'd been here once before, many
years ago, with Dennis. After a marathon twenty-four hours
of partying with his roommates in his apartment, on a Sunday
morning we suddenly had the brilliant idea to drive to the Bronx
Zoo. When we got to the zoo it was terribly hot, and the park was
jammed with people.

We went into the monkey house—this was long before they
remodeled—and were hit by an ammoniac smell that could have
knocked out a rhinoceros. We tried to retreat, but the crowd
pushed us forward, as if we were on a subway platform at rush
hour. We had to keep shuffling toward the exit at the far end of
the long, narrow building. The poor monkeys stared out listlessly from overlit, cavelike enclosures with glass fronts. Between
the gibbons and the gorillas stood a ceiling-to-floor mirror with
prison bars stenciled on it, with a sign at the top that read THE
MOST DANGEROUS ANIMAL ON EARTH. Dennis and I read the bottom of the sign before being pushed on. It said something like
THERE ARE ALMOST FIVE BILLION HUMANS ON PLANET EARTH,
AND WE ARE THE ONLY ONES WITH THE CAPABILITY OF WIPING
OUT THE ENTIRE PLANET.

Right behind us, a woman with one of those New York voices
like a police siren read the top of the sign aloud, "THE MOST DAN-
GEROUS ANIMAL ON EARTH . . . gibbons?" she said in wonder.
"And so small! Who would of thought?"

Dennis made his eyes cross so that his irises almost disappeared behind the bridge of his nose. "And we want to write

literary novels?" he muttered. I was overcome by such a bout of existential angst, I wished I'd never been born.

But here I was, with Kevin and Eyrna, taking in the day among the other families, and I had one of those moments of perfect joy, realizing that this was *me,* here, just standing in a crowd, one normal mom among other normal moms and dads, part of the human race. I had never been a part of anything when I was drinking, always an outsider, looking in. And none of these people knew that, really, I should have been dead and had no business being among them, having been given this extraordinary reprieve, a chance at life.

Finally we stepped into the gorilla exhibit, came around a dark corner and found ourselves in a wide, arching glass tunnel that made us feel that we were the ones enclosed and the gorillas were outside and free. Farther into the tunnel, a few feet from the glass and eye level with Eyrna, a mother gorilla was holding a tiny baby to her breast. The mother was regurgitating some kind of corn and vegetable mix and eating it again with great delicacy, a normal gorilla thing to do, but the boys just ahead of us screamed and laughed and made gross barfing sounds. Eyrna was too little to be grossed out, and as we approached the mother gorilla, Eyrna stopped and pressed both hands against the glass. I stood behind her and started talking to the gorilla, as I would to an interesting foreigner with whom I shared a good deal in common.

"Yes, you are a beautiful gorilla and your baby is a beautiful baby. I have a baby too, see my baby?" I laid my hand on Eyrna's shoulder.

The gorilla gazed at us for a while without expression, then ambled closer to the glass. She peered at Eyrna, then up at me, with bituminous eyes that seemed as wise as an old priestess's. Then she pressed both her palms against Eyrna's, and left them there.

"Oh, my God, Kevin, look!" I started to feel choked up. He

approached behind us and slowly lowered himself to his knee on the other side of Eyrna.

"She saying hi," Eyrna said quietly, as if sensing that to move her hands or raise her voice would break the spell.

"Yes," I said, blinded by tears, "she's saying hi to us."

I sat down on the ground. "You're better off here," I told the gorilla. "At least you're safe and your baby's safe. They'll feed you and take good care of you." The noise of children shouting and laughing and babies crying all around us was deafening.

"Is she safe, Daddy?" Eyrna asked.

"Yes, she's safe," Kevin said, his voice breaking.

"Oh, Mommy, why you crying?"

"Because she's so beautiful and so intelligent. I don't understand why she's in there and we're out here."

And all the while the mother gorilla continued to gaze at us, her palms pressed against Eyrna's on the other side of the glass.

PART III

To hate injustice and stand on righteousness is a difficult thing.
Furthermore, to think that being righteous is the best one can do
and to do one's utmost to be righteous will, on the contrary, bring
many mistakes. The Way is in a higher place than righteousness.
This is very difficult to discover, but it is the highest wisdom.

—YAMAMOTO TSUNETOMO,
HAGAKURE: THE BOOK OF THE SAMURAI

"Mon mari est en chaleur"

Here is my mother's favorite story about her troubles with the French language. Everyone who knew her well heard this at least two dozen times.

→≻   ≺←

Upon first arriving in France, Jim bought an adorable Mercedes two-door sports convertible, which he loved very much. When I was born at the American Hospital in Neuilly, he drove Gloria and me, their brand-new miracle baby, home to the newly decorated apartment on Île Saint-Louis. He made Gloria sit in the back, which was not really even a backseat, but a storage shelf. She sat there, folded practically in two with the bundle on her lap, her neck bent at an excruciating angle because of the low convertible roof. He drove so slowly that he almost caused several car accidents because the French, being highly impatient and volatile drivers on their best days, were honking and shouting and giving them the "up yours" arm signal the whole way.

Gloria pointed out that maybe it was time to buy a different car, now that they had a family. This thought had apparently never crossed my father's mind.

A few weeks later, as they were driving in the city, they got into a heated argument—about what, Gloria could never remember. They yelled at each other, she told him to go fuck himself, and punched him in the arm. At a red light, he pulled the emergency break, got out, slammed the door, and walked away.

Gloria slid over into the driver's seat, but she had never driven the little car, and it stalled out. The light turned green, and now the French drivers behind her were really pissed off, shouting and honking up a storm. The commotion brought over a spiffy young policeman, who bent down to the open window, saluting, and politely asked my mother, *"Alors, qu'est-ce qui se passe, madame?"* Basically, What's the problem, madam?

Gloria, harried and upset, responded, *"Mon mari est en chaleur,"* my husband is in heat, instead of, *"Mon mari est en colère,"* my husband is angry.

"Et bien, vous en avez de la chance, madame. Rentrez vite chez vous!"

Well, you're very lucky, madam. You'd better get home quickly!

And he doffed his cap and walked away.

CHAPTER FOURTEEN

→→ Self-Defense ←←

WHEN EYRNA WAS ALMOST FOUR years old and just about to start her second year of preschool, we heard that Richard Chun was offering a great deal on his peewee tae kwon do classes, so Kevin and I decided to sign her up. On a morning in early September, while Eyrna was with her babysitter, I went to the Korean martial arts school on East Eighty-sixth Street, which I'd been passing for years on my way across town on the bus. As I waited for the manager, I looked at the photos and placards along the walls. Some had yellowed with age, their corners curling, the silver award placards spotted with stains and rust. There were pictures of men and women, and even small children, flying through the air, their feet only inches from their opponents' faces, their legs so far off the ground that the photos seemed to be digitally enhanced.

I looked into a large, white room beyond a glass partition, which had a gleaming, amber-colored parquet floor, where a children's class was in progress. The students must have been between four and eight years old. I watched through the glass as they practiced, lined up in perfect rows. Clad in matching white uniforms and wearing belts that ranged from white to black, their arms and legs moved in fluid unison. Their young voices let out ferocious shouts, which seemed so full of confidence they made my heart swell with admiration.

I didn't have that kind of confidence as a child. I'd never had it as an adult.

The manager, a woman with a weather-worn face and cropped platinum blond hair, hurried in and sat behind the desk. She wore a white uniform with a black collar and a black belt.

When it came to my daughter, I felt very confident and sure of myself, and I displayed my impeccable mothering skills as I asked the woman about the dangers and risks of tae kwon do, the fees, and the purchase price of a uniform. A man in a uniform that had once been white appeared out of nowhere and was now standing a little to the side of the desk, tall and stately and commanding, his dark brown skin shining from a recent workout. The collar on his tunic and his belt were pale gray—I'd never seen this color before.

His body emitted a strong masculine odor that reminded me of the smell that used to waft out of the men's locker room in my college gym. "I regret that I never did this myself," I said, more for conversation than because I really meant it. "Now I'm too old." I gave a little laugh.

"What do you mean, too old?" the man chided. "You're a spring chicken compared to me. I'm sixty-two." He barely had any gray in his short-cropped hair, his stomach flat as a door. He looked about fifty, which convinced me it was worth a try; it might knock ten years off without the plastic surgery my older—and richer—girlfriends had all done in one form or another.

"I was thirty-nine when I started," he said. Then he added with a devilish smile, "You, you probably barely thirty."

I know flattery when I hear it. But he made me laugh. I signed up both Eyrna and me for six months. I had to buy everything—uniforms, sparring gear (I looked quite mad in my red foam helmet, gloves, and boots), white belts, patches to be sewn on the breast of the tunics. I shelled out more than fifteen hundred dollars. I walked out into the hot September day sweating, saying to myself, What the hell were you thinking?

I kept hearing in my head, Klutz, klutz, klutz . . .

What a klutz. That's my mother, laughing with her girlfriends during my first piano recital, in Paris. I was not the youngest of Madame Odile Budan-Daniel's students, but I was the worst, and that meant I had to play first, on a shiny and imposing black grand piano up on a stage, in front of a roomful of elegant Frenchpeople. After the scattered and unenthusiastic applause, I went back and sat down beside my mother, my face burning. I wouldn't look at her.

"Klutz," she said, and giggled. Her breath smelled of scotch, sweet and cool.

After that, I told my parents I wanted to quit piano. My father threw a fit. "You will not quit piano!" he bellowed. "I quit piano when I was a kid, and I regret it every day of my life!" So I was forced to endure five more years of lessons with Madame Odile Budan-Daniel, who came to the house every Saturday morning at ten, in her gray tweed suit and sensible walking shoes, smelling of talc. When I finally started to like her and began practicing in my free time, we moved back to the States, to Miami, where I found out I would have to learn new American names for the notes, and I simply quit. Strangely, giving up piano is not something I have regretted all of my life. I had quit everything I'd ever started: piano, ballet, gymnastics, tennis, yoga, aerobics, weight lifting. As soon as it didn't go my way, I went for the door. I hated to be made to feel a fool.

When Eyrna was three, she'd invited my mother to her first peewee ballet recital at Ballet Academy East. Gloria took the Jitney in from Long Island.

The little ones, clad in pink leotards, slippers, and tights, flitted around on the shiny floor, arms flailing. When it was Eyrna's turn to dance alone, my mother, sitting beside me, murmured, "What a klutz."

I felt blood rush to my neck, and my throat close up. "She's three years old, Mom," I managed to say, my voice sounding all wrong in my ear.

"She's still a klutz," said my mother with a laugh. I got a slight whiff of something pungent—a sweet, fermented fruit smell that was slightly nauseating—Binaca Blast? Or Listerine? They had alcohol in them. Should I warn her not to use them?

In any case, I felt like beating her to a pulp. I breathed deeply, calmed my heartbeat, as I'd learned to do in the mindful meditation I'd recently learned. I was so busy trying to calm down that I forgot to take out my camera and completely missed Eyrna's dance. *Am I responding to some old, atavistic wound? Does this have anything to do with Eyrna at all?* I had to talk myself down from the edge of calamity, because I felt capable of great emotional violence toward my mother. I told myself, *She can't hurt you anymore. You're the grown-up now.*

I told myself, *Let it go.*

Eyrna's first peewee class and my adult tae kwon do class were on a Tuesday, and by 9:00 A.M., I was already freaking out. Kevin was home, having coffee in the living room. He'd recently left the airline business to pursue a career in Internet search engine marketing and his hours were no longer as stringent as they had been.

This was the morning of September 11, 2001, and it wasn't long before we heard about the terrorist attacks. I decided to pretend everything was fine and packed us up for tae kwon do.

The studio was empty except for Geraldine, the platinum-haired manager, who was rushing around, trying to close up. She had a tiny black-and-white TV behind the desk, and the images of the Twin Towers collapsing were playing over and over again.

"The worst terrorist attack in U.S. history and you show up for class?" she said to me, shaking her head.

"I figured if I didn't show up today, I never would," I replied with an empty laugh.

"Come back on Thursday," she said. "We'll be here. Unless they nuke us or something. Been here for thirty years." She led us out and locked the door behind her.

"What's going on, Mommy? What is it?" Eyrna kept asking. That afternoon would have been the first day of her second year of preschool.

"Some very bad people crashed an airplane into a big building. But we're all right up here. Everything is all right."

"It smells funny," she said. Indeed, the air smelled of an electrical fire, of burning asbestos and . . . something else.

For five minutes I stood on the sidewalk, with Eyrna in her stroller staring up at me. I was paralyzed. I didn't know what to do. Everyone wore the same wide-eyed look of disbelief, as if we'd collectively been punched in the face by a total stranger.

From a pay phone I tried to call Kevin at home, but it rang busy, over and over. No one's cell phone seemed to be working, either. I decided to go looking for Nora, who lived in the East Sixties and would probably go to our favorite Greek coffee shop, ten blocks down First Avenue. Pete the Greek was behind the counter, and for once, he was speechless, looking down, shaking his head. Five minutes later, Nora came in, even paler than usual, so that her freckles stood out sharply against her white skin, thick red curls, and green eyes. We asked Pete for an order of dollar-size pancakes for Eyrna, and Pete made her a stack so tall it started to collapse on the way over to the table.

"Eat, little girl, eat. Is good for you."

Outside on First Avenue a constant stream of people kept drifting by the window, their clothes, faces, hair covered in white ash. No one was talking. They looked like an army of ghosts, their eyes wide with shock, arms and legs moving as if by rote. Pete grabbed some bottles of water and took them outside, holding them out to people as they passed.

The next morning, we were still glued to the TV set and to Peter Jennings, who'd rolled up his shirtsleeves and stayed up all night reporting the news as it came in. The phone rang—our land line—startling us.

"Hi, it's Matt." He was a firefighter I'd met at the Caron Foundation rehabilitation program for children of alcoholics. We'd been put in the same group. When we'd acted out his family, he'd asked me to play his older brother; when we did mine, I asked him to play my father. On the way back to New York on the Martz public bus, he told me that every male in his family back four generations had been a New York City firefighter, and that his mother had died in a fire, passed out drunk in bed with a lit cigarette. Then his eyes filled with tears, and he admitted that he was still drinking; he thought it was keeping him from committing suicide.

I looked right in his eyes and said, "Matt, if you don't stop drinking, right now, you have no chance at all. For us, quitting is the *only* chance we have."

Matt nodded slowly, then said, "So, can you help me?"

"I can," I said.

He stopped drinking and believed I was responsible for his recovery, though I never thought so. He'd been ready to stop, that's all. And yet, I had the same feeling about Gianna, and nothing she could say or do would ever change my opinion, because I knew I would not have stopped drinking without her.

"Matt!" I shouted into the phone, into the noise of sirens and machinery grinding and whining behind him. Kevin looked up from the TV. "Is he okay?"

"Are you down there, Matt? Are you all right?" I shouted.

Matt had retired from the FDNY a few years ago, due to a

back injury sustained during a fire rescue. He'd moved to California but happened to be back in New York that week for a family wedding. As soon as he heard, he got his old firefighter's helmet out of storage and rushed down there, to Ground Zero. "I'm losing it," he now said into the phone, his voice breaking. "Can I come up and see you guys for a few minutes?"

"How're you going to get here? The whole city's shut down."

"There's cops all over the place just standing around with nothing to do. They *want* to help. I'll ask one of them to drive me up."

Ten minutes later, as Eyrna and I sat on the front stoop waiting for Matt, we heard a police siren wailing and getting louder. A cop car with its lights flashing came flying down our street and screeched to a halt in front of our door. Matt, dressed in his firefighter's helmet, a thick blue jacket with the reflective yellow stripe, and boots, was covered from head to toe in that gray ash. He slowly pulled himself out of the backseat, his movements labored. We started to cheer, for Matt and for the cop who'd brought him, who now saluted us. Matt had clean streaks from tears or sweat running down his ash-covered face. He thanked the cop, closed the door, and came toward us, sitting there cheering and clapping. I felt choked up.

"Trust me," he said, "you'll never see that again in your life— a fireman getting a friendly ride from a cop!" He sat down next to Eyrna on the steps and said, "Have no fear, little Eyrna. Fireman Matt is here, and you are safe."

Eyrna jumped up and threw herself into his arms.

"Why is the teacher's belt gray?" I asked a lady Red Belt with impressive muscles on my first day of class, that following Thursday, September 13, in the locker room. I'd been feeling fearful since the attacks, but now I felt sick to my stomach with fear. She told me dismissively, as if I were an idiot, that Mr. Bill is a Sixth Dan Black Belt and that his collar and belt had faded from age. "It's a cool thing," she said with a slightly condescending smile. "You never wash your Black Belt." I thought of my dad in World War II, who, along with the other wounded foot soldiers sent stateside to recover, would never wear their medals in public, only their Combat Infantryman Badges. It was a matter of pride. No one needed to know how much they'd bled for their country, or how brave they'd been, or any other goddamn thing about them.

We lined up in front of Mr. Bill, the master. Mr. Bill turned. He looked surprised to see me there, hiding in the back row. I didn't even know how I was supposed to stand.

He came and stood about two feet in front of me and said, "First of all, learn to tie your belts properly. Excuse me, ma'am, may I?" He pointed at my belt. I'd tied it like the belt on a robe, with a jaunty knot on the side. I nodded, and in a flash he untied it and repositioned it, looping one end under the first layer in front and tying a tight knot at the center, just under my navel.

"This ain't anything like your step class, ma'am, you know what I mean?"

"I don't go to step class."

"Sir."

"I don't go to step class, sir."

He moved away, relaxed his shoulders, faced the class, around eight of us, ranging from Black, Brown, and Red Belts in the front row, Green, then Yellow, then me, alone in the back. He stood with flexed arms ending in fists, and looked into each pair of eyes. Finally he shouted, *"Joon-bi!"* and everyone snapped to attention. He said to me, in a distinctly Oprah-like voice, "You stick around and listen to me, pretty soon you gonna have a whole new attitude toward life."

"Yes, sir!" everyone shouted but me.

"This is not an exercise class to make you thin and beautiful," Mr. Bill continued. "Tae kwon do is a philosophy. A way of life. Understand?"

"Yes, sir!"

He talked and I listened, having no idea what he was saying.

"In our society," Mr. Bill said, "we're taught not to yell. But yelling is good. It gets the anger out, it empowers you. And, most important, it frightens your opponent. See how lions and elephants they make themselves big when they gettin' ready to fight?" Suddenly he made himself big. "Why you starin' at the ground? Walk with your head up, not starin' at the ground like you have no self-confidence."

I laughed emptily and grumbled, "Self-confidence. What is that? Okay, self-confidence."

Mr. Bill shouted, "What is *okay*? A slave word!"

He bellowed that his uncle had been a champion boxer, a Golden Gloves winner who'd become a professional, and he himself was coming all the way from "uptown" to teach this class and expected our full attention. I presumed he meant Harlem but wasn't about to ask. Suddenly the air in the room went still. Not a sound.

"Yes, sir!" I shouted, catching on. That part wasn't hard for me, being that I'm the proud daughter of an ex-soldier. My dad first taught me to handle a pistol when I was five, then came the boxing lessons. After we moved to the States and no longer had a full-time maid, he taught Jamie and me how to wash and dry the dishes. Then he'd go around the sink with his index finger wrapped in a paper towel, checking for spots. He called it "the white glove treatment."

Even if I could connect with the discipline, during the exercises I had that horrible feeling of blood rushing to my throat and head, my heart pounding out of control. *Klutz, klutz, klutz.* The kicks were the worst. I felt like I had two cement blocks for feet.

At the end of one of the most painful sixty minutes of my life, as we were walking toward the locker rooms, Mr. Bill kept me back.

"I think I made a mistake," I blurted. "I'm a klutz. This is not for me."

"You have excellent balance and hand-eye coordination."

"I've quit everything I ever started," I said. "I haven't had a drink in nine years, and I haven't smoked a cigarette in eight, and those are the only two things I ever quit that I'm proud of."

"You don't look like a quitter to me," he said, and slapped me hard on the shoulder blade. "You ain't gonna quit this."

So stupefied was I from the experience, I walked out in front of a cab on Eighty-fifth Street. The cabdriver came to a gentle stop, smiled at me, and didn't even honk his horn. He waved me on, even though he had the light. I smiled back and thanked him. Tuesday's terrorist attacks had done something weird to New Yorkers. They were all being nice to one another. When I got home I found Kevin cutting a page-size U.S. flag out of the *New York Times*, which he taped to one of our front windows.

He didn't take it down until the day our country invaded Iraq.

Within three weeks, I'd learned the first form, *Ki-Cho* 1, and was shakily practicing side and front kicks, high and low blocks, and shouting out deep, guttural belly-yells with my punches. I still felt like an absolute fool, but nothing was as terrifying, or paralyzing to me, as sparring. When confronted with a blow or a kick aimed in my direction, I cringed or giggled uncontrollably, and froze. I couldn't seem to get past this weird paralysis, which was similar to what I experienced when I felt under attack from my mother.

Once, I got a bruise the size of an orange on my bicep, from cringing in the wrong direction during a sparring exercise and accidentally encountering Mr. Bill's brick of a foot. I really liked that bruise. I wore T-shirts to show it off. And when other moms at Eyrna's preschool asked, "My God, what happened to your arm?" I responded proudly, "I got kicked in tae kwon do."

After three months of attending twice a week, Mr. Bill told me that Eyrna and I were ready to test for our Yellow Belts.

The promotion test was on a Friday evening in early December, and the studio, which they called the *do-jang*, was crowded with people—grown-ups, children—from Black Belts to lowly White Belts. Kevin had to be in Las Vegas on business, so Eyrna and I went by ourselves.

Eyrna was not afraid to test; but me—my heart was pumping too fast, my mouth dry, hands sweating. I watched Eyrna stand up and take her place with the other children. I couldn't believe how brave she was. Where had that courage come from? Not from me, that's for sure. Before I quit drinking, I couldn't give a reading without taking Inderal, a beta-blocker prescribed to me by Dr. Ellen. I called it Endure-All. I wished I had an Endure-All now. I wanted to run away.

Eyrna passed her Yellow Belt test with a plus mark and sat down coolly beside me, crossing her legs. Then it was the adults' turn.

"I'm scared to death," I whispered to Eyrna. "I feel like I'm going to throw up." *You could quit right now, walk away.* This comforting thought kept running through my mind, and I was seriously contemplating it. But what would my daughter think?

"What are you scared of, Mommy?" Eyrna asked.

Now I felt my throat tighten, my eyes beginning to sting. "I'm scared of failing. I'm scared of making a fool of myself. I'm scared of being a klutz."

"What's a klutz?" Eyrna regarded me with her luminous eyes.

"A klutz is a person who's not good at sports," I explained, swallowing hard.

"You're not a klutz, Mommy. If I can do it, so can you." She squeezed my hand. My palms were wet with sweat. It was also trickling down my back. I was starting to hyperventilate. God, please don't let me fuck this up, I thought.

"You're right," I said.

"White Belts!" shouted one of the stern-looking Black Belt judges at the front. He began to read off names from a list.

When my name was called, I stood up quickly and ran to the second line, in front of the Black Belt judges, six of them, and bowed. There was Mr. Bill, his face quiet as a mask. Dr. Richard Chun, Twelfth Dan Black Belt and onetime Olympic champion, owner of the *do-jang*, sat straight-backed and unsmiling in a black suit and somber tie, taking notes behind a table covered in a white cloth.

Mr. Bill turned his eyes toward me and blinked once, almost imperceptibly, and I remembered to breathe.

I didn't ace the test at all, but I did pass.

Elated, we went home and called Kevin in Las Vegas, then my mother.

"Guess what, Mom? Eyrna and I passed our Yellow Belt test!"

Silence. "You're nuts," she finally said. "And don't you think that's dangerous? She could get hurt, you know."

In Adult Children of Alcoholics parlance, calling my mother on this occasion was like going to the hardware store for oranges. And maybe I *was* nuts. As Gianna had once told me, *insanity is doing the same thing over and over again, expecting different results.*

"Catching Your First Millionaire"

Recently, I had dinner with my good friend Beverly Donofrio from the Columbia writing school, and we talked about my relationship with my mother.

"Your mother was *mean*," she said to me. How strange, I thought. When Bev knew Gloria, my mother and I were getting along pretty well. During graduate school, I had become my mother's best drinking buddy. I knew I could only go out to dinner with her on nights when I didn't have a morning class because the next day would be a total loss.

Then Bev reminded me of this story, which I'd completely forgotten.

When we were graduate students at Columbia, in the summer of 1982, Bev came out to Sagaponack one weekend. The house was filled with people—my mother's beau, Walker; my brother and his friends; the cousins; and even a famous courtesan visiting from France. During dinner the first night, under the grape arbor, my mother turned to Bev and said abruptly, "Why are you friends with my daughter? She's at least ten years younger than you."

Bev, stunned, stared Gloria down and said, "So what?"

My mother recognized an Italian fighter when she saw one and immediately backed down, for while she loved to antagonize people, she was loath to get into direct confrontations.

The next day my mother got it into her head to drag Bev and me to a dinner party at our friends the Woods' in Watermill. They had seven wealthy, erudite, and well-traveled sons and stepsons whose ages varied from mine to Bev's. The last time I'd been to a party there, I'd gotten plotzed and ended up in the pool house with a French count, a misadventure I was not fond of recalling.

"It'll be good for you," Gloria assured us.

God, did I dread those parties. I always felt sick afterward from drinking too much, and from comparing myself unfavorably with every successful person at the scene. But I didn't want to antagonize my mother. After all, it was only Saturday, we still had to get through Sunday. After bracing ourselves with several margaritas, Bev and I piled into the back of the car, Walker behind the wheel and Gloria riding shotgun.

As we were driving along Montauk Highway, my mother turned to us in the backseat and said, "Girls, here's some advice. Catching your first millionaire is the hardest. After that, the rest come easy."

Bev turned to me, her eyes wide, and after a moment, she burst out laughing. I started laughing too, nervously, for I feared my mother wasn't joking in the least, and in her opinion, my inability to *catch* a rich man was a major character failing on my part.

CHAPTER FIFTEEN

⤜ Accountability ⤛

IN FEBRUARY 2003 I'D HELD a Yellow Belt for more than a year and had no intention of moving up. That's when Mr. Bill told me I could skip the next level, High Yellow, and test for a Green Belt.

"You can't be serious," I replied, quickly adding, "sir."

"Serious as death," he said. "For your test, you'll have to break a board just like this one." He gripped a three-quarter-inch-thick pine board vertically in his hands and said, "Break it with a side kick."

"You must be joking. Sir," I replied.

"Do I look like I'm joking?" His tone turned hard and scary. "Look through the board to the end of the movement. Practice once. The board is not there. Don't judge yourself, *do* it. Yell."

I stood back. I breathed. I imagined the side kick passing through air between Mr. Bill's hands. I practiced once, aiming and setting up. I felt adrenaline pumping through me, and I'd never felt anything like it, except for the time in Paris when I fell through the plastic skylight of Sterling Hayden's barge, seven feet down, to the kitchen floor.

Bam. The board split easily. The outside edge of my foot ached. Mr. Bill handed me the two pieces. "Keep it," he said. "Don't talk back. Relax your shoulders. If I tell you you can do it, you can do it."

I took the split board home to show Kevin.

· · ·

For the test, I performed four forms by myself. I also had no trouble with the self-defense moves and kicking and punching combinations. My troubles, naturally, began when it was time to spar, and I couldn't stop myself from freezing up and giggling like a fool. Yet I passed my Green Belt test with a plus mark. Now I started considering the possibility that I might want to move forward, aiming for higher and higher belts.

The Tuesday after the test, Mr. Bill told me I was judging myself and that was why sparring was so difficult for me. He explained that when we judge ourselves, we can't react cleanly. "Face every obstacle without fear," he said, "because obstacles are gifts of learning."

His words stayed with me all day. I did not feel free of self-recrimination, but at least I was now aware of its constant presence.

After class once during the early summer, Mr. Bill asked Eyrna and me if we'd like to have lunch with him and George, another Green Belt, who was in his midfifties.

We went to Pizzeria Uno downstairs, one of Eyrna's favorite places in the world because they have an extravagant dessert of brownies topped with vanilla ice cream, Oreo cookies, and hot chocolate fudge. Before we even ordered lunch, Eyrna wanted to know if she could have this dessert. I said no, it was too much, but Mr. Bill volunteered to split it with her, and winked, and George said he'd help too, so they were now her new best friends, and she gave them one of her smiles that could melt an iceberg.

As lunch went on, Mr. Bill told us a few things about himself. His family had come from St. Croix three generations ago. His uncle's name was Lee Canegata, aka Canada Lee. He was a boxer turned actor, who'd played Bigger Thomas in *Native Son* on Broadway, and was in Hitchcock's film *Lifeboat*.

"My God, he's famous!" I said. "My dad saw Canada Lee in *Native Son*. I remember him talking about how great he was."

Mr. Bill told us that early on in Canada Lee's boxing career, an announcer, while introducing a fight, couldn't pronounce Canegata, and kept stumbling over the PA system, "Lee Cana . . . Lee Caga . . . Ladies and gentlemen, Canada Lee!"

Mr. Bill lived uptown with his mother, Evadne, who for forty years had been a customs agent at JFK Airport. "You couldn't get *nothin'* by that woman!" Mr. Bill said with a laugh. She was now in a wheelchair and needed constant care. After lunch, he told us he was off to buy adult diapers.

I went home and looked up Canada Lee on the Internet. Canada Lee refused to bow down to racism and fought against it all his life. He wouldn't enter the theater through the back door like he was told to. In the Hitchcock movie *Lifeboat,* he changed his dialogue because he refused to be made into a two-dimensional, humorous stereotype. He wouldn't give up his left-wing politics, even when the producers pressured him. He ended up in jail several times and was on all the FBI pinko watch lists. He died just before he was to appear before the House Un-American Activities Committee, his honor intact.

That evening, my mother called.

"I miss *Urna*. I love her more than I've ever loved any child in my life," my mother admitted, and my first reaction was to chuckle. Then I suddenly realized I had no air left in my lungs. At once I felt a pang of guilt for not calling her more often, for not having visited her in a month. "Since you're teaching out here this summer anyway, just stay with me and put *Urna* in a summer camp. It's much, much nicer out here. Why stay in the city if you don't have to?"

I told her I'd talk to Kevin about it and let her know. "We'll come visit as soon as we can," I said.

Then I listened to a five-minute accounting of her health problems. She was having trouble breathing again. When she'd been drinking, she had terrible sinus allergies and infections. I had been convinced, and had told her years ago, that she was allergic to alcohol. She had not wanted to hear that. As soon as she stopped drinking, her breathing cleared and the infections stopped.

But she wasn't drinking. She hadn't had a drink in four years, so what could be wrong?

After hearing Mr. Bill's advice, I began to try to fight in earnest, but only against him, defending my space with my best kicks and punches, which sometimes he'd allow to land against his stomach. Kicking him was like kicking a closed door. He told me not to look into my opponent's eyes, nor at his arms and legs, but at the whole picture, the circle of space around him. He said people attack out of fear, and freeze out of fear. One must train the mind to turn to stone, to allow no fear, no judgment, no thought to penetrate. To learn to watch is the goal.

"You can't fight angry," he told me. I stared at him, speechless. Was there another way to fight? Was there even any other *reason* to fight?

Kevin thought that moving out to my mother's for the summer was a terrible idea. I kept insisting that my mother needed us. She was showing signs of her age. She was suffering from her old sinus infections and breathing problems. I was worried about her. Maybe having us around would ease her ever-growing anxiety and loneliness.

I'd been invited to teach a four-week summer course in the MFA program at Southampton, and to be a teacher at the week-long intensive Southampton Writers Conference. It seemed logical to stay out there for at least that period of time, and Kevin did not argue with me. Much later, when I asked why he hadn't tried harder to stop me, he cryptically said, "You had to do what you had to do."

He came out on weekends and worked on the garden, trying to hold at bay the engulfing weeds that had again grown as large as trees between the 150-year-old lilac bushes. The house was in such disrepair that it would take much more than us to begin to tackle the problems of rotting window frames, broken wooden steps, moldering cedar shingles, and angry wasps' nests.

On the first night of the summer session, I had to go to a reception at the college, so I rented *The Sound of Music* for my mother and five-year-old Eyrna. I remembered seeing the movie with my mother in Paris when I was a little girl. We'd both loved it then. I figured, long movie, Julie Andrews, good for kids, what could go wrong?

I put on a pale blue linen dress, cut on the bias, calf length, and sandals, and walked out of my room. My mother and Eyrna were sitting in the library in front of the TV as I passed.

"That's a terrible dress," my mother said. "You look like a fat old lady in that dress."

"I'll be back around nine," I said woodenly.

"And you're a mean fat old lady too," Eyrna said to my mother.

"You're right," my mother said to Eyrna. "That was a mean thing to say."

I kept walking, struck dumb by this exchange. I never would have stood up for myself like that. And my mother never would have admitted to being mean—not to *me*.

At times I'd heard her say mean things to Jamie, such as, when they were getting ready to play poker, "Sit down, you dumb shit, I'm going to kick your ass." If she'd said this to me, I would've retaliated with some abuse of my own. But Jamie would just giggle delightedly in his charming way and reply, his eyes shiny and his face pink with mirth, "Watch out, old lady, in a minute I'll have you whistling 'Dixie'!"

I admired and was astounded by his ability to step away from her jabs. Me, I took them all head-on, chin first, or right in the chest.

When I returned three hours later, Eyrna came running toward me through the long kitchen. "Mommy! Mommy! You know those Nazis?" I saw my mother approaching through the doorway behind her.

"You mean the Nazis in the movie?"

"*All* Nazis!" Eyrna explained. "They're a pain in the ass!"

One afternoon I heard Eyrna screaming in the living room and ran from my bedroom to find my mother standing in the middle of the bald, piss-and-mildew-stinking Persian rug, cordless phone in hand, and Eyrna a few feet away, sitting on the rug, gripping the side of her head, howling.

"She hit me with the phone!"

"She wouldn't shut up," my mother said. "I'm on the phone here."

"Are you crazy? You can't hit a child in the head with a phone!"

I picked up Eyrna and carried her back into my room, and eventually outside to the swing set. Once she had calmed down, I drove us to a clothing store to get Eyrna some new shorts.

"Eyrna, what's going on here?" I said, angry and flustered as I tried to snap shut the size 8 shorts. At five years old, she suddenly couldn't fit into a size 8. I had to go get a size 10.

"What are you eating with Grammy that I don't know about?"

"Grammy says you're mean to me. Grammy says you're much too strict."

"That's not true, and you know it."

"Grammy says she loves me more than you do."

Suddenly I had the urge to smack my daughter. I forced myself to walk out of the changing room and breathe for a solid minute before I was calm enough to face Eyrna and resume being a good mom. All right, I thought, I'm the adult here. My mother is trying to get between us. I am not the child here. I am the mother. I can handle this.

But, five minutes later, having entirely forgotten the incident, Eyrna tried to hug me, and I turned away from her.

"What's going on with Eyrna's weight?" Kevin asked me the next Saturday. He wanted to know what I was feeding her. I was feeding her exactly the same foods she ate at home—vegetables, fruit, a little chicken, fish, rice, and pasta once in a while.

Gloria came into the kitchen and told us she was taking Eyrna to lunch in Sag Harbor and then to the toy store.

"Thank you," Kevin said, "but we're going to the beach." My mother left in a huff, without saying another word.

At the beach, Kevin said: "You can't let her take Eyrna to the toy store and to lunch every day. I mean, look at her." Compared with all the other children cavorting in the shallows, I could see now that she was much too big around the middle, her belly hanging over her bikini bottom. Why hadn't I noticed this before? And why did we never go to the beach anymore?

"Are you okay?" Kevin asked me searchingly.

"I don't know," I said.

"Why don't you come back to New York with me?" He took my hand and held it in his. His hands always felt a few degrees warmer than mine, and usually this was hugely comforting, but today, on the beach, I was too hot and I felt trapped. I pulled my sweaty palm away.

"We paid for camp. She's got two more weeks."

Kevin didn't say anything.

On Sunday evening, he went back to the city, and I felt bereft. I wanted to leave with him. But I was afraid of angering my mother.

On Monday morning, after I dropped off Eyrna at camp, I approached my mother in the kitchen, calmly and reasonably, about Eyrna's weight. "You can't let her eat anything she wants, Mom. She's too little to make those kinds of decisions." My mother didn't respond.

Ten minutes later, she knocked on my door to tell me she'd pick up Eyrna after camp, since she would be in Sag Harbor anyway. I had to go to Southampton College to hand in my grades, so I didn't say no.

Later that afternoon, Eyrna came home with three Barbie dolls in their colorful boxes, and had chocolate all over her face. "I had a hamburger and french fries and then we went to Carvel and I had an ice cream dipped in chocolate," Eyrna told me. "And we had two Hershey bars."

I felt as though a giant wave had knocked me down. Exhaustion took hold of me. As if caught in a sudden riptide, fighting to get my bearings, to get air into my lungs, I felt like I was being pulled under. I wanted to go lie down in my cool room and sleep.

My mother meanwhile was having an asthma attack, leaning against the butcher block island in the middle of the kitchen, a hand to her chest. She took out her inhaler, pumped two big shots into her mouth, then lit a Marlboro Red. Like a sleepwalker, I walked out of the kitchen and through the little vestibule-hallway whose walls were covered with family photographs.

I heard my mother say to Eyrna, "What's the matter with you? Don't *tell* her, you dope." Then my mother chanted in a high-pitched, teasing voice, *"Who's Fat, Fat, the Water Rat?"*

A memory came charging back from my own childhood, and all at once I was seized by rage. My vision began to close in on me as I remembered that miserable chant—that teasing, horrible voice! I charged back into the kitchen, a bull drawn by a red cape.

"I'm not fat, Grammy! Don't say that!" Eyrna had already started to cry, her mouth contorted into a rictus of shock and despair. Kids have no defense. No defense at all, I thought. Her face, I saw with horror, mirrored exactly what I'd always felt and had learned over the years to hide so well—so well that I could no longer even recognize when I was in pain.

I heard Mr. Bill's voice in my head: *You can't fight angry. You gotta fight calm, without judgment.* "Why did you say that to her?" I asked my mother, trying to keep my voice under control.

"Say what?"

"Why did you tell Eyrna she was fat?"

My mother sat down in an old wicker rocker and looked up at me, perplexed. "I didn't tell *Eeer-na* she was fat. I was singing a song, that's all."

"You sang that to me too, when I was little, and I didn't like it either." My voice was tight, stretched like a rubber band about to snap.

"You just don't have a sense of humor," she said dismissively, vaguely, and tamped her cigarette out in a large pewter ashtray. Her head was completely enshrouded in smoke. Yes, I thought, around my mother I am stiff, wooden, unbending, lazy, humorless—in fact, I'm the very person she always accuses me of being. And then it occurred to me that someone must have sung those words to *her* when she was little.

"No," I said slowly, the brittleness gone from my voice. "No. That isn't just a song. You hurt Eyrna's feelings. It made her feel like you were telling her she was fat."

My mother stared at me as if I were speaking Swahili.

"Who sang that song to *you* when you were little?" I asked her. Her eyes grew wide, suddenly anxious, as if, for a brief moment, a light had flicked on in her mind. My heart leapt with hope.

But just as quickly, her eyes turned vague again. "You're a pain in the ass, you know that?" she said. "You've always been a pain in the ass."

"If you continue to overfeed Eyrna," I said to my mother in my new, adult, calm, equable voice, "we'll go back to New York and stop coming out here to see you."

Then I turned to Eyrna. "Come with me, baby," I said, "let's go for a swim."

The next day, I left very early and took Eyrna back to New York with me so we could attend Mr. Bill's noontime class. He could see I wasn't well. He sensed my self-recrimination and paralysis as he stood before me, looking me over like a drill sergeant. "Relax your shoulders."

"I can't."

"*Yes, sir* is the only answer I want to hear," he corrected, his voice sharp.

Oh my God, did I not want to be here. "I can't, sir."

"You got to relax in order to fight," said Mr. Bill. I felt like Aurora in *Sleeping Beauty,* waking up from a hundred-year coma. Even my muscles were having trouble adjusting to Mr. Bill's demands.

"*Yes, sir!*" the whole class shouted.

Relax in order to fight? That's an oxymoron, isn't it?

"You can't fight in anger," Mr. Bill reminded us.

He's out of his mind, I thought. I shouted, *"Yes, sir!"*

I thought of the fights I'd had with my mother over the years, how I always ended up capitulating, because I was so much angrier than she. Because she had always been a much better bluffer than I. Because I was too serious and too earnest and too weak. How come my brother was able to just laugh it off? How come everything she said just went straight through me like a poisoned spear?

"You're going to take your Blue Belt test in September," Mr. Bill announced.

"What? I can't take my Blue Belt test in September! Sir. I've been away almost all summer."

He pretended I hadn't responded, and strutted off, his back perfectly straight, his head held high.

Afterward, sweaty but calm, I left Eyrna in the children's park with her friend and her friend's mom, and I called Nora and asked her if she could meet me for coffee. She could probably tell by my voice that it was an emergency.

At Pete the Greek's, I recounted to her, stumblingly, guiltily, our last four weeks at my mother's.

She said, shaking her head with a laugh, "Still busy rearranging the deck chairs on the *Titanic*."

After a moment, I laughed too. I'd met Nora when I'd been sober around two years. She'd been in exactly the same kind of relationship I'd been in with Dennis when I'd first stopped drinking. She couldn't see the forest for the trees. She'd been as jumpy as a cat in a cage surrounded by playful dogs.

While we had something to eat, Nora told me the following story.

Nora's father—a terrible drunk—had sexually abused her older sister, Mary, who was a year older than Nora. He then began to focus his attentions on Nora when she turned fifteen. Nora fled and never lived at home again.

Many years later, her older brother, Patrick, had two step-daughters, twins of fourteen. Patrick told Nora on the phone from Vancouver that he'd sent both girls to spend a weekend alone with his father, in his cabin in the woods. Nora, apoplectic, asked Patrick how in the hell could he have left the girls alone with their father, when he knew perfectly well what had happened to Mary and Nora at that same age. Patrick, after a silence, responded that he couldn't refuse his father's invitation, because the old man would throw a fit and fly into a rage.

Now Nora looked at me with her green eyes, which had seen way too much, and concluded with somber resignation, "My brother was more afraid of my father's anger than he was of his daughters getting abused."

I felt a chill crawl up my back despite the blaring heat from Pete the Greek's grill. I began to feel like I wasn't getting enough air.

"Are the girls okay?" I asked in a murmur.

"I don't know if the girls are okay. Patrick died of a heroin overdose four years ago, in a public park in Vancouver. An eight-year-old boy found him. Patrick was leaning up against a tree with a needle sticking out of his arm."

I was aware that two of Nora's three brothers had died from drug overdoses. But she had never told me this before.

At once the fog cleared in my mind and I saw a new truth: my mother had turned her relationship with Eyrna into a *Romeo and Juliet*–style epic tragedy, with Kevin and me as the evil parents keeping them apart. And she'd fed this romantic notion to Eyrna and conscripted her into her army of two. And I'd let it happen. Because I wanted to please her. Because I wanted her to be happy. Because I wanted her to love and respect me. Because I was afraid of her wrath. Isn't that what children are supposed to do, respect their parents and allow them access to their grandchildren?

And, of course, I was afraid that without Eyrna, my mother would drink again.

I went home, held Eyrna tight for a long time, then called my mother. Scared, my mouth suddenly dry, I told her we wouldn't be coming out for a while. There was a dead silence. She lit a cigarette and said pointedly, "New York City is no place for a *child* to be in the summer. It's *wrong* of you to keep her there, suffocating in the heat. It's plain *wrong*." I could hear her sucking on her inhaler. Jesus.

"We won't be here all the time; we're going to visit friends," I replied weakly. Of course, this was an unnecessary statement on my part, because, after all, it was not in the least about Eyrna suffocating in New York City, but about my mother suffocating out there, alone, with no one to play with, with no one on whom to focus her attention. And why was I explaining myself to her anyway? *"No,"* Gianna used to say, *"is a complete sentence with a period after it."*

My God, I thought, what if she starts drinking again? It never occurred to me, not for a moment, that she'd been sneaking booze all along.

That night, late, I had a dream in which my mother's house crumbled in on itself and rolled down the hill in an avalanche of wood and bricks and cedar shingles.

I called Nora in a panic. "I feel so guilty," I said.

After a moment of silence, Nora responded, "I presume you're not familiar with the saying: *If you feel guilty, then you're doing something right?*"

We'd been back in the city only three weeks, recuperating from the summer, Eyrna having just started first grade, when my mother was once again rushed to Southampton Emergency. She had pneumonia and encephalitis and was completely delusional. There was a general panic as to what had caused the encephalitis and the delusions. Many strings were pulled by Barbara Hearst (now reinstated, to some degree, after her years of exile) to get Gloria admitted to a private room at New York Hospital. There, Gloria was put under the care of Dr. Paul Smith, an infectious diseases specialist, brought into the fray by the power of the Hearst name. Dr. Smith discovered that on top of pneumonia, Gloria had contracted West Nile virus from a mosquito bite, which had apparently caused, or exacerbated, the encephalitis.

She kept trying to escape from her hospital room, rolling herself out of the bed and falling, so they strapped her down. Jamie and I stood helplessly by her side. Her face would change quickly, the muscles going from placid to pinched and belligerent, focusing suddenly on me with intense and vicious rage, as if I were the one who had somehow gotten her into this condition, and strapped her into a straitjacket with my own hands.

"Because of you I'll be remembered as a drunken bitch. You're a nut," she said with finality.

My mouth opened to speak, but I couldn't. The needy child voice inside me said, *If she says you're a nut, then you must be a nut. She's your mother, the one who always tells the brutal truth.* But then the fighter, the rageful furious one awakened, and I felt in my gut the first prickly sparks of an explosive rage igniting. I could feel its cold fire burning down the fuse within me. Who would pay?

"You're in the hospital, Mom," Jamie said, trying to keep his voice from shaking. "You really need to calm down."

I kept thinking of that scene in *The Exorcist* when the old priest warns the younger Father Karras not to listen to a thing the Devil says. "The Demon is a liar," he tells him. Father Karras enters the room, and on the bed, the child has assumed the voice of his dead mother. "Why you do this to me, Dimi?" she says plaintively, in her heavy Greek accent. "Why?"

My mother's blue eyes had ceased roaming and now turned on me once again with the intensity of a helicopter searchlight. "That's a nice sweater. Cashmere? Too much black, though, you need to put on some jewelry."

I went home and looked at myself in the mirror. "Do you think I wear too much black?" I asked Kevin.

"I think maybe you should call the therapist," he said.

. . .

Gloria spent three weeks in the hospital, half the time strapped down in the straitjacket. *"You fucking cunt! You whore! You're never going to get my money! Help! Help! My daughter has kidnapped me!"* She looked at me with such venomous hatred it made me shudder. Was it me she was seeing? As much as I logically understood that she was sick and her brain was not functioning properly, I felt certain that she truly despised me and would annihilate me if she could.

Dr. Smith told me one morning that my mother had attacked her nurse's aide from St. Lucia with racial epithets. "Your mother is a racist."

My mother? A racist? "She's . . . out of her mind," I stammered. After all, this was the woman who'd marched with James Baldwin for civil rights!

That night, she had a mild heart attack, and they rushed her up to the cardiac care floor. For several hours, my brother and I stood at the foot of her bed, watching the heart monitor beep above her head.

"How *dare* you do this to me? How dare you . . . I know you're trying to kill me." Tied down to the mattress, with straps at her hands and feet. "You're a nut." She was looking straight at me.

What I couldn't understand was, why *me*? Why not Jamie or anyone else?

I'm not trying to kill her, I thought guiltily. But I want her to die. Is that the same thing?

God, I prayed, let it end now. Let it all be over.

After two days, she was moved back to Dr. Smith's floor. He stopped in during his rounds. "How are you today, Mrs. Jones?"

Betty Comden was visiting. Well into her eighties, Betty had her own private attendant and was sitting in a wheelchair beside my mother's bed. Gloria was not in the straitjacket this day and seemed almost lucid, except if you looked too long into her eyes.

"You have no idea who I am," my mother said to the doctor, her chin jutting out. "And you have no idea who this lady is, I bet. Because you're too young and you don't know anything. This is the most famous lyricist in the world!"

Betty protested but giggled delightedly at my mother's accolades.

Dr. Smith, pale with exhaustion, checked Gloria's chart and then stepped out into the hall. I followed him, so I could ask about the West Nile virus. Eyrna and I had spent the summer with Gloria, and if she was infected, perhaps so were we. Dr. Smith rolled his eyes and sighed deeply, then lit into the media for causing a completely unnecessary panic over this virus, which was absolutely no danger to anyone, except people who were already debilitated by illness, or had severely compromised immune systems. In other words, people like my mother.

Slowly, he lifted his hand and patted me on the bicep. "You poor thing. How did you survive, with a mother like that?"

I was stunned, for no one had ever said such a thing to me before. My first reaction was to jump to her defense. "She . . ." Then I just gave up. "I don't know," I said.

On the day she was discharged, Eyrna and I walked behind her wheelchair as a hospital nurse rolled her down the hall. They couldn't wait to be rid of her, it was clear from the battered look on the nurses' faces. Gloria shouted at everyone she passed, "You can all go fuck yourselves!" Elbow on the armrest, hand in the air, her middle finger proudly extended, Gloria waved slowly from side to side, as if she were Queen Elizabeth II parading before her subjects in an open car.

Gloria did not remember her three-week stay in the hospital. Once home, she remained bedridden for months, telling her visitors that the local news crews were in a frenzy to find out who, in the Hamptons, had contracted the extremely famous West Nile virus. According to Gloria, the ambulance that carried her home from the hospital was chased down Montauk Highway by several news vans with their cameras sticking out of their windows. "I'm a local legend!" she'd tell her company. "This is a very *famous* disease, you know, and *I* had it! The phone rang constantly, but I didn't talk to them. They parked down at the bottom of the driveway for days!

"Can you imagine?" she'd say, "*I* was the only one who got it!"

In March, now a Blue Belt, I went to a Saturday-morning class, one I didn't usually attend. To my great dismay, the teacher, Mr. Andy, told us this was going to be a sparring class. Frightened, I tried to move to the back, but Mr. Andy called me out and pitted me against a seventeen-year-old male Blue Belt. As soon as we'd bowed to each other and taken our fighting stances, I started giggling. The boy began to circle me, stepped in for a front leg front kick, and I reciprocated with a back leg round kick but was so nervous I forgot to pivot my standing foot. I heard a snap and felt a pain in my right knee that was almost as bad as childbirth. I fell to the floor with a scream. My stomach flipped over itself, and I thought I was going to throw up right on the golden parquet floor. For the next couple of days, I waited to see what would happen. The swelling abated, but I had lost all control of the lateral movement in my knee. On Tuesday I went to a sports surgeon and learned that I'd completely pulverized my ACL—the anterior cruciate ligament—in my right knee. Dr. Silver recommended surgery as soon as possible. I had the choice of "harvesting" the central third of my own patellar tendon, or doing an allograft, a "harvest" from a cadaver. Dr. Silver said with the cadaver "harvest," recovery took about half as long.

"I want to get back to tae kwon do as soon as possible," I told Dr. Silver. "So let's go with the cadaver."

On the day of my surgery, Kevin took off from work and waited with me. As I lay in the rolling bed prepped for the operation, I began a litany of all the things Kevin would have to take care of if I died, and he talked me down, right up until I was wheeled into the operating room. I awakened to a searing pain in my knee, and his smiling face peering down at me. I was wheeled to a recovery room, where four of us were settled into recliners with our legs in the air and ice packs on our knees. We were given fruit juice and cookies.

It took me three months of rehabilitation to be able to walk without a limp, at which time I resumed tae kwon do classes. It took me another three months to be able to pivot at all on my right leg, wearing a brace.

When I returned to see Dr. Silver for my follow-up visit, he walked me down the hall and stopped in rooms along the way, pointing me out to patients and other doctors and nurses in the practice. "Three months," he told them, "and she's back doing tae kwon do!"

"Take That, You Son of a Bitch!"

Here is a story my mother never told anyone. The tale, however, spread like wildfire through Sagaponack and neighboring Bridge-hampton. Employees of the post office and general store and other witnesses each had their own version, which when pieced together, created the following scenario, told to Jamie and me by our cousin Michael Mosolino, some two years later.

→→   ←←

After Gloria recovered from her first bout of cirrhosis in 1999, she traded in her two-door Dodge behemoth for a minivan, which she took to calling The Fat Lady. Gloria was imagining the wonderful outings she would organize for Eyrna, in which we would fill up the minivan and head to the beach for picnics, or for garden parties with her friends who also had grandchildren Eyrna's age.

Every morning Gloria drove to the Sagaponack Post Office at exactly eleven to get her mail. She knew her mail would have been sorted and placed in her box by then, and she wouldn't have to wait. The post office was half a mile from her house. On this day, in the spring of 2004, she got into her minivan with her dog Lily, the obese German shepherd, in the seat beside her, and pulled into one of the parking spaces in front of the little village general store and post office. In the two minutes it took her to go inside and collect her mail, a large delivery truck pulled into the driveway just behind and perpendicular to The Fat Lady, blocking the way.

Gloria got back into her car and honked the horn several times. The truck driver did not appear.

"Well fuck you, then, you asshole!" she shouted out the window, put the car in reverse, hit the gas, and plowed The Fat Lady into the truck. At the appalling sound of twisting metal and shattering glass, a small crowd gathered on the porch of the old post office–general store, including the truck driver. They watched impassively as she repeated this maneuver several times. The delivery truck suffered no damage whatsoever, but the back end of The Fat Lady was completely smashed in, the rear bumper hanging by a thread. "Take that, you son of a bitch!" she shouted out the window, to the amazement of the gathered crowd.

She swung a U-turn and lurched home, the back end of the minivan caved in, the bumper dragging and making sparks on the ground.

The Fat Lady was totaled, the damage irreparable. Gloria was forced to trade her car in for scrap and buy a brand-new minivan.

CHAPTER SIXTEEN

→→ Your Own Private Omaha ←←

In June 2004, two months after my knee surgery, I attended a seminar of American writers in Caen, Normandy, to commemorate the sixtieth anniversary of the D-day landings. I was still wearing my imposing neoprene and metal leg brace, but I wasn't about to turn down this opportunity. If I could walk, I could go. So I went.

Richard Price, my teacher from Columbia, was also invited. I hadn't seen him in several years, but now he called me a few times to make sure I was still going. He seemed nervous about being in a strange French city without his French publisher or a translator or a guide. I told him he had nothing to worry about, that I'd translate for him if the need arose. By now, Richard was hugely successful. He'd written a number of bestselling and critically acclaimed novels, including *Clockers*, which was made into a Spike Lee movie, as well as several screenplays that had become box office hits.

The Centre Régional des Lettres de Basse-Normandie in Caen, our host, did not have a lot of money to spend on accommodations, but the hotel, which had once been a monastery, was a quaint, nicely appointed space with small, low-ceilinged bedrooms. The local Calvados was flowing freely in the evenings, and many strange, disjointed political discussions took place. I translated for our French hosts, as did Jérôme, our representative from the Centre Culturel, who was the only one besides me drinking pear juice.

On our last day, the Centre hired a tour bus with a guide to take us to Omaha Beach. I took two seats for myself so I could stretch out my right leg in its brace. Apparently it was the guide's first day on the job, and his English was far from fluent. He started out the tour with a garbled lecture on the centuries-old friendship between our two nations. Having grown up with French and French accents, I could decipher some of what he was saying, but most of the American writers were straining, mouths agape, their faces frozen in expressions of total incomprehension, as the guide waxed forth with grand gestures and words like *Lafayette, Jefferson*, and the *Independence Declaration*.

Richard was stirring impatiently in the seat behind me. He grumbled through the first twenty minutes of this and then said to me, "Go up and tell him we don't want a lecture on American history. Tell him to talk about D-day and the landings."

The guide must have been pushing forty, and he had a wide-open, innocent face with big blue, sad eyes. I felt sorry for him, but I got up and moved through the rows of seats to the front of the bus, and told him in French what Richard had said. *"Ils veulent que vous parliez du débarquement."*

The poor man looked positively petrified, but he bravely launched into his speech.

He stretched a hand out flat, making a horizontal motion and declared, "We 'ave a French bitch." He placed his other hand a few inches above the first. "Ze Nazis are on top of the bitch. Under ze bitch are the *Américains*. And they are fighting over zis bitch."

"What bitch?" asked Richard from behind me.

"He's saying *beach*," I translated, caught up suddenly in one of those fits of laughter that only escalates the more you try to swallow it.

"So vey are fighting and fighting over zis bitch. It is a long fight for ze bitch. And finally, ze *Américains* win ze bitch."

"Good, I can't wait to hear what they do with her next," muttered Richard.

"Vey 'ave now the bitch under control, so now it is ze time for to make in ze water large erections all around ze bitch. Vey do this . . ."

"I had one of those once, as I recall," Richard called out, and the busload of American writers erupted into howls of laughter. By now I was laughing so much I could barely breathe to translate. I figured the tour guide was talking about the temporary floating Mulberry Harbors that had been constructed around Omaha and Arromanches beaches so the Allied ships could disembark their matériel. I tried to stop laughing long enough to figure out what the guide was now trying to explain.

"And vey do this because why? Because vey 'ave too many nuts. Vey must to 'ave sree nuts or less."

"I thought it only took one nut, although two is better," Richard offered.

"I think he's saying knots. Knots. The ships carrying the matériel were too fast. They had to slow them down to three knots or less in order to dock."

"How can you understand what he's saying?" Richard asked suspiciously, poking his head through the space between the seats. "I think you're just making this up." I knew about the floating ports from my visit to the beaches with my father in 1973.

"And now we will present to you an emu," our guide pronounced.

"An emu? Where?" Richard stood up and looked out the windows in all directions. "They have emus in France?"

The tour guide, opening a pamphlet, blew out his chest and began to recite:

"Onward, Christianne soldiers, marching as to war,
Wiʒ ʒe cross of Jesus going on before . . ."

Hymn, I thought. He's trying to say *hymn. Ee-mu.*

"Is he . . . is he reading 'Onward, Christian Soldiers'?" Richard asked in horrified disbelief. "Hey!" he shouted toward the front of the bus. "Hey! There were Jews there, too, you know. And they sure as shit weren't singing that *emu!*"

My stomach ached, and I had tears streaming from laughing.

By the time we disembarked at the American military cemetery in Colleville-sur-Mer, which lies at the top of the cliff leading down to Omaha Beach, all possibility of decorum and solemnity was lost. It was a hot, sunny, beautiful day. I tried to compose myself as I walked slowly toward the lines and lines of white crosses and intermittent Stars of David that spread out in perfect symmetry, shrinking into the distance in their even rows, but the tour guide's speech kept interfering. I still felt oddly light-headed from laughing so hard; I hadn't laughed like that in years.

We were there two weeks after the June 6 sixtieth anniversary festivities, which had been attended by many heads of state, including George W. Bush. On French TV, a news clip had shown the U.S. president failing to stand for the old veterans until President Jacques Chirac leaned over and quietly urged him to his feet.

Now, dozens of buses were disgorging tourists into the parking lot, many of them German. Inside the cemetery people were talking loudly, joking and smiling and horsing around, taking pictures of themselves in front of the American soldiers' headstones.

When I was growing up in France in the sixties, the war was still strong in everybody's mind. There were whispers among the shop owners on the Île Saint-Louis that the concierge a few doors down from us had been a *collaborateur* and had helped the Nazis round up Jews. So many people said they'd been in the Resistance that it seemed the whole country had been fighting against the Germans. The black-and-white war films I'd watched on TV as a child had left me with nightmares of Nazi jackboots marching down cobbled streets, the sound growing louder and louder as they came for the good guys, holed up in some dark apartment.

The American tourists were cavorting around as much as the Germans. There seemed to be a lot of kids and teenagers on vacation. Annoyed, I wandered off by myself to the farther reaches of the cemetery, where the hordes rarely ventured. I suddenly felt very old.

I remembered how quiet the cemetery had been on that cold December day in 1973 when I'd come here with my parents. We were the only visitors. The landscape—the cemetery's grass, the trees, bushes, and the beach—had seemed washed of colors, all blending in sepia tones like an old photograph. The tide had been out, and the beach seemed to stretch for miles toward England, where the choppy sea and dark, cloudy sky merged on the horizon. The rusty iron antitank barriers, shaped like giant Xs, had still marred the vista, a frightening reminder of what had taken place here. I wondered if they would still be visible today at low tide.

Finally I looked down the path through thick, flowering shrubs to the beach below, now bustling with chattering tourists. My knee was aching and I did not want to limp all the way down there, but I felt I had to. I made my way with mincing steps down the steep path. It was high tide and the beach was just a narrow, rocky strip that looked very much like any other beach in the area. The tourists seemed to be standing around, waiting for something to happen. I tried but could not conjure up a picture of the scene in 1944.

I'd also been to Omaha Beach once before our visit in 1973. When I was nine months old, in 1961, my mother and I accompanied my father on a business trip. He was writing dialogue for the American sections of the screenplay *The Longest Day,* based on the book by Cornelius Ryan. My father's friend Romain Gary, the renowned French author, soldier, and diplomat, was writing the French dialogue; Erich Maria Remarque, the German author of one of the greatest antiwar novels ever written, *All Quiet on the Western Front,* was in charge of the German scenes; and David Pursall and Jack Seddon took on the task of writing the British dialogue, after Noël Coward declined.

My father combed the D-day beaches and tried to imagine what it must have been like. This was only sixteen years after the war ended, and nothing much had changed in the landscape. The German fortifications were still intact, and from his position on the beach, the pillboxes stared down ominously from the bluffs. I'm certain he could still hear the explosions and the shooting, the shouting and crying of the wounded.

When we visited the beaches in 1973, my father told me, his eyes watering from the cold or from emotion, that in 1944, after he'd recovered from his ankle surgery in an army hospital in Memphis, he'd received orders to return to combat duty with a regiment that was soon shipping out for Europe. He knew he would have been part of the invasion force and was certain he would not survive. "I knew my luck had run out," he told me. So he went AWOL and pretended to be insane—or perhaps he really was a little insane—and started fights in bars until the army saw fit to give him an honorable discharge.

There is a photograph of him on the set of *The Longest Day* with Peter Lawford, looking down the barrel of a rifle, perhaps checking it for authenticity. Another photo shows my father talking with Darryl Zanuck, whose back is turned, only a cigar extending from his mouth. My father is smoking a cigarette and grabbing a bottle of French wine by its neck.

As research, my father toured the Normandy shore from Utah

Beach, ten or twelve miles farther east, to Omaha Beach. He had no trouble imagining what the men must have felt, facing German artillery and machine-gun fire. There is a wonderful description of it in his nonfiction book, *WWII*, which re-created the war from the soldiers' points of view; it is a synthesis of his own recollections, analysis, anecdotes, and graphic art from the war. In his words, D-day looked and sounded much like Steven Spielberg's version in *Saving Private Ryan:* "The terror and total confusion, men screaming or sinking silently under the water, tanks sinking as their crews died inside, landing craft going up as a direct hit took them, or grating ashore to discharge their live cargo into the already scrambled mess, officers trying to get their men together, medics trying to find shelter for the wounded, until out of the welter a certain desperate order began to emerge, and men began to move toward the two bottleneck exits. I sat there until my friends began to yell at me from down below, and I fervently thanked God or Whomever that I had not been there."

There were more artists at Normandy than at any other battle in World War II. The Germans may not have known where the Allies planned to invade, but the Allied photographers and writers did. Paintings show men with their arms shot off; bodies slung over the iron crosses on Omaha Beach, like casual crucifixions; a battlefield execution of a German soldier, blindfolded and bound.

My father described some extremely graphic carnage in *The Longest Day*, but the Hollywood censors were displeased. His final assessment of the film was that it did not honestly portray war and warfare, especially the carnage suffered by the Americans on Omaha Beach. They removed all of the soldiers' language, which my father had already softened in an attempt to pass the Production Code board's litmus test. Geoffrey Shurlock, the Production Code administrator, objected to the "casual profanity" and vulgar dialogue: *crap, stuff it, motherlover, SOB, bastards, jeez, damn, puke;* all had to go. Shurlock's conclusion: "We are concerned with what seems to us to be an excessive amount of slaughter in this story. We realize that it is impossible to tell the story of the invasion of Normandy without indicating the staggering loss of human life. We do urge you, in those scenes you stage, to minimize the dramatization of personal killings. We think that such an effort on your part would avoid the 'bloodbath effect.' "

My mother, in order to lift my father's spirits, took to calling the administrator No-Shit Shurlock. My father's response to No-Shit Shurlock's letter: "What the fuck do they think war is? What did they think Omaha was, if not a 'bloodbath'?"

Ultimately, my father wrote a blistering ten-page memo to the studio criticizing the final script of *The Longest Day*, demanding that his name be removed from the credits. Cornelius Ryan, however, wanted full screenwriting credit anyway, and fought the producers to have his name appear alone on the screen. He won his case, so my father's little revolt against the Hollywood machine was moot.

My father wrote the following in 1963, in an article for the *Saturday Evening Post*, as a result of his experience on the set of *The Longest Day*: "Most deaths in infantry combat are due to arbitrary chance, a totally random selection by which an unknown enemy drops a mortar or artillery shell onto, or punches an MG bullet into, a man he has never seen before—and perhaps never does see at all! Such a death is totally reasonless and pointless from the viewpoint of the individual, because it might just as well have been the man next to him. It only has meaning when it is viewed numerically from a higher echelon by those who count the ciphers. And for that very reason it is a much more terrifying death to the individual soldier and to an audience seeking 'meaning.' "

My father would have been outraged by the message of *Saving Private Ryan*, that the just and fair U.S. government would expend the energy and manpower to locate Mrs. Ryan's last surviving son—one man among the myriad soldiers whose lives were at stake that day. He believed that war and warfare turn most men into animals, not heroes. And the individual, in warfare, does not count, never did count, and never will. And anyone who says otherwise is lying. But people in general would probably rather believe a Spielberg film over the soldier-writers who dedicated their lives to trying to debunk such glorifying myths. It is much safer, and more comfortable, to believe in the notion of "the good war," and that no American soldier killed, or died, in vain.

Our modern society has managed to turn a good many legendary battles into successful films and video games. Herodotus wrote in his *Histories* about three hundred Spartans, who in 480 B.C. held off a Persian force of 80,000 for three days at the Thermopylae pass. But why read the difficult Herodotus when we can now experience this famous battle in a graphic novel called *300*? And if we don't want to read at all, there is a film based on the book, complete with supernatural creatures—a huge commercial success. There is even a video game of the Omaha Beach assault, created in the wake of *Saving Private Ryan*, in which we may virtually experience killing Nazis, getting blown up, deploying Bangalore torpedoes, storming the German pillboxes, and saving the day.

My friend Ray Elliott, former president of the James Jones Literary Society, writer, and former marine, had a cousin, Bruce Elliott, who participated in the Omaha Beach landing. A neck injury Bruce received during the war bothered him for the rest of his life, and he suffered from post-traumatic stress disorder and depression. He was able to hold down a job until his last few years, when he was forced to go on total disability. Bruce Elliott eventually shot himself, on D-day 1982—a statement heard loud and clear by his family. Ray visited Omaha Beach on several occasions; in 1994, for the fiftieth anniversary, he attended the ceremonies on a D-day pass granted by the Pentagon, thanks to Bruce's service. During that visit, Ray noticed a number of young faux soldiers in vintage

U.S. military garb and medals, tooling around the countryside in World War II U.S. Army jeeps—boys playing war.

Ray went back in 2004, just a few weeks before I did, and was stunned by the changes he noted in just ten years. Pointe du Hoc, a mile farther down the beach from Omaha, where Army Rangers had clambered the sheer rock face under heavy machine-gun fire, now looked like a Disney World ride, with state-of-the-art observation towers and panoramas. I was reminded of a recent attempt by some commercial-minded entrepreneurs to turn an infamous Virginia Civil War battlefield into a Civil War–themed amusement park. This plan was actually considered seriously until many notable historians and writers—including William Styron—vehemently spoke out against it and put a stop to it.

But every war has had its great writers, soldiers who witnessed the ugliness and were not fooled by lies of grandeur. I thought of Stendhal, who survived Napoleon's retreat from Russia; and Tolstoy, who survived the battle of Sebastopol, and read Stendhal to understand how to write about war; all the way down to my father, James Jones, who read both Stendhal and Tolstoy, and laughed his head off at their gallows humor and their elegant descriptions of young men's hunger for glory.

For several years now, I'd stopped writing. I'd lost hope in the literary novel. In the midst of this crisis, in 2002, I spent the month of June in Paris with Kevin and Eyrna, organizing the James Jones Literary Society yearly symposium, which was held at the American University of Paris on June 22. Norris Church Mailer, George Plimpton, and Norman Mailer came and performed their play, *Zelda, Scott, and Ernest,* before a crowd of hundreds at the American Church on the Quai d'Orsay, to raise funds for the Society. A well-known French literary journalist, François Busnel, wanted to interview Norman for French radio, and Norman asked me to be his translator.

Busnel's first question was about the September 11 terrorist attacks. I was so stunned by Norman's response I could barely translate. Norman laughed and said he was amused that the French were more interested in his opinion of 9/11 than the Americans. He said, with a bemused smile, that literary writers' opinions no longer held any sway in America. The time of the great American novelists had passed. In the forties, a few writers thought they could change the world. And perhaps they did. James Jones's novel *From Here to Eternity*, for example, changed the U.S. Army, Norman said. "I still think that's the role of literature: to try to change the world. But that's no longer what preoccupies American writers, unfortunately. If I had to do it over, I'd be a film director."

But, he explained, this did not mean that we could stop taking a stand, and stop hollering when it was time to holler. I thought Norman was fantastically brave, because people in the States were being called "unpatriotic" if they opposed the Bush administration's intention to invade Iraq. As *patriotic Americans*, we weren't even supposed to be in France, which refused to back the U.S.'s invasion plans.

Busnel and Norman looked at me, expecting my simultaneous translation. I was so busy listening and thinking that for a moment, I'd forgotten what I was doing there. I quickly resumed.

And what genius, Norman continued, to hit the Twin Towers, the greatest American symbol of globalization and financial greed!

After Busnel and his crew left, I told Norman I thought the Tower card in the tarot deck was eerily descriptive of what had happened to us on September 11.

"How interesting," he said. "Do you read tarot cards?"

I told him I did and had been studying the tarot for years. He asked me if I had my cards with me. I didn't. They were back at my friend's apartment.

"Oh, too bad. I read cards too," Norman added, after a pause. "I find them fascinating. I used to read my cards every day, but it began to obsess me, so I stopped. We should trade readings sometime."

"Norman," I blurted, "I haven't written a word in ages. I was so depressed over the fate of literature in the U.S. that I felt completely useless. But now, listening to you, I see it's not an option. I *have to* write. I see it's more important than ever."

"Yes, it is," he said. "Even more so if you do it without any expectation of success."

Now I looked up the green cliff face to the top, where on a white esplanade tourists had crowded to gaze down at the beach. Why did everyone look so joyful? I was thinking of Norman's words and wondering if I would have become a novelist if I'd known, back in 1981, that the literary novel would hold so little sway in the years to come. Well, too late now, I thought. I don't know how to do anything else. Not a fucking thing, except teach.

Time to start writing again.

I limped slowly back up the steep, uneven path to the cemetery, and made my way through the crowds to the parking lot, where our bus was waiting.

As I approached the bus, I saw Richard standing a few feet away, looking pensive. "I didn't feel what I thought I would feel," Richard said, his voice hollow. "I don't know—it was strangely unemotional."

"I was here before," I replied awkwardly. "My father brought me. It was so quiet. There was no one here."

Richard nodded. In silence, we made our way back to our seats on the sunny bus.

"It's Just Like Driving Miss Daisy—in Reverse"

Here is a story Mary Johnson, my mother's housekeeper, told me.

→>―   ―<―

The next vehicle my mother bought after she smashed up The Fat Lady was a Dodge Caravan, another minivan that was only slightly less fat, but easier to maneuver. Apparently, sometime in the summer of 2005, driving home from a liquid lunch at Dockside restaurant in Sag Harbor, she hit the stone embankment of the narrow train overpass on Butter Lane and totaled the passenger side of the Caravan. It was no longer possible to open the passenger door, and the side mirror was ripped right out of its casing.

Every day, at around eleven, Mary, who was three-quarters blind and could no longer keep house, accompanied my mother on her outing. First they would go to the post office, then to the shopping center, where my mother and Mary played Lotto and picked up booze. Once or twice a month they drove to the Shinnecock Reservation in Southampton to buy cartons of discounted, tax-free cigarettes.

After the passenger door was smashed in and could no longer be opened, Mary was forced to sit in the back, and that's how they drove around town. One day, Mary said in her dreamy Georgia drawl, "It's just like *Driving Miss Daisy*—in reverse!" and let out her deep, rumbling smoker's laugh.

My mother was not amused. After that, she stopped driving and had Vladimir—the drunken Russian artist who'd moved into the attic—drive her and Mary around town, both of them now in the backseat.

CHAPTER SEVENTEEN

⤻ Heart ⤺

My mother threw us out of her house one last time in mid-July 2004. By then we were visiting rarely, and stayed only for one night. Her fit of rage was triggered by a phone call from Max Mosolino, who told her that Kevin and I were trying to undermine her.

We had called Max, who was a builder, earlier that morning to ask for his help with the house's most urgent and serious problems, like the crumbling porch steps and the wasps' nests inside the steps' wooden posts. The bigger issues, like the rotting window frames, would have to wait. Kevin told Max he was very concerned about my mother's state of mind, and repairs were absolutely necessary or someone was going to get hurt. Max, after a thoughtful silence, told Kevin that Gloria should sell the house and move into a manageable condo. Yes, Kevin said, of course, but she won't move. Max did not offer to come help, and Kevin said something like, After everything she did for you, it wouldn't kill you to take a couple of days to fix the more urgent problems.

I don't know how Max reported this to Gloria, but it was an easy conversation to spin any number of ways. I can understand, on some level, Max's loyalty to his aunt, and his refusal to accept that she was in serious trouble. But the result was that Gloria returned from her friend Liz Fondaras's yearly Quatorze Juillet luncheon bash and stormed into our downstairs bedroom. Eyrna, now six years old, was changing out of her wet bathing suit, the three of us having just returned from the beach.

"You and I are finished. *Finished*," she said to me. "Get out."

I stood there, stunned, staring at my mother, who had gained quite a bit of weight recently, and I got a strong whiff of that weird, pungent, fermented fruit smell emanating from her. And yet my mind refused to compute what should have been patently clear. Instead, I felt a surge of unbearable guilt and tried to determine what I'd done wrong. I realized immediately that Max must have called her.

She turned to Eyrna, whose face was already twisting in horror and pain. "*You* can stay," she said.

"Don't be ridiculous," I said, my voice quivering. "She's our child."

"You see," she said to Eyrna, pointing at us, "this is all because of them. This is *their* fault. *They*'ve done this to us." She turned and walked out of the room. Eyrna started to howl.

I felt as if I'd exploded from within as my vision closed in around me. I charged up the stairs behind my mother, shouting at her in a voice I did not recognize. I called her a fucking bitch. I kicked open her bedroom door with a perfect front kick and raised a fist to knock her down. I could still hear Eyrna howling downstairs. My mother cowered before me, cringing, and I saw not a colossal Hydra but a frightened old lady, and I was able to hold myself back. Instead, I picked up a heavy glass ashtray and threw it at the wall, putting a dent in the sheetrock.

I shouted, out of breath as if I'd run six miles, "You're a monster. Our relationship as you know it is over. And you've just lost your privileges as a grandmother. I am *never* going to let you do this to us again, you fucking cunt."

We took everything of ours we could fit in the car, until there was not an inch of room left, and drove away. We left all our winter clothes in the attic. Kevin, behind the wheel, was shaking and breathing shallowly, attempting to get control of his anger. Eyrna cried the whole way back to New York and was still so upset she couldn't go to her summer camp the next day. By Tuesday, I felt it necessary to take her to my therapist, Sherrye, who was an expert in treating children of alcoholics. Kevin came as well, and we let Sherrye tell Eyrna that her grandmother was not in her right mind.

I felt I had completely let my child down, not to mention my husband and myself. But never did I think that Gloria had been drinking.

We tried to maintain our stable, normal, daily routine. Eyrna was enrolled in a summer day camp on the Upper East Side that took the kids to Westchester every morning by bus. I continued to attend my tae kwon do class. We had not been going to my mother's for weekends as we used to in the past, so the change wasn't so radical. Every person I spoke to who was sane thought Gloria had been undermining Kevin and me as parents, and the relationship between her and Eyrna had to change. I would not let Eyrna call her.

That July, I read Eyrna *Harry Potter and the Order of the Phoenix*.

When Harry returns to Hogwarts Academy after witnessing the murder of his friend at the end of the previous book, he sees for the first time that the school's carriages are not self-propelled but are pulled by cadaverous, black-winged horses. He learns they are called thestrals, and they have always been there, but the only people who can see them are those who have watched someone die. At first, they are terrifying, but Harry learns to appreciate their peculiar beauty.

At this point, I started to feel choked up and had to stop reading.

"*You* could see the thestrals, Mommy," Eyrna said in a quiet voice.

"Yes," I said, "I could." And I added, "And so could your daddy."

I love the way J. K. Rowling describes the line between those who have looked death in the face and those who have not, allowing children who have suffered such a loss to feel special, part of an exclusive club. My father witnessed death at the age of twenty, the day Pearl Harbor was attacked. My mother was much younger; she was four when her sister Kitty died of polio. But my mother seemed to have spent her life trying to pretend the thestrals weren't there.

"When you can see the thestrals, you're very special," I said to Eyrna, my voice warbling.

I knew that soon enough, Eyrna would be able to see them too.

Mr. Bill began to look unwell. From one day to the next, his skin seemed to lose its luminous sheen, and all at once his hair appeared to go gray. He breathed too hard during class and moved as if he were aching all over. He could barely lift his legs to demonstrate the kicks.

"What's wrong with Mr. Bill?" Eyrna whispered to me as we were changing in the locker room one Saturday, after class.

"I don't know," I whispered back.

Everyone was afraid to ask him.

The next Tuesday, I asked Mr. Bill to join me for lunch. I told him what had happened with my mother, and how Eyrna was suffering. I asked him if he thought I was wrong to keep Eyrna away from her grandmother.

"Kids raised in violence only know violence. They confuse it with love," he elliptically said.

"Mr. Bill, are you okay?" I asked him.

"I got prostate cancer," he said without emotion. "I took all them tests. CAT scans, MRIs. I hadn't been to see a doctor in years. It already spread to my bones." He placed his hand flat against his sternum. "Right here, they say."

Thirty years ago I watched my father die slowly, and I was not afraid of illness. I wanted Mr. Bill to know that, but I also didn't know how to tell him.

"What can I do to help you?" This was the only response I could think of.

"Just keep showing up."

"I won't quit," I said. "It's a promise."

He nodded. Then he ordered a margarita, and after it arrived, he took a delicate sip and said, "I'm not scared of dying. I'm scared of leaving my moms alone. Ain't nobody else to care for her."

"I used to flirt with death," I said. "I used to drive drunk, too fast. Now, I'm scared of dying because I can't stand the thought of Eyrna having to face this world without me."

He nodded, took another sip. We sat in silence for a moment.

Then Mr. Bill told me he didn't get paid much to teach at the *do-jang*. He saw it as his spiritual duty. He had his VA check, and they took care of his medical, but of course that was hardly enough. His moms had some dough, he said. That took care of her bills, as long as he was the one caring for her, not a nurse.

He had two sons, almost the same age, from different women; one lived in California, and one was away at Bard College. The one at Bard was majoring in Japanese studies and was a tai chi expert. I had met the Bard student when he'd come to meet Mr. Bill for lunch at the *do-jang*. Mr. Bill didn't want his sons to know he was sick.

"They need to know, Mr. Bill," I said gently. He didn't respond.

"Now I got to do that chemo shit," he finally said.

When the bill came, he pulled some crumpled twenties out of his pocket and wouldn't let me pay my share.

"If that don't work," he added, almost as an afterthought, "then I'll just have to learn how to die."

On the way to pick up Eyrna at the camp bus stop, I went into an upscale health food store and asked the man behind the counter what was good for prostate cancer and chemotherapy treatments. He recommended green tea extract and phellinus linteus extract, a Chinese mushroom. They were almost as expensive by weight as marijuana. I got both for Mr. Bill and brought them to class on Thursday.

He looked at me somberly and bowed in thanks.

"When you run out," I said, "tell me and I'll get you more."

At first Mr. Bill lost a good deal of weight. But as soon as he started his chemo and hormone treatments, his hair started falling out in great clumps, and his face grew bloated right up to his eyes. But he still showed up, and worked slowly and laboriously, teaching us as he always had.

He couldn't do the kicks or stretches anymore, but we still responded to his commands as if he'd lost none of his strength and form. This was exactly the way we treated my father as he weakened and grew thin and shrank before our eyes. We pretended he could still manhandle us.

I told Mr. Bill, "You look great. You always do." This was tricky, for Mr. Bill hated to be patronized, or to have anyone feel sorry for him. I watched my father weaken, drowning slowly as his lungs filled with water, and yet I never felt sorry for him, only helpless to ease his discomfort. Mr. Bill did look great. And he kept showing up. I realized, with a jolt, that the *do-jang* was the center of his life. While it was not the center of mine, I hoped to make it the new foundation from which I could proudly move forward into an unknown and terrifying future.

. . .

Eventually, my mother and I had a slight rapprochement. I went out to her house toward the end of October, dreading every moment, so I could pick up our winter clothes. I didn't call ahead. I knew the house would not be locked, and she would probably be out to lunch. No such luck. She sat at her usual place, on a high stool at the butcher block island in the center of the kitchen, smoking.

"Hi, Mom. I came to get our winter clothes. I'll only be here for a minute."

"Eyrna hasn't called me," she said.

"It's not up to her to call you," I said calmly. "You threw us out of your house, in front of your six-year-old granddaughter. She had to go see a therapist because of it."

"No-o," my mother countered, as if I'd just told her a spaceship had landed in her backyard.

I ran up the two flights to the attic and retrieved our plastic bags, rolling them down the narrow stairs, one after the other. I was in the house a total of four minutes. On my way out carrying the last two bags, I said, "If we're unwelcome in your life, so is she. She's just a little girl."

On Halloween, my mother finally called our apartment; it was nine days before Eyrna's birthday. Giving in for Eyrna's sake, I invited her to meet us to celebrate—in neutral territory—for tea, at the American Girl Doll Store on Fifth Avenue. I made reservations in the restaurant, where girls could bring their dolls, and the dolls would be served their own tea and cakes in miniature cups and plates.

"What a gimmick, this place," said my mother under her breath as we walked around, looking at the dolls in their delicate, colorful, historically accurate rooms. The Native American doll, Maya, had a faux buffalo hide teepee with furs for a bed and a spotted pony with a travois. Eyrna was carrying Felicity under her arm, dressed up for the occasion in a black velvet and white satin ball gown.

My mother made a twisted-mouth face. "They have all these people fooled, but not me."

"Eyrna loves this store," I said, "that's all I care about." I had a strange realization: in the past, her words would have hurt me, but now, what she thought no longer mattered to me in the least.

We had fancy high tea with a triple-decker arrangement of little sandwiches and pastries that cost me eighty dollars. Eyrna was delighted. To anyone seeing us, we looked like a television ad. Three generations of attractive, well-groomed, healthy, loving women. Sitting at the table with my mother, I caught a whiff of that terrible fermented fruit smell. Could she be drinking? No. It was impossible. I dismissed the thought as a case of nerves on my part.

My mother bought Eyrna a new doll—one she'd wanted for a long time. Coming out of the store in the chill November afternoon, there were no cabs anywhere, and my mother couldn't catch her breath, so she hired a bicycle cab to carry us and our bevy of shopping bags back uptown to Cecile's apartment.

"You know, not too long ago I was driving and I had the radio on and they played that song by Beethoven, remember? 'Da, da, dada, da . . .'"—she sang in her low, raspy voice that still always managed to be in tune—"and I thought of you" . . ." Her voice trailed off.

"Beethoven's Sixth," I prompted. I felt like reminding her that it was a symphony, not a song, but held my tongue. Apparently she wasn't going to continue. "What did you think when you thought of me?" I wanted to know.

"I just thought of you, that's all," she curtly replied.

Was she trying to say she was sorry for the terrible scene she'd caused last July? Was she trying to say she'd missed me? In the old days, this would have been enough to make me drop my armor and prostrate myself at her feet. Not anymore. My heart was not even quivering.

She had hurt my child. She had burned the last bridge back to me.

. . .

I knew Mr. Bill had his chemo treatments on Wednesdays, and he missed class on Thursday. That night I looked up his mother's phone number in the big phone book and called him at home.

"Hi, Mr. Bill, it's Kaylie. How're you doing?"

There was a dead silence.

"KJ," I said quickly.

"How's Shortstop?" he said, his voice turning warm and light.

"She's good. She sends her love. I know you had your chemo yesterday. How do you feel?"

Talking in a murmur, he said he felt okay. He said he was whispering because he didn't want his moms to worry. He said his moms was failing now and didn't have long to go. He asked me if I'd be coming to class on Saturday, and I said absolutely.

"Do you need any more of that green tea extract or the mushroom stuff?"

"I like the green tea extract. That seems to help."

"I'll get you some tomorrow."

He thanked me, and then after a silence, I said, "I'm honored to be your student, Mr. Bill."

We didn't have anything else to say, so I told him I'd see him on Saturday.

Saturday I showed up for class, and a new fellow was behind the desk. He said his name was Mario, and he was taking over the *do-jang*.

Over the course of a couple of weeks, he took down all the old, yellowing photographs and removed the dusty, peeling trophies. Mr. Bill continued to teach the lunchtime class, straight and tall and dignified, and didn't say a word about it.

The *do-jang*, under the new management, quickly transformed itself into a large conglomerate called Premier Martial Arts.

They completely remodeled the place, painting, putting down a blue rubber mat floor, and knocking out some walls. Everything looked new and seriously professional now, even the equipment. They started a mixed martial arts curriculum—tae kwon do, ju-jitsu-style grappling, as well as Muoy Thai–style fighting, which is much less elegant and much tougher on the joints, and boxing.

Then, one Tuesday, a new teacher showed up to teach the noontime class. His name was Mr. Sevilla. In his late twenties, from Miami, tall and pale, with a handsome patrician profile, he was charismatic and self-confident. Mr. Bill stood in the back, behind us, and didn't say a word. About halfway through the class, he went into the men's locker room, changed, and left the *do-jang*.

After class, a few of us regular students stayed behind to ask Mr. Sevilla what was going to happen with Mr. Bill. Mr. Sevilla said he didn't know. I said I would leave the school if they didn't respect Mr. Bill's long-standing relationship with Master Chun's school and the old noontime students. The others agreed.

Mr. Sevilla said he'd pass that on to Mr. Mario.

Mr. Sevilla, who held a Third Degree Black Belt in tae kwon do from the legendary Master Joon Ri's school in Miami, was an honorable man. On Thursday, when we arrived for class, Mr. Bill was already there, dressed in his yellowing uniform with his gray collar and gray belt. Mr. Sevilla told us that Premier Martial Arts would be offering lunchtime classes five days a week from now on, and that in three months, in June, we would take the promotion test for Red Belt, and Mr. Bill had volunteered to continue to teach us the old tae kwon do forms. We needed to perform *Palgue* 1 through 6 to pass the test.

Mr. Bill told me a few days later that even though he had been one of Master Chun's oldest students, Master Chun hadn't called him to tell him they were selling the school.

Friday, near the end of the session, Mr. Bill, who'd been sitting hunched over on the sidelines, suddenly pulled himself up, breathed in deeply, gathering his strength, and threw himself into the first move of *Palgue* 6, demonstrating a double knife-hand back stance followed by a sharp and perfect back leg front kick. He looked like a champion.

"Face the form with an open heart," he told us. "As if you're facing a deserving opponent."

After class, looking extremely uncomfortable, Mr. Bill asked me quietly if he could borrow twenty bucks. I told him sure but I had to go to the bank. We walked to the corner of Second Avenue, and he waited outside while I went in to use the cash machine. I folded two twenties up small in my palm, and when I got out into the street, I slipped them to Mr. Bill while we were shaking hands.

"I'll get you back next week," he murmured.

"I don't want it back. Don't even think about it."

On Monday, the regulars all decided that from now on, we would pay Mr. Bill on our own for teaching us the forms.

I took Eyrna out to Sagaponack for Easter weekend, for she remembered with deep happiness those chilly early-spring Sundays of egg hunts in the greening garden. I didn't want to go. Cousin Anne and her husband had moved to Pennsylvania, so there was only Gianna's daughter, Nina, now eleven, playing along as they hunted together for the colorful eggs.

At dinner on Saturday night, my mother poured herself a glass of red wine. I couldn't believe what I was seeing. I suddenly realized there wasn't any Diet Coke in the pantry or food in the fridge. Tonight's dinner had been brought over by Michael Mosolino's catering shop. I had to say something to her and dreaded it. I waited until she was alone in the library and approached her. I suddenly felt exhausted.

"Mom, if you continue to drink, you're going to die." My voice was calm and devoid of judgment.

"Don't be silly," she said dismissively. "I'm not drinking, anyway. I have a sore throat, and it helps with the pain. I'm not swallowing it."

I realized, of course, that if she was drinking in front of me, she must have been drinking for quite a while. Last summer's episode began to make a weird kind of sense, and at once, everything began to fall into place.

The emergency bell had been tolling for a long time, but I had not heard it. She would not go quietly, and she would take a great deal down with her. I tried to steel myself as best I could for the oncoming disaster.

I went into my room and called Cecile. "My mother's drinking again," I said, my voice hollow and unfamiliar.

"I know," Cecile said. "But she seems to be in control of herself right now."

"If she could maintain control of her drinking, she wouldn't be an alcoholic."

Dead silence.

There was no point in playing Cassandra and prophesying doom and gloom. I said good-bye, and slowly began packing up the few things in my old bedroom that still mattered to me—photographs, books, old letters. I did not think I would be staying here again.

I fell into a depression that kept me bedridden for several weeks. Everything felt difficult, as if I were buried up to the neck in a stinking mud swamp. I rose in the morning to get Eyrna off to school and to walk our little dog; I pulled myself together in the afternoon to pick up Eyrna at the school bus; the rest of the time, I slept. For close to three weeks, I didn't go to tae kwon do or call anyone from the *do-jang*.

Kevin grew concerned and asked me to return to Sherrye, the therapist, which I did. She asked me if I wanted to do some anger work. She handed me the foam bat and told me to hit the pillows. I couldn't even lift it; it hung limply from my hand like an extension of my arm.

I had been full of expectations until I realized my mother was drinking again. I'd still believed in the notions of justice and retribution. I'd thought that because I'd gotten ahold of myself, because I was being forced to face my demons, she should be forced to face hers and to be accountable for her actions. She had to *pay*.

Was it true, what James Baldwin had said, that "people pay for what they do, and still more for what they have allowed themselves to become. And they pay for it very simply; by the lives they lead"?

I'd never blame a person with cancer for being sick. I'd never try to reason with a madwoman in an insane asylum—so *why* did I still expect my mother to understand the consequences of her actions, and despise her for not taking responsibility?

And where does one draw the line, ultimately, between mental incompetence and accountability? Between madness and sanity? When is personal choice removed from the equation? We still revile and punish drunk drivers who kill people, as if they were morally inferior to us and had a *choice* in whether or not, with their judgment completely impaired, they got behind the wheel of a car. The law sends those people to jail, not to insane asylums or rehabilitation centers.

Mr. Bill called. I had not missed as many weeks of tae kwon do in a row since my ACL surgery.

"My mother is drinking again, Mr. Bill," I said. "I don't know what to do."

"There's nothin' you can do," he replied. "Except take care of your daughter and your husband. But especially you got to take care of yourself."

Eyrna asked me that night as we snuggled together in her soft loft bed, "Are you quitting tae kwon do, Mommy?" Her eyes were big and shining.

"Never. I'm going to get my Black Belt." I'd never said this out loud, and I didn't quite believe it myself.

She nodded solemnly. "So am I going to get my Black Belt, too."

The next day, I dragged myself back to the *do-jang*. Mr. Sevilla, who is charismatic and funny as hell but not one for emotional displays, looked at me for a long moment in silence.

"Ladies and gentlemen, get your gloves out. After warm-up, we're boxing!" he shouted.

I loved hitting the mitts and practicing body punches on the heavy bags. I had quickly become one of the fastest female boxers in the school. Mr. Sevilla once asked me where I'd studied boxing before. I told him I'd never studied boxing in my life, but my dad had taught me to punch and parry when I was a little girl. This talent had come as a surprise to everyone—except Mr. Bill, who knew my father had been a boxer in the army; he believed such abilities were inherited.

Now, commenting on my weak and uninspired warm-up and my despondent condition, Mr. Sevilla yelled that at this rate, I'd never be ready for my Red Belt test in June.

"Jones! Over here!" he shouted.

"Yes, sir."

Mr. Sevilla had on his own personal mitts. "Hit it. Jab, cross. Give me six. Go, go, go, go! Jab, cross, hook! Jab, jab, cross! Cross, hook, cross! Cross, hook, uppercut! Uppercut, I said! Now, jab, cross. Give me six!" Over and over and over, until my arms ached and then lost their strength and I let out a fierce, rage-filled scream.

"Feel better?" Mr. Sevilla asked under his breath.

I was folded over double, panting hard. "Yes, sir! Thank you, sir."

Mr. Bill sidled up to me after class. "This is only one realm of existence," he murmured. "You understand?"

No, I really don't understand, but what does it matter? I'll show up anyway. That's what matters.

"It's your karma. You fix it this time around, next time you won't have to."

"Yes, sir."

"Come on, let's work on those *Palgue* forms."

Toward the end of July, I got a call from Vladimir, the Russian who lived in my mother's attic. He had been a nurse's aide/companion to a well-known aging artist in my mother's neighborhood. He'd moved into my mother's attic about a year ago. Vladimir had driven her into the City and checked her into Columbia Presbyterian Hospital. She had pneumonia again, and was completely delusional. Her friend Liz Fondaras had pulled many strings to get Gloria admitted under the care of a lung specialist who'd been President Clinton's doctor. Eyrna and I took a taxi up to Washington Heights to see her. The resident on the floor was quite upset because he felt she didn't belong here; he thought she should be in the alcohol and drug detox center.

We went into her private room. She was sitting up in bed, staring at us petulantly, her eyes following us as we walked toward her. I stared right back, amazed that I no longer feared her.

"They tried to lock me up but I kicked the doctor in the shins," she told us proudly. "I'm not staying here with these idiots."

Outside the huge window the Hudson River steamed. In the distance, the George Washington Bridge, ensconced in haze, was undulating in the heat. The resident came in and told us my mother's tests wouldn't be back for four hours. Meanwhile, he wanted me to convince her to go to the detox center. Kevin, Eyrna, and I were supposed to be leaving on a six-day camping and white-water rafting trip that afternoon, a Thursday.

"Oh, we're not staying," I said. He looked troubled. He sent for the social worker, a young, nervous woman with a pale complexion and flyaway hair. I wasn't up for this discussion, so we left her with my mother and went and stood out in the hall. The social worker lasted five minutes.

"I don't know what to tell you," she said to me when she came out, even paler than before. What I had come to accept, which she apparently had not yet, was that a person in my mother's condition was no longer able to make a sane decision on her own behalf. She'd passed that fork in the road some time ago and no longer had the mental capacity to look back, or forward, with sound judgment. But the law states that unless the person is an immediate danger to herself or others . . .

"You don't have to tell me anything," I replied. "I'm no longer taking responsibility for my mother's drinking. My daughter and I will deal with our own issues in therapy. We're leaving now. We're going on vacation."

And we walked out, holding hands, without looking back.

In September 2005, Anna, George, and I—the three of us who had started this journey together—took the candidate for Black Belt promotion test, judged by Mr. Sevilla and Mr. Mario. Mr. Bill sat in the back, his face devoid of expression. It was an endurance test that lasted an hour and a half. I was not afraid. Anna, my age, has the temperament of a Valkyrie. She is the type of person who gets stronger and more aggressive the more she's challenged, and that helped me to stay focused and strong; and George, well, George was in it for the long haul too, now. He didn't complain or say a word, he just performed the tasks in silence. After being pounded, boxed, kicked, run aground, and hollered at for an hour, we performed the *Palgue* forms 1 through 7, in front of the rest of the students. I was moved by a vehemence and control I never knew I possessed. Mr. Sevilla and his new assistant, six-foot-five, 240-pound Mr. Acosta, a karate and capoeira master, held my rough pine boards for me. On my second try, I broke two three-quarter-inch boards with one reverse side kick; I broke another with a back fist punch on my first attempt.

Afterward, I saw myself in the mirror, in my sharp, black *gi* and my new candidate belt, which was red with a thick black stripe along the center. I stared at my reflection, standing calmly, shoulders relaxed, and I thought, That is the person I want to be.

I began to walk around the city with a spring in my step, my eyes up and looking out and around, not down at the pavement. I noticed things. When a gang of kids walked brazenly in my direction down Eighty-sixth Street, I did not flinch or move out of the way. They must have seen something in my eyes because they silently split up and moved around me, like river water flowing around a boulder. I still didn't believe I would be able to survive if I were seriously attacked, but I knew I'd never let anyone tie me up, and I would never quit or back down. An attack like that is never personal, Mr. Sevilla said—well, I would make it personal, and I'd make the guy pay.

The nasty blind man I saw around the neighborhood was standing one day by himself at the light, listening for cars. I asked him if he wanted help across the street. He turned his head in my direction, his blind eyes rolling up under his eyelids. "Yes, thank you, that would be nice," he said peevishly. I took his arm and walked him slowly across the avenue.

I let an old lady pass before me in line at the supermarket (she had three items and I had a million). At first she looked at me in fear, as if I were a nut. It seemed to take her twenty minutes to count out her change, but I didn't even huff or sigh loudly.

I felt as if I suddenly had a new purpose in life: to get my Black Belt in tae kwon do, and to act like a martial artist, even if I didn't feel like one. Mr. Bill always said, *Face your greatest opponent with an open heart.*

I wanted to live my life with that kind of open heart.

"And Me, Vice Versa"

My mother liked to shock elegant guests with this story, which I heard her tell innumerable times at dinner parties.

→→   ←←

Jim had some literary business to take care of, and an important New York lawyer came to Paris to meet him. He and Gloria threw a dinner party for the lawyer, and no expense was spared. They invited the fanciest people they knew and out came the good silver, dishes, wine, et cetera. The lawyer was an extremely proper and elegant Harvard-educated gentleman and had a much younger wife who had been a famous model. During the dinner party, his beautiful wife, after having sat silently, snubbing everyone for an hour, turned to Gloria and said, "I made my fortune on my face."

And Gloria answered in a deadpan voice, "And me, vice versa."

The ex-model's husband, the important lawyer, blanched, and my father started to howl with laughter and couldn't stop.

CHAPTER EIGHTEEN

⤜⤜ The Power of Good-bye ⤛⤛

MY BROTHER CALLED AT 7:00 A.M., November 9, 2005. It was Eyrna's eighth birthday. Apparently Bobby Geisler—the shady producer who had first optioned *The Thin Red Line* for Terrence Malick—had just called him from Southampton Hospital. Flat broke and on the run from debtors and lawyers, Bobby had been hiding out at my mother's house. Last night, according to Bobby, Gloria misjudged the distance to her bed and had fallen and shattered her hip. Her prognosis wasn't good. She was profoundly malnourished and dehydrated, severely delusional, and so intoxicated they could not operate on her hip until she stabilized. Jamie was driving up tonight, after work.

That Bobby had moved into my mother's house was not good news.

In 1999, Bobby Geisler and his partner John Roberdeau's main investor, Gerald Rubin, had sued them for the $6 million seed money he'd invested in their company, and won. Rubin's lawyer, Barry Goldin, obtained judgments against Geisler and Roberdeau for extortion, fraud, breach of fiduciary duty, misappropriation, contempt of court, and bad-faith bankruptcy proceedings. John Roberdeau had died of a heart attack in May 2002, and Bobby had not only managed to stay out of jail, but he had also continued to con innumerable people into investing money in his now nonexistent, bankrupt company. Gloria had not worked in years and was now living off of her capital, and the money was dwindling quickly. Bobby had convinced her that he was two steps away from signing a huge Hollywood deal on *Whistle*, which she'd let him option for free, with no binding legal attachments.

A few minutes after Jamie called, the phone rang again, and it was Bobby. "It's that Russian in the attic, Vladimir. He's a nightmare," Bobby said. "They drink together, and then he yells at her for being a drunk. Last night I thought he was going to hit her, I swear. I feared for her safety."

An hour later, Vladimir called, almost hysterical with concern. "You must to get Bobby Geisler out of house. He is bad influence. He drink vith Gloria all night then she fall down and break hip. Soon as possible, he must to go."

On a Monday, I was in Southampton to teach my writing class, and I visited my mother in the physical rehabilitation center. She had finally had surgery, and a pin had been inserted into her shattered hip. Lying in bed, she looked at me as if I were a Nazi officer arrived to interrogate and torture her. Bobby Geisler, with long, wispy gray hair and glasses and a big bulging belly, was sitting to her right in a utilitarian metal chair with armrests.

"How are you doing, Mom?"

"I fell off my horse, you see," she said primly.

"You fell off your horse?" I repeated.

"Yes. She's always been a little wild."

"What's your horse's name, Mom?" I asked.

"Mary-Margaret O'Hara," she said without losing a beat. Then she told me she was being held prisoner against her will. "You can't imagine what they're doing to me here. This place is horrendous. Last night this big black nurse kidnapped me. She took me to a whorehouse."

"A whorehouse?" I repeated in stupefaction.

"Yes. And everyone was black."

"And what did you do there?"

Her gaze wandered off, blank, unseeing. After a while, she focused on me and said, "You don't know how to have fun." Then she pointed to Bobby with a limp hand. "He's fun. Jim was fun. Remember when . . . the woman said, 'This is not the Chesa Grischuna?' and then I got into bed with the German couple and . . . 'This is not the Chesa . . .' we always had so much fun . . ." Her voice trailed off, then came back, sharp. "You are a cruel, cruel woman to keep an old lady in prison like this. You have no idea what they're doing to me. They're trying to kill me."

Then she began to cry. I told her, without emotion, that it wasn't up to me. She had a broken hip, and the doctors wouldn't let her go home.

She stopped crying immediately, her mouth agape, as if I'd slapped her.

As I drove to the campus, I thought of my friend Pat, who'd been sober quite a few years longer than I. We'd met when I used to go to bodybuilding classes. Pat could talk a blue streak about the sales at Bergdorf's, or who the best plastic surgeons were in New York. Once, sitting over thick, green health shakes after our workout, she'd been telling me about her abusive father who now had Alzheimer's, when she suddenly said, "Have you ever met a victim who wasn't absolutely certain they were right? You can't talk to victims, because no matter what, they're right, and therefore, their own cruel behavior is always justified."

"Wait . . . ," I said, quickly reaching into my bag for my notebook. "Wait, say that again."

"What?"

"What you just said. About victims." But she'd already moved on to worrying about what to buy for dinner. As she discussed a recipe for a Greek fish dish cooked with feta cheese, her words bounced and echoed through my head. My mother was a victim, and I was her cruel oppressor. This was the role she had set for me, and I had unwittingly accepted it all of my life.

Now as I drove toward the college, the red sun was setting to my right, and the shadows of the dark, bare trees stretched across the narrow back road. I felt gloom descend upon me as rage was once again ignited in the pit of my stomach and would not burn itself out. I felt poisoned, as if I'd just spent two hours in a toxic waste dump.

The day after Christmas, Jamie called me to say Gloria had tried to escape from the physical rehabilitation center and broken her other hip while falling out of her wheelchair. He said she'd screamed at him on the phone, insults you couldn't believe. Oh, I could believe, I replied.

"Yes," Jamie said somberly, "I guess you could. I'm sorry. I never understood before." I didn't blame him in the least. It was only at the Caron Foundation that I had understood for the first time that Jamie and I had not had the same relationship with our mother. Up until then, I'd always thought he was simply in denial about her cruelty. But that wasn't true. He had never experienced it. I never had that kind of easy, joking, back-and-forth relationship with her that he did. I was the dark and moody one, the one with no sense of humor.

"The rehab center wants her out. I'm driving up tomorrow and taking her home," he said resignedly. "I think we better hide the Calders and whatever else of value is left in the house."

"Well," I suggested, "we can always put the good silver and stuff like that at Cecile's." A few years ago, Gloria had been robbed of most of her table silver—platters, bowls, candlesticks. The house's doors still didn't lock from the outside.

My mother had no valuable jewelry left. But I decided to take what was there and keep it in my apartment, where it would be safe. Vladimir took the Calder prints to an art dealer in the city to be appraised and restored.

I didn't think she'd survive a month.

A hospital bed was set up in my old bedroom downstairs. Gloria was happy and grateful to be home. For two days. Then she grew antsy. She wanted to drink. She wanted Bobby to call the liquor store. She kept on him and her nurses about this. She confused night and day and hollered for liquor at 4:00 A.M., insisting it was cocktail hour. No one could calm her down.

When I came to see her the following Monday, Bobby was sitting in a wicker armchair beside the bed, laughing and joking as if they were at some cocktail party.

I was reminded for some reason of *The Lord of the Rings*— Wormtongue, envoy of the evil Saruman, hovering, hunched and solicitous, over King Théoden, who has been bewitched and can no longer think or see that his world is collapsing around him. His own son lies dead in the next room, his favorite nephew banned from the kingdom for standing up to Wormtongue . . . I tried to shake this image from my mind.

My mother glared at me accusingly and shouted, "What have you done to the hallway that leads upstairs? How dare you remodel my house without my permission!"

She spotted a bottle of rubbing alcohol on the bedside table and reached for it greedily, trying to twist off the top as she brought it toward her lips, craning her neck forward. Horrified, I made no move. Her nurse came running and wrested the bottle from her grip.

The first week in January, I went to the biyearly, weeklong residency at the MFA program at Wilkes University in Pennsylvania, where I taught fiction, but my mind was not on my work.

Students and faculty must have seen the stricken look in my eyes because they treated me with deference and kindness. Bobby Geisler called me on my cell phone while I was in the middle of a class, to say my mother had called a limousine service and, for $250, had gotten a driver to come pick her up and take her to the liquor store in Bridgehampton. How was this possible? She couldn't even dial a phone.

Desperate, I called Nora, who told me: "If she wants to go out that way, who are you to tell her she can't?"

Nora called again, the next day. She wanted to know how I was doing. I told her I was not doing so well. "You're going to have to make amends to her," she said bravely.

"Amends?" I shouted. "What the hell did I ever do to her to deserve this?"

"It isn't for her," said Nora. "It's for you. If she dies this week, or next week, or in a few months, you'll never be free of it. You have to clean up your side of the fence."

Dan, one of the graduate students I taught, came from Pottsville, where my mother grew up. I told him my grandparents were buried in Pottsville but I had no idea where. His mother worked for the Catholic Archdiocese in Pottsville and had access to all the records. He asked if my grandparents were Catholic. My grandmother was, and my grandfather, while raised Catholic, believed the Church was corrupt and worthless. You know, Dan said, Pottsville is less than an hour from here.

I'd had no idea. This seemed providential, so I asked Dan to call his mom.

Within an hour, Dan's mother had the exact location of my grandparents' graves in the Catholic cemetery. Dan volunteered to drive me there the next morning, before classes.

We left just before sunrise and drove through the mountains. On the highway, the sun shone, weak and watery, but down below, a murky fog hung over the valley like a white sea. We went down into Pottsville, the hilly town so ensconced in fog we couldn't see ten feet ahead. I didn't recognize a thing. We drove up Mahantongo Street, where the rich people's imposing mansions stood on a steep hill, gazing quietly down on the rest of the town. I had an approximate idea of where my grandmother's house should be, right across the street from the Yuengling Mansion. There was a redbrick Victorian standing behind a tall iron fence, with black chimneys and white trim, on a frozen green lawn shrouded in fog. "This must be it," I said to Dan. Gone were the wild gardens and tall trees that had hid the house from the street in my grandmother's time.

When we were twelve, Jamie and I had stayed with Gertrude for a week. We wanted to visit our Mosolino cousins, but apparently things weren't going so well over there, and she wouldn't take us. I needled and pressured and pushed her until she spat out, "You're just like your mother, a stubborn little bitch. I bet you lie just like her too. A teller of tall tales. And I bet you show the boys your butterfly, just like she did." I was so aghast I couldn't even formulate a response beyond, "What are you talking about, Grandma?" And I remembered now, my mother telling me that as a girl, she used to suddenly lose her breath and faint the minute she walked through the doors of the church. No number of beatings from Gertrude could cure Gloria of this malady, which caused Gertrude endless shame before the priests and nuns.

Dan's mother met us at her office. She had taken out the original leather-bound volume that listed my grandfather, Mark Anthony Mosolino, as having died of "indigestion" on New Year's Eve, 1947.

Dan drove me to the cemetery with his mother's hand-drawn map. The pale gravestones on both sides of the narrow asphalt road drifted in and out of sight through the fog. The road curved, and Dan pulled to a stop. We got out and began to search the headstones. Who was this woman who had given birth to me? I wanted to find some connection, some way back to who she had been, in the hope that I might better understand who she had become.

We found the Mosolino monument, a marble rectangle with both my grandparents' names engraved on it: Mark Anthony Mosolino; Gertrude Mosolino Dietman. In middle age, she'd married a sullen, nasty old man with webbed fingers on both hands, who wouldn't let us watch TV in the living room.

I took out my cell phone with a shaking hand and called my mother.

"Mom?" I called out, as if reaching out to her across a great distance. I took a deep breath. Dan politely wandered off down the path. "Mommy, I'm here in Pottsville! I'm standing in front of your parents' graves."

"You poor thing," she said, slurring, as if waking from a deep sleep. "You had such a terrible mother."

"This is Kaylie," I said, baffled. "This is your daughter."

"You had a terrible mother. Kick her grave for me."

"Are you talking about Gertrude, Mom?"

"Gertrude . . . ," she said vaguely. "Spit on her. For me." My mother had run away from this place and never come back; and yet, she had never truly left it behind.

I made a spitting sound, pretending. "There," I said to my mother. "Done."

We giggled together breathlessly, like naughty children. Then I started heaving deep, painful sighs that caught in my throat. "Mom, I'm so sorry. I'm so sorry for everything I ever did that hurt you." Tears cascaded from my eyes, as if a dam had suddenly cracked open.

"Oh, honey . . . ," she said, crying as well. "You had a terrible time."

"I had a terrible time? Do you know who I am?"

"Yes," she said, "you're Gloria."

The jackals started to circle, smelling the death struggle, and a free meal. She was hemorrhaging money. The nurses' aides alone cost over $3,500 a week, and Gloria was shelling out a small fortune on liquor and food. And meanwhile, Bobby told her they'd be getting a check soon for *Whistle*, hundreds of thousands of dollars; soon they'd be picking out her dress for the Oscars.

Jamie and I had been growing increasingly concerned about Gloria's financial situation. We called a lawyer to see if we had grounds to petition the county court to have our mother declared incompetent.

I took Eyrna out to see her grandmother for a few hours on Presidents' Day. Jamie and I both had power of attorney from the last time she'd almost died, and every week, one of us needed to pay Gloria's bills. Vladimir wanted $960 for the groceries and house necessities he'd bought over the last month. Michael Mosolino wanted $750 for the groceries he'd also bought, over the last few weeks. Who was eating all this food? I wanted to know. Vladimir secretly told me it was Bobby. Michael secretly told me it was Bobby, but also Vladimir.

A big man I didn't know wearing work boots entered the kitchen. He said he was ready to start. He said he wanted a down payment on the agreed sum of $5,000.

"Start what?" I wanted to know.

"I want that big tree cut down," my mother told me, "pay him." She flung her arm out indifferently, the Red Queen giving an execution order.

"I think we need to discuss this," I said, my hand out to slow everything down.

"Oh, shut up. You're an asshole," she said to me.

"Get your coat, sweetie," I said to Eyrna, "we're going."

"What?" said my mother, surprised.

"We're leaving. I won't be spoken to that way in front of my daughter."

"Oh, come now, you don't have to go," her nurse's aide said to me as if she were talking to a five-year-old. She turned to my mother. "Say you're sorry, Gloria. Say you didn't mean it."

"But I did mean it. This is my house. I can do what I want!"

I had tried so hard to accept that she was not in control of her faculties. But a hurricane of emotions was raging within me, and I felt on the verge of incredible verbal violence. But this raging crazy person inside me was no longer me—not the person I'd become—and I knew the only way I would survive intact was to get out.

I calmly put on my coat; I helped Eyrna with hers. "I'll call you tomorrow," I said in a low voice. They all stared at me in stupefied silence.

On the way west, driving along curving and treacherous Noyack Road, teal blue inlets sparkled through the dense, dark, leafless trees. I turned and saw that Eyrna was asleep in the back. Conked out from the strain, I guessed. I felt ill, as if I had the flu. But I didn't. I switched the radio on low. A sad, strange, complex orchestration with a kind of New Age techno instrumentation filled the silence. I recognized Madonna's voice immediately, though I'd never heard the song. It was about the ending of a relationship, the end of trying to make things work.

"There's no greater power than the power of good-bye."

An orchestra of string instruments took up the refrain and grew in intensity until it reached a vibrating pitch. But then a lone guitarist strummed a few chords, and the song came to an end, dead in its tracks, in the middle of a measure. Astonished, I turned off the radio and pulled off the road at a boarded-up marina.

I decided I would not go to court to have my mother declared incompetent. I would not fight. I put the car in drive and hit the gas. I felt as if I'd jumped off a sinking ship and was in a life raft with my little girl, my face turned away from the horror, rowing, rowing, as fast and as hard as I could in the opposite direction.

Two days later, the phone rang. I thought it was Kevin on his way home from work. *"This is your mother."* No one could spit out the word *mother* like she. It was pulverizing in its power to degrade and insult. *"You are a vicious little cunt,"* she went on, *"and I'm going to kill you, do you hear me?"* Her voice was low and filled with venom. *"How dare you try to steal my money!"*

I shouldn't have picked up, and I immediately cut her off without saying a word. I turned off the ringer and sat there, shaking, unable to get my adrenaline under control. I could feel my hand inching toward the phone to call her back and say I was sorry. But sorry for what?

The answering machine clicked on and her shouting filled the apartment. *"You fucking bitch, how dare you hang up on me! I'm going to bury you, you fucking whore. You're a thief and a liar. I'm going to cut your heart out with a knife . . ."* I ran past Eyrna, who was playing in the living room, to the answering machine in the kitchen, and turned that off too.

Someone had told my mother about the petition to have her declared incompetent. It could only be one of two people—Michael or Bobby—both of whom my brother had apprised of our plans. I felt my blood pressure crash, as if I were about to faint. I went into the bathroom, locked the door, closed the toilet lid, and sat down with my head between my knees. A hard rain began to pelt the window. I heard Eyrna's small feet padding toward the door.

She turned the knob, slapping the door with her palm. "Mommy? Are you all right?"

Still trembling, I unlocked the door and let her in. I couldn't look up. Eyrna's hand gently patted my back. I forced myself to turn my face toward her. She tried to read my eyes. I couldn't stand when my mother used to look at me that way, because she always knew what I was feeling and made a joke.

"Why did Grammy say those things?"

"Oh, honey." My voice shattered. I didn't know what to do. "She's insane, honey. She's poisoned her brain with alcohol."

For two days I refused to answer the phone, so Gloria called the Southampton police and told them I'd robbed her. Jamie immediately called the police and faxed them our power of attorney papers. The officer who'd shown up at my mother's house told Jamie over the phone that she had offered him a drink at nine in the morning. He was concerned about the two individuals who were goading her on, a certain Bobby and a certain Michael. Did he know these characters? Jamie was horrified. How were they goading her on? Well, said Officer Cavanaugh, they were telling her she's absolutely right, that her daughter's a thief. Mark my words, said the officer, those two are trouble. Next thing they'll do is bring in a reverse mortgage for her to sign. You'd better watch your back.

Having no idea what else to do, I walked over to my lunchtime tae kwon do class.

Mr. Sevilla took one long look at me and said, "What's wrong now?"

"My mother called the police. I'm afraid they're going to come arrest me. She says I stole from her."

He threw his head back and exploded into laughter, showing his back molars, as if he hadn't heard anything so funny in his life. "Ah, that's a good one!" he said gleefully and slapped me on the shoulder. Every time the doorbell rang during class, Mr. Sevilla shouted to the girl behind the front desk, "Don't answer it! It's the police coming to take away Ms. Jones!"

Two days later, Michael gave Gloria a million-dollar reverse mortgage contract to sign. Jamie drove out to Sagaponack from Washington in the middle of the night to stop her.

On Wednesday, March 15, my brother called at nightfall to tell me my mother had taken away my power of attorney and signed a new will in which I'd been disinherited. She'd left my share of the estate to Eyrna and had cut Michael Mosolino in for 10 percent. I felt a piercing pain through my chest on the right side, as if I'd been speared. I called Kevin at work. "Kevin . . ."

"Are you okay, my love, what's wrong?"

"She cut me out of her will." My mouth was completely dry, and I was hyperventilating. "I can't breathe."

"I'm coming home."

"It's okay."

"I'll take a cab," he said and hung up.

Kevin gave me a muscle relaxant and a eucalyptus rub and attempted to talk me down. He made me promise to call our doctor first thing in the morning.

In a panic, gasping for air, I said, "If you want me to, if you think it's the right thing to do, I'll go out there. I'll apologize to her. I swear, I will."

"To hell with her and her money. We don't need it. We never needed it. All we ever wanted was to be able to provide for Eyrna a private school education and an Ivy League college, if that's what she wants. And she'll have that. We'll be all right." Kevin held me in his arms, rubbing my back where my right lung seemed to be in some kind of spasm. "It's okay, my love. You didn't do anything wrong."

. . .

I must have dozed off just before dawn. I awakened with a start, only a short while later. Feeling as if I had a hundred-pound weight pressing down on my chest, I wondered if the solution would be to find some heroin somewhere and kill myself. But where did one find heroin, anyway?

I turned over, and there was Eyrna, gazing down at me in the pale light, her eyes shiny. Ah, my only child, my greatest gift . . . She jumped on me and kissed my neck. I opened my arms to her, and she folded her warm body into mine. I smelled her clean, fruity hair.

"I love you, Mommy."

Suddenly I couldn't breathe, and I wanted to push her off.

Help me, God, I thought. Let me get through this. Let me accept whatever you put in my path. But really, I was thinking, underneath that soft and gracious prayer, God, how much longer are you planning for this to continue? Could you let me know? Is this going to go on for a year? Five years? Six months? If I knew, I could hold on . . .

"And I love you, too, baby girl," I choked out, "more than anything in the world." The alarm buzzed loudly, and it was time for Eyrna to get ready for school.

I waited with her for the school bus to come, watched her climb aboard, her heavy backpack hanging from her shoulders. I waved good-bye as she sat in a window seat and blew me a kiss. I took our little dog down to the East River esplanade. The sun was bright for late winter, and warm on the stone walk. The river seemed quite blue, a dark mirror of the sky. By nature I'd never been brave, unless faced with an absence of choices. That's when I could act bravely, like a rat with its back against the wall. My mother had disowned me. She'd done the very worst thing to me she could think of. That was really the only thing she *could* do, to punish me for turning my back on her. I had a moment of perfect clarity: she'd done her very worst, she'd fired off her last, best cannon, and I was not dead. She had nothing left. My father's work was safe, because by law the copyrights already belonged to Jamie and me as well as Gloria. She couldn't cut me out, and no one could touch James Jones's work without my consent.

Have you ever met a victim who wasn't right?

The only power I had was the choice to no longer be a victim. "God," I murmured out loud, to river and sky, "I give this up to you."

My soul went quiet within me in the bright sunshine. I realized that for today, for right now, everything was all right. My daughter was safe. My husband loved me, and he was safe. My home had not burned down. I was not sick. We had money in the bank. The bills were all paid. The dark carrion bird of guilt and shame suddenly loosened its talons and lifted off from my shoulders and flew away.

It was over. And I was free.

She lived for another ten weeks. Her violent messages on my answering machine did not stop. Who dialed the phone for her? Jamie's and my lawyer told me to save Gloria's messages and record them. I couldn't listen to them, so I asked Kevin to do it, even though her words made Kevin's face turn the color of ash.

Less than a week before she died, Bobby and Michael threw her a birthday party that cost her more than $10,000, catered by Michael's own company.

I had no premonition or feeling of loss on her last night on earth. Kevin and I made love that Thursday night, quietly but fiercely. It was the first time in months. He held me in his arms as we slept, and I felt safe and protected and deeply loved. The next morning, I took Eyrna to the school bus, and when I returned to our apartment, the phone was ringing. Of course, I didn't pick it up until I heard my brother's shattered voice. What now? I thought, my heart pounding as I brought the receiver to my ear.

"Kaylie, Mom died," Jamie said. "Bobby found her at six this morning. She had a heart attack." He started to cry. I hadn't heard Jamie cry since he was eight years old.

"My poor Jamie," I said. "I'm so sorry."

I felt terrible for my brother, but no sense of loss, no regret, no sadness for her. Like the survivor of a terrible war coming out of hiding and finding a silent world of swirling dust, I felt nothing but relief. Jamie took some deep breaths, then told me he'd be driving out to Long Island late tonight. I said we'd meet him there tomorrow.

When we disconnected, I called Kevin at work. Eyrna's Candidate for Black Belt test was that night, June 9. She also had two girlfriends sleeping over, a party she'd been planning and looking forward to for months. My mother had fallen and broken her hip on Eyrna's eighth birthday. She had taken so much from us already that I decided I would not tell Eyrna until tomorrow.

Two days later, on Sunday afternoon, Jamie called Michael Mosolino to try and sort out Gloria's new will, which Jamie didn't think was valid. We were sitting at the round, wrought iron and glass table in our mother's garden. Michael had somehow gotten himself into the will for 10 percent of his aunt's estate. Michael was also named successor executor and trustee for Eyrna's share, if anything ever happened to Jamie.

I didn't trust Michael. He'd charged his aunt more than $3,500 for the food alone at the birthday lunch, and he'd fed the guests lamb that was left over from a wedding he'd catered the day before. He admitted this unabashedly to our cousins Kate and Joanie.

Jamie kept telling me that my mother had been insane, that nothing she'd done made sense. She'd been coerced into making this new will, and we had the medical papers to prove it. We would most probably win in court, Jamie said; but it would take years and cost hundreds of thousands of dollars.

"I'll do whatever you want to do," I told Jamie. "I will never fight with you over this. Ever."

Jamie, always the diplomat, told Michael he'd pay him his 10 percent from the proceeds of the sale of the house and whatever other cash there was, which was not much, but Michael would have to renounce his position as successor executor and trustee for Eyrna's share. And he had to abandon any claim to our father's literary works.

As he listened to Michael's response, my brother's eyes widened slightly and the color drained from his face. Then his mouth slowly hardened, and he began to concentrate. It was his poker face—pure, cold calculation. He was a great poker and chess player, and whatever Michael was saying, it was not sitting well. My heart started to palpitate, my mouth went dry again. How could we have allowed ourselves to get into this position?

But I continued to watch my brother, reassured by that calculating, calm, ruthless look. Jamie was preparing to go to war. But his was going to be a tactical, quiet war, one that would have scared the shit out of me if I'd been on the other side. Michael did not know Jamie well if he thought he was going to bully him. He did not know Jamie well if he thought Jamie would cave in.

"I'll get back to you on that," Jamie said calmly and put the portable phone down on the table.

He sat in silence, thinking, and I asked, "What did he say?"

"He said, 'I'm a businessman. How much is it worth to you?'"

I thought, And this is who my mother chose to protect Eyrna's assets if anything ever happened to Jamie? Jamie sighed, and, in a resolute tone, added, "We need a really good lawyer. And I'm never speaking to that greedy son of a bitch again. He has no honor."

I felt immensely grateful to have this decent, intelligent man for a brother.

Two weeks later, back in Washington, my brother mentioned to me on the phone, in passing, as if it were common knowledge, that Gloria had been drinking for at least the last four years of her life. At first I didn't believe him. I thought he had his dates wrong. If I'd been asked to swear under oath, I would have sworn she had not been drinking.

In my mission to be uncompromisingly honest, I tried to look back, unflinchingly, to find the truth. When did she start drinking again, exactly? I wanted to know.

So I called Jamie again and asked him.

"If she was sober two years, that would be generous," he said.

So, from about, say, 2002 on—all that time—she was hiding bottles? Secretly drinking? Why didn't I smell it? Why didn't I notice?

But I did smell it. Every once in a while I'd get a whiff of that strange, cool, fermented, sugary smell. Kevin had often commented on my mother's lack of physical affection. He'd never met a less physically demonstrative person than Gloria. Was that why, in the past four years, she'd never hugged or kissed me? Because she was afraid I'd smell it? I had thought it was because she hated me.

"I didn't know," I said to my brother, at a loss for words. "How could it be that I didn't see this?"

"I don't know," Jamie said equably. "She was drinking. I could always tell when she called me."

So perhaps that was why she so rarely called *me*. She did not mind so much if Jamie knew, but did, terribly, if *I* knew. Was she afraid I'd keep Eyrna away from her? I would have done what Jamie did—come for a few hours on holidays. But I would never have moved in with her for the summer, or spent so many weekends there, or let her drive around with Eyrna in the car. I would not have left them alone together.

It now occurred to me that she had perhaps not meant to be cruel by not calling me but simply had not remembered my birthday and other important dates. In my silent, righteous anger at this injustice, I'd sat and stewed, waiting for her to call *me*.

"But why didn't you tell me she'd started drinking again?" I asked my brother.

"I thought you knew."

How could it be that Jamie and I never discussed this? It seemed inconceivable. Yet I realized now that Jamie and I had barely spoken to each other over the past four years. And we shied away from such painful topics as the condition of the house, or our mother's health.

Jamie would rarely spend even one night in the house he had worked so hard to hold together as a young man. While he called our mother several times a week, and he brought his wife and kids over for Christmas Day and sometimes Easter, they came from his in-laws' home in Westchester and left before trouble brewed.

I was the one who stayed. And what a torment it must have been for Gloria to have Kevin and me in her house, being assailed constantly by the desire, the *need*, to drink, and being forced to hide it, like a criminal. No wonder she was in a constant rage.

As it turned out, no one had been more in denial than I. I had attributed all of her inconsistencies, her weird rages, vicious attacks, and mood swings to my belief that she was suffering from untreated depression and anxiety. I thought she hated me, and of course, Kevin, because we were the only obstacles standing between her and Eyrna. Clearly she had not wanted to be with us in the least but had to tolerate our presence because we were Eyrna's parents. And I had tolerated her behavior because I thought it was important for Eyrna to have a relationship with her grandmother, and that Eyrna's presence in her life—Gloria professed to love Eyrna to distraction—was keeping her sober.

Stunned by this news, I immediately called Cecile and asked her the same question. "When did my mother start drinking again?"

"Well," Cecile said, and sighed. "She never drank in front of me, but people called me and told me she was drinking. I really knew it when I realized she'd been watering my scotch. I don't drink scotch, but someone came over for dinner, and I offered him a scotch. He said, 'This is terrible!' and I realized Gloria had just stayed overnight, and had watered down a brand-new bottle."

"But *when* was this?" I persisted. Cecile was not sure.

"And why didn't you tell me?"

After a pause, Cecile explained, "Because I knew you'd lose your mind over it."

No one told me. Apparently no one wanted to trigger my mother's ire. And I've always prided myself on my ability to smell alcohol from five feet away. I could always recognize the telltale signs of a person in trouble. So what does this say about me, about the writer with the acute talent for observation and bottomless memory for detail?

I began to doubt my own sanity all over again. How could I have been so completely shut down from reality that I failed to notice the blaringly obvious signs? I had never believed the psychology textbooks that described the human mind's capability of completely shutting out what it did not want to accept. But now I saw that not only was this possible, it had happened to me.

The same day I called Cecile, I picked up Eyrna at the school bus with our little dog Natalie, and we walked down to the East River promenade. It was mid-June; we were coming to the end of the school year. The sky was a warm blue and summer had set in, a mild, light breeze blowing off the water. Keeping my voice gentle and devoid of recrimination, I asked Eyrna, "Did you know that Grammy was drinking? I just need to know, honey. None of this is your fault."

She looked at me with her tawny eyes. "I knew," she responded, calm and serious.

"Do you remember when it was that Grammy started drinking again?"

"I don't remember how old I was. We went out to lunch and she had this stuff in a green bottle and it smelled really weird."

Eyrna said that soon after, Grammy was hiding bottles all over the house—in the pantry, behind certain books in the bookshelf. She put vodka in her Diet Coke. When Eyrna confronted her, my mother said, "Don't worry about it. I can handle myself. Your parents are the crazy ones. They don't know anything about it. But don't *you* tell them. If you tell them, they'll take you away, and we'll never see each other again."

How could it be that I didn't see it? Around my mother, I lost all sense of direction, self-discipline, self-esteem. I completely lost my sense of self.

Memorial

Gloria's memorial service took place in her garden on July 2, 2006. The blue hydrangeas were in full bloom, large and round as children's heads gathered in tight clusters, as if quietly conferring. Here is what Eyrna wrote and read aloud to the gathered company.

→→   ←←

Dear Grammy,

I miss you very much and I'm sorry you had to go the way you did. I think you went the way you wanted to but I'm sorry it had to be that way. I love you very much and I'll miss you every day.

Love always,
Eyrna

→ Epilogue ←

IN AUGUST 2008, JAMIE AND I drove out to visit our storage unit in Bridgehampton, hoping to organize fifty years of family photographs—a task we had not felt ready to tackle until now. Cecile invited us to stay at her house. She had stood by us through all of it, never veering from her conviction that Gloria's mind had been poisoned by alcohol.

Jamie and I had driven out to Riverhead once before, to be deposed in our court case against Michael Mosolino. Seeing that we had a good case, Michael eventually caved in and renounced any claims to our father's literary estate, as well as his role as successor executor for Eyrna's trust. But Jamie had been obliged to pay him 10 percent of proceeds on the sale of my mother's house. Jamie called it blood money.

By the middle of July 2006, just a few weeks after Gloria's funeral, her credit card bills began to arrive, and we learned that Bobby Geisler had been making forays in the City using Gloria's Visa and Amex cards. Jamie was left with a $15,000 credit debt, and receipts for elegant New York City hotels, fancy restaurants, designer food stores, and even a brand-new laptop computer. Around $4,000 had been charged to her cards after her death. When questioned, Bobby said he was working for Gloria as a producer and had permission to use her cards. The police did not pursue the case—they felt that legally it was a "gray area" and not worth their while.

Jamie, who was driving, asked me if I ever dreamed of our dad.

I told him I'd had three dreams about our father over the past thirty years, perhaps one every decade. In the first, I was a freshman in college, and while I was having a quick nap one afternoon, there was a knock on my dorm room door, and it was my father. I walked him around the campus, pointing out my classrooms, and it felt like a holiday until suddenly he said he had to go, and I woke up covered in sweat, calling out to him to come back. In the second, I was living in New York, writing my second novel, and I dreamed he'd married another woman. I went to him and begged him to go back to our mother, but he solemnly shook his head no and turned his back on me. Our mother tried to kill herself by jumping out a high window of a white hotel, onto a shimmering green lawn. In the third dream, which was much more recent, I was visiting our mother in Sagaponack and learned that our father had never died; our mother had told us he was dead because he'd left her for another woman, and now he and this woman had three kids and lived happily somewhere down the street from our mother's house. When I went and knocked on his door, he stared at me blankly, as if he no longer remembered who I was.

It felt cozy and safe to be in a car with Jamie driving. He was the best driver I knew—fast, but completely alert. Our dad had taught him on lonely back roads, as he'd taught me, a small gift in the last months of his life. We had been talking for an hour straight, comfortably, as if we'd always done this. Getting to spend twenty-four hours alone with Jamie felt like a holiday, despite the nature of our trip. It was never easy for us to go back there, but I was not afraid.

I'd passed my Black Belt test on December 9, 2006, six months to the day after our mother's death. Mr. Bill, too ill to suit up, had watched from the sidelines, dignified, quiet as a statue. Anna the Valkyrie, George, and I shared the floor with several younger and stronger men; two were from another branch of the school. During the one hundred push-ups, my arms began to shake and I thought I would not make it, that I was going to pass out. I heard Kevin's and Eyrna's voices shouting from the sidelines, "Come on, you can do it!" And a cold, calm fire ignited within me. I decided I would die before I quit.

After the push-ups, I knew I'd passed the worst of it. One of the young men from the other branch of the school, in his twenties, had to take a break to go barf. *I am not my thoughts, I am my actions.* I said this to myself as a mantra, over and over again. Toward the end of the ninety minutes of grueling endurance exercises, we each had to pick our best *Palgue* form and perform it alone in front of the judges. Then I had to spar against six-foot-five, 240-pound Mr. Acosta, who kept yelling at me to hit him harder. I gave him all I had, and he didn't even flinch.

Mr. Sevilla handed Mr. Bill our Black Belts with our names embroidered on them in gold—in Korean and English. Mr. Bill stood at the front of the *do-jang* and tied the belts around our waists and bowed. I took his hand in both of mine and bowed deeply, holding the bow several seconds longer than required.

"I've had only one dream about Dad," Jamie told me after a few minutes' silence, keeping his eyes on the road. I'd learned that if I pushed with Jamie, he'd recoil. He had to be given space and quiet to talk intimately about his feelings.

Around fifteen years ago, Jamie had dreamed that he was sitting in the kitchen of the Sagaponack house, when our father walked in the door. The rest of us were in the house, but not in the kitchen. Jamie thought, Thank God, everything is going to be all right now. He jumped up to pull out a chair for our dad.

Jamie wanted to ask him where he'd been, but it didn't seem like the right time. Our dad sat down at the long, dark, beautifully waxed wood table, and everything continued normally, as if we were whole again and his death had just been a horrible nightmare. But our father didn't speak.

Jamie finally asked, "Where have you been, Dad?"

But our dad still wouldn't say a word. He got up and started walking around the house, Jamie following. Our dad looked around, inspecting things—the pulpit bar, the books on the coffee table and shelves. Everything was exactly as it had been before he died. He climbed the stairs to his attic office and shut the door. Jamie realized something was wrong, but he wasn't sure what, the feeling of relief leaking away.

He had awakened, lying in the darkness, heart pounding, aware that it was only a dream.

I did a slow, silent breathing exercise to get ahold of myself, for Jamie had never appreciated my emotional displays.

In February 2007, I'd finished emptying our mother's house. I left Eyrna in New York with Kevin, because I wanted her to keep her good memories. Many friends came and helped me, and I was amazed and stunned by their generosity. The only object left in the end was the imposing pulpit bar. On the last day, I waited for my friend, who was a carpenter, to come and take it apart, because there was no other way to get it out the door and move it to storage. I stood in the empty, echoing living room and stared at it as the edges of the long room darkened in the afternoon gloom. The prayer stools, its longtime companions, were gone now, and the bar looked forlorn, like the prow of a galleon shipwrecked on a shallow reef.

When I felt pulled together, I told Jamie that recently, in the magazine *Time for Kids*, there was an article about a planet that astronomers had discovered that they believed might support life. A planet, like ours, but circling a red dwarf sun. Eyrna was amazed when I got choked up while reading it. "My daddy always believed there were other planets that could support life!" I told her. Years ago he'd already thought it was absolutely egomaniacal to believe ours was the only inhabitable planet in the entire universe.

I said to Jamie, "Remember how he used to watch the Apollo missions, and said he couldn't believe men would get into those tiny capsules and go out into space? He said imagining all the things that could go wrong would make a job like that totally impossible for him."

Jamie smiled. "I loved watching *Star Trek* with him. He thought Mr. Spock was the coolest character ever. He used to analyze every show!"

We fell silent once again, and I continued to think about all the things—good and bad—our father had missed. I turned to my brother now and said, my voice coming out raspy, "He would be so proud of you, Jamie. What a brave and strong man you are."

I looked out the car window and saw new buildings going up in what had once been beautiful green fields. Tonight, I would not be home to put Eyrna to bed and stretch out beside her until she fell asleep. On many nights she still wept for her grandmother, shoulders shuddering. She'd turn to me and murmur, "Grammy didn't love me enough. If she'd loved me more, she would've stopped drinking."

"There's nothing you could have done, my angel. She was very sick and couldn't help herself. She loved you more than anything." I had not managed to keep the disease away from my child, and my heart felt cleaved in two.

Eyrna, my brave girl, passed her own Black Belt test on June 9, 2007, on the one-year anniversary of her grandmother's death.

Watching her test was harder for me than getting through my own. I almost jumped up and pulled her out a couple of times, but the other mothers and Mr. Bill held me back. Eyrna did not want to quit, never even considered it, even as tears streamed down her cheeks. I was so proud of her I cried myself. As a child, I'd been nothing like her. I was afraid, and if something was hard, I ran away.

Mr. Bill was not running away. He still came to the *do-jang* almost every day, weak and in pain, to teach us our advanced forms. Anna, George, and I had learned the *Koryo* and *Bassai* forms and performed them in front of all the Premier schools, in Mr. Bill's honor, at the last promotion test.

I know now that if I see my father again, in a deathbed vision, I will tell him I was not able to keep my deep-sworn vow to him to stop my mother from drinking. But I am not sorry. I could not have stopped her. It was never my responsibility.

Perhaps for me heaven is a well-lit, shining room with a long, beautiful table piled high with delicacies. On both sides sit all the writers I have admired and loved, even Nabokov, that persnickety snob. But here, their egos and earthly problems have left them, and all they do is eat, and drink the nectar of the gods, which doesn't get them drunk. And they talk about books. My father is sitting next to Tolstoy, whose eyes have lost their hounded look. They're comparing the battle scenes in *War and Peace* and *The Thin Red Line*. Stendhal is listening in rapt attention.

I approach, a little uncertain, and my father turns to me. His fifty-five-year-old face breaks into a warm smile, his eyes bright with recognition. He stands, introduces me to the gathered company, pulls out a chair for me, and welcomes me to the table.

ACKNOWLEDGMENTS

I owe a huge debt of gratitude to Laurie Loewenstein Moyer and Nina Solomon, my first readers, who gave me more time, kindness, and encouragement than a writer has any right to expect.

Megan Thompson and Larry Kirshbaum saw a rough manuscript and understood how to organize it and shape it as only true aficionados with a vision could, and for that they have my eternal thanks.

I have the best editor, Henry Ferris, who took it a step further and "cleared the excess furniture out of the overfurnished room."

For their help with research on the life of James Jones, I am indebted to Thomas J. Wood, archivist, Special Collections, University of Illinois at Springfield; Robert Taylor, archivist, Harry Ransom Center, University of Texas at Austin; and J. Michael Lennon, PhD, Norman Mailer biographer and bibliographer.

For generously sharing their memories and knowledge of my parents' life and times, I wish to thank Cecile Bazelon; Helen Howe; Doug Lawhead; Don Sackrider; Kate Mosolino Sotiridy; Kathy Stillwell; Joan Mosolino Wall; and Kathryn Weissberger. Ray Elliott, USMC, ret., graciously helped me with issues of war and warfare.

David Andreas, Anna Bahceci, Cecile Bazelon, Meg Bennett, Tom Borthwick, Dan Burda, George Krzyminski, Kathy Stillwell, Barbara Taylor, Theasa Tuohy, and Renette Zimmerly volunteered as readers and gave me invaluable feedback.

I must especially thank Susan Cheever, the first and the bravest of "the second generation," who suggested this book was a memoir and taught me by example not to be afraid.

Love and thanks to Julia Murphy for sharing her profound wisdom and kindness.

Lastly, this book would not have been possible without Kevin and Eyrna Heisler, who waited every day, with good humor and aplomb, for me to return to them from the great distances I traveled.